Business Strategy and Information Technology

Edited by
Ewan Sutherland
and Yves Morieux

ROUTLEDGE

London and New York

First published 1991
by Routledge
11 New Fetter Lane, London EC4P 4EE

Simultaneously published in the USA and Canada
by Routledge
a division of Routledge, Chapman and Hall, Inc.
29 West 35th Street, New York, NY 10001

Printed and bound in Great Britain by
Biddles Ltd, Guildford and King's Lynn

British Library Cataloguing in Publication Data

Business strategy and information technology.
1. Organizations. Management. Applications of computer
systems
I. Sutherland, Ewan *1956–* . II. Morieux, Yves *1960–*
658.05
ISBN 0-415-04336-0   6 b003b1006

Library of Congress Cataloging-in-Publication Data
Business strategy and information technology / edited by Ewan
Sutherland & Yves Morieux.
p. cm.
Includes bibliographical references and index.
ISBN 0-415-04336-0
1. Strategic planning – Data processing. 2. Management – Data
processing. 3. Information technology – Management. 4. Management
information systems. I. Sutherland, Ewan, 1956– . II. Morieux,
Yves, 1960–
HD30.28.B865   1990
658.4′012′0285–dc20   90-39727
                                                                   CIP

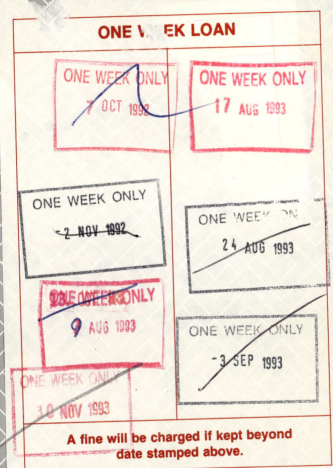

ONE WEEK LOAN

ONE WEEK ONLY
7 OCT 1992

ONE WEEK ONLY
17 AUG 1993

ONE WEEK ONLY
-2 NOV 1992

ONE WEEK ON
24 AUG 1993

ONE WEEK ONLY
9 AUG 1993

ONE WEEK ONLY
-3 SEP 1993

ONE WEEK ONLY
10 NOV 1993

**A fine will be charged if kept beyond
date stamped above.**

10013

Business Strategy and Information Technology

Contents

Contents

Part III Implementation

Part IV Value Added Networks

Part V Conclusion

Contributors

Yannis Bakos is assistant professor at the University of California, Irvine, USA. His research interests are in the strategic use of information technology and inter-organisational systems. He recently completed his PhD at the Sloan School of Management, Massachussets Institute of Technology.

Lynne Baxter was a research assistant at the University of Glasgow and a member of the Centre for Technical and Organisational Change. She has moved to the Heriot-Watt University in Edinburgh, Scotland.

Per Blenker is a researcher in the Department of Marketing of Handelshøjskolen I Århus (Århus School of Management) in Denmark. His research interests are in decision theory, philosophy and information technology.

Robyn Chandler was a lecturer at the Polytechnic of Central London, UK, before which she worked for five years in systems analysis in Australia and the UK. She has recently completed an MSc in Information Systems at the London School of Economics. She has recently returned to her native Australia to undertake commercial work in systems analysis.

Mark Ebers is a lecturer at the Universität Mannheim in the Federal Republic of Germany. His research interests are in organisation theory and public administration.

Jo van Engelen is the manager of the business analysis department of Océ Nederland BV, a leading European firm in copying, printing and publishing. He is also a part-time Assistant Professor of Marketing and Systems Research at the Universiteit Twente.

Contributors

John Fripp is assistant director of Studies at Ashridge Management Centre where he divides his time between teaching and research into the use of IT. He is also actively involved in the design and use of business games for educational purposes. Before joining Ashridge he worked from the United Kingdom Atomic Energy Authority as a physicist and with Rolls Royce and British Gas as an internal operational research consultant.

Bjarte Frøyland is marketing manager for Computer Associates Scandinavia, based in Oslo. He has previously worked in marketing for Bull Norway and as a management consultant for Arthur Andersen and Company.

Hans-Dieter Ganter is a lecturer at the Universität Mannheim in the Federal Republic of Germany. His research interests are in information technology and cross-national studies.

Filip Ivanov is head of information technology at the Shipping Research Institute, Varna. His research interests are in the application of information technology for the shipping industry.

James McCalman is a lecturer in management studies at the University of Glasgow and manager of the Centre for Technical and Organisational Change. He is currently researching the objectives behind applications of new technology. He has published *The Electronic Industry in Britain - coping with change*, Routledge, 1988.

Gillian Marcelle worked as a researcher at the Institut für Weltwirtschaft, Kiel in the Federal Republic of Germany. She has since moved to work for British Telecom in London where she is involved in economic and strategic analysis.

Marie-Christine Monnoyer is maître de conférence at the Université de Bordeaux I, France and is editor of the review 'Tech de Co'. Her research interests are in the development of small firms and in the strategic use of information technology.

Yves Morieux is a senior consultant with Groupe Stratema in Paris, a public policy and management strategy consulting practice. His work is focused on helping senior executives mange the transitions leading up to and after mergers and acquisitions. He previously worked for Arthur D. Little International for four years. He also teaches business policy and strategic management at the Paris-Grignon Institut National d'Agronomie.

Contributors

Nikolai Petkov is a researcher in the Shipping Research Institute, Varna. He previously worked for twelve years in the commercial department of the Shipping Corporation, Varna. His research interests are in methods for the investigation and forecasting of freight markets and in the management and investment policies of shipping companies.

Jean Philippe is a research engineer at the Centre d'Economie Regionale of the Université d'Aix-Marseille III, France. He is also editor of 'Notes de Recherche', a publication of the CER.

Andrea Pontiggia is a researcher in the management department at the Università L Bocconi, Milano, Italy. He teaches in the SDA Business School and researches in CRORA (Research Centre on Organisation). His research and teaching focus on the organisational use of information technology and organisational information systems.

Juliet Sheppard is head of operations management and quantitative methods at Kingston Business School. She has previously worked at the London Business School. Her current research interests include organisational decision processes and the management of IT investment decisions.

Ewan Sutherland is a lecturer at the University of Stirling. He has previously worked at the European Business School and at the Polytechnics of Central London and Wolverhampton. He is deputy editor of the 'International Journal of Information Resource Management'. His research interests are in strategic use of information technology, telecommunications and office information systems.

Arjen Wassenaar is a senior lecturer in the Universiteit Twente, Enschede, in the Netherlands. He has previously held posts as information analyst, project manager and information management consultant working in industry. His current research involves leading a project on information management.

Foreword

The chapters of this book have been developed from papers presented at the First and Second Workshops on Information Technology and Business Strategy held in Brussels at the European Institute for Advanced Studies in Management (EIASM). The Workshops arose from our perception of the growing popularity of 'Strategic Information Technology' which had spread to Europe from the United States of America. It was clear when planning the First Workshop that interest in this area was beginning to take off. That message has been reinforced ever since, with strategic issues relating to information technology currently established as a major issue on the agenda of business strategists.

The Workshops drew together available experience in Europe in order to see whether the relationships between business strategy and information technology were as significant issues here, as in the USA, and to see how they were developing. The book is able to achieve that goal in an integrated way; rather better than the Workshops, though in a much less personal way. The authors have taken the opportunity provided by the presentations and discussions at the Workshops to revise their thoughts in the light of each other's work and the comments made by the other participants.

The first three chapters provide our introduction and the framework with which to approach the rest of the book.

The chapter by Ewan Sutherland is an introduction to the issues at the intersection between information technology and business strategy. It attempts to put the issues raised into their appropriate contexts. It also identifies a wide range of works which readers can follow up in particular areas should they require more detail.

Yves Morieux examines the influence which the use of information technology has on strategic analysis; the basis of the formulation of all good business strategies.

Bjarte Frøyland, from Norway, looks at a very different area. He examines how information technology is affecting the operation of political activities. Here, the strategic viewpoint is in marked contrast to that taken in commerce and industry. It is an area which may have a significant effect on us all, and one in which Scandinavians have played a leading part in identifying and voicing public concerns.

The following four chapters consider issues related to the selection of information systems and to the planning processes involved.

Arjen Wassenaar examines the links which can be achieved between a business strategy and the process of information systems planning, in order to help formulate plans.

Robyn Chandler looks at the traditional techniques of systems analysis and shows how and why these fail to accomodate the fast changing demands of strategic action in business.

Jo van Engelen examines the influence of information systems on the success of a product in a particular market. He presents a very elegant model, drawn from physics, which he uses to explain the complex relationships and to measure the likely effect of information systems.

Reviewing current practice in the UK, Juliet Sheppard describes the different approaches taken by senior managers to the management of IT at the strategic level.

The next section of three chapters looks at the implementation of information systems for strategic advantage.

John Fripp describes a range of uses of strategic information systems which match the popular image. He also provides an insight into the other issues in the firms which have contributed to their success.

Mark Ebers and Hans-Dieter Ganter discuss the complex issue of integrated information systems.

Lynne Baxter and James McCalman show how the application of IT has affected the means of control and the organisation structures in multinational entreprises.

The next section deals with value adding activities including networks.

In the only contribution from the USA, Yannis Bakos explains how information systems, which extend beyond the conventional boundaries of organisations, can be used for strategic purposes. These interorganisational systems are seen to be creating markets for the more efficient exchange of information. This work is based on case studies from the USA, but this is understandable given that national as well as organisational boundaries are being eroded.

A well known area of innovation in the use of information technology is in the French Minitel service, and this provides part of the background to the chapter by Marie-Christine Monnoyer and Jean Philippe. They demonstrate how French companies have created new business activities through the use of value added networks.

Gillian Marcelle reports on work from the Federal Republic of Germany where political deregulation of the telecommunications industry is combining with new technological openings to create many commercial opportunities. She explains how three German companies are coping with, and adapting to, these strategic opportunities in the value added network market.

Value added networks provide an important element in the chapter by Nickolai Petkov and Filip Ivanov from Bulgaria. They explain how they use remote database systems and local expert systems to help in the process of strategic planning in the shipping business.

The final chapter, our conclusion, is presented by Per Blenker and Andrea Pontiggia. It is based on a complex and wide ranging discussion at the Workshops on whether information technology has a 'dialectical' relationship with business strategy, i.e. that the two are fundamentally opposed to one another. They were therefore set the task of closing the book by determining whether this was true, showing the extent to which IT could be seen as a benefit or a curse for business strategists, and how this affects the role of managers of information systems departments.

Taken together these chapters represent a broad spectrum of activities from a range of countries, which adds to our understanding of the development of strategic information technology in Europe.

We would like to acknowledge the important contribution made by the participants who are not listed here, and by Gerry van Dyck and the other administrators of the European Institute for Advanced Studies in Management in Brussels.

Ewan Sutherland   Yves Morieux
Stirling   Paris

Part I
Frameworks

1

The Meaning of Strategic Information Technology - an analysis of the literature

Ewan Sutherland

There has been rapid growth in the use of the phrases such as strategic information systems and competitive advantage through IT. These are used by consultants, suppliers and even some firms to signify a new set of applications of IT demonstrably linked to business strategy. However, it is clear that the term strategic is being used in ways which are inconsistent and sometimes misleading, perhaps even willfully so.

The reasons for the interest in strategic information technology are many and varied, they include the almost insuperable difficulties of cost benefit analysis, and the misalignment between expenditure on IT and organisational goals. Many firms feel that their information systems departments cannot continue to function in isolation from their business strategy because of the effect that the use or misuse of IT might have, and because of the high cost of many IT programmes. Mechanisms to link the use of IT and business strategy are not new, and in some cases have been around for many years. [104,149] What is new, however, is the emphasis on the contribution of IT to business strategy.

Business strategy

Over many years, an increasing importance has come to be attached to the use of strategy in business. [26] The idea of strategy is most closely associated with warfare, exemplified by Clausewitz; Napoleon and Wellington had strategies for the conduct of their military campaigns. The idea of strategy was utilised for business, for example, by Chandler [42] who showed its connection with the growth of industry in the USA. Levitt went on to show the necessity for strategic vision in business. [153]

3

Frameworks

 A corporate strategy is a pattern of decisions determining and revealing the objectives, purposes or goals of a company. It gives rise to the major policies and plans for achieving those goals and defines the range of business activities which the company intends to pursue. It also covers the kind of economic and human organisation the company is or intends to be and the nature of the economic, social and cultural contribution it intends to make to its shareholders, employees, customers and the communities within which it operates. A distinction can be drawn between a corporate and a business strategy in the level at which they are applied; the overall strategy of a corporation compared with the strategy used in a strategic business unit (SBU).

Many methods and approaches exist for the formulation of a business or corporate strategy. [1,4,8,9,81,100,126,185,204,227,231,239,240,250, 263] Quinn *et al.* have brought together much of the current literature on business strategy. [214] Taking regional views, Ohmae [197] has examined business strategy as seen from a Japanese perspective, while Hunsicker [119] has looked at practice in Europe.

A number of populist authors have drawn on specific aspects of business strategy, or given strategy a more important role in achieving business success. Peters and his co-authors put great stress on strategy as part of general guidance for managers. [204,205,206] Porter devised and applied the value chain for analysing businesses. [207,208,210] This extra boost to the significance of business strategy has influenced the importance attached to business strategy in the arguments for IT.

Links with information technology

 It is possible to identify four major categories of overlap between the use of information technology and strategy (used in its widest sense) [6,13,14, 70,83,122,146,243,249,251]

- IT considered in the formulation of business strategy
- IT used in the implementation of business strategy
- strategic planning within IT functional units
- IT used to help in the formulation of business strategy

Of course, there is also the case where there is no overlap, where decisions concerning IT are *ad hoc*, in that they are dealt with one at a time. Decisions about whether requests for new systems or changes to existing systems can be met are decided on availability of resources and whether the IT department wants, or feels obliged, to meet them.

It is necessary to justify the technological perspective used in this classification, since an alternative basis would be information, e.g., information resource management (IRM). Apart from its less than spectacular success, IRM still has a strong technological aspect. Indeed, the whole field of information systems has a considerable technological bias and is, to a very large extent, driven by technological forces. Moreover, there is no satisfactory information-based framework. [64,65,235,248,253]

Many of the problems which arise in relating information technology to business strategy, and vice versa, have already been considered in the application of other technologies - mainly industrial process and product research and development. [5,11,12,20,21,33,67,79,80,84,85,89,90, 91, 105,115,128,161,165,186,213,230,236,238,254,256,257,258,266,272] Porter has applied his value chain to the general area of technology in business. [209,211] Regional perspectives have also been produced. [30, 196,198]

Earl identifies four ways in which IT can be used strategically; to improve productivity and performance, to enable new ways of managing and organising, to gain competitive advantage and to develop new businesses. [70] This range of applications is indicative of the problem of defining strategic information technology.

[margin note: 4 points IT use strat.]

IT planning

IT planning describes those circumstances where planning of the allocation of resources is made within the information systems (IS) department without regard to the overall business strategy, perhaps, even in ignorance of it. That is, individual requests from departments or managers for new systems or modifications to existing systems are treated on their own merits within total resources allocated to IT, rather than in some framework which reflects corporate objectives. The emphasis is on the building infrastructures and on ensuring technical compatability of systems. [97]

[margin note: def]

These problems of coordinating uses and users of information technology result from the merging of different technologies and application areas. The main targets are cooperation and consolidation between the departments and individuals responsible for conventional information systems, office automation and telecommunications. McFarlan and McKenney have warned of the organisational problems of having islands of IT within a firm having different and, frequently, conflicting responsibilities. [179]

The reasons for resource planning are: the scarcity of resources, high cost, the complexity of IT, the need to control the uptake of IT (especially the tendency towards diversity of systems), the desire for greater diffusion of IT and the ever shortening replacement cycles. There is also the recognised need to project technological trends into the future in order to anticipate developments [16], e.g., artificial intelligence. [217]

Perhaps the greatest problem at this level, or any other, is financial control and particularly cost benefit analysis, which bedevils so much of IT. Without charging or equivalent mechanisms it is almost impossible to control the operation of an IS department and the use of IT. [43,194]

McFarlan has advocated a portfolio approach to applications and developments of IS in order to achieve a spread of risks. [176]

An important and as yet unresolved issue is how to fit information systems to the requirements of individual and collective users [34,46,52, 157,189]. There have been many attempts to review the post-implementation success of IS, usually focusing on organisational rather than technical issues. [59,110, 111]

This category of planning is inherently limited by not being linked to business strategy, it can go in the wrong direction, or can give the wrong emphasis.

Strategic implementation

The intention of linking IT planning to business strategy, to the extent of using the strategy to formulate guidelines for IT expenditure, arises from several problems; the possible effects on strategy of the use of IT, cost, long lead times, and the need to reinforce business strategy, e.g., low cost production.

Where the business strategy is explicitly known in the information systems department it can be used to develop a plan for the implementation of information systems, including reviews of existing systems and the identification of opportunities for the use of information systems. Often this planning is undertaken in conjunction with senior managers in order to ensure that there is a strategic fit.

McKenney and McFarlan have devised a matrix of the strategic importance of current applications and the the strategic importance of applications under development. The framework indicates how information technology should be managed. [178]

A series of methodologies exist to link the selection of IS applications to business goals, notably IBM's Business Systems Planning (BSP). [120] There are a number of other such techniques [93,200], e.g., Business

Information Control Methodology (BICS) [136,273], Strategic Information Systems Planning [23] and James Martin's strategic methodology for databases. [173] Methodologies also exist for telecommunications planning. [40,44,113,133,155,244,264]

Perhaps the best known is Rockart's Critical Success Factors Methodology, which was developed to allow senior managers to play a greater role in devising plans for the development of IT. Individually, it aimed to overcome the problem of pumping information indiscriminantly at managers. [2,52] Collectively, it aimed at identifying the critical success factors of these managers and converting them into prioritised lists of information systems. [18,170,171,172,188,219,220,222,224,237] The success of the CSF's methodology has resulted in a number of assessments of the approach. [24,57,190,274]

Strategic Value Analysis is a methodology developed at Arthur D Little Inc. [46] It is a structured methodology for the the design of information systems based on strategic business units (SBU's) using structured analysis. It recognises the need for an overall systems planning methodology because of the use of integrated databases, distributed data processing and end-user computing. This has since been enhanced, renamed Strategic Information Value Analysis (SIVA), and is used in a variety of industrial and commercial sectors. Eastlake, a consultant with Logica, has devised a similar methodology. [77]

Competitive advantage

It is possible to go a stage further in the integration of the application of IT and business strategy. This occurs where the formulation of the business strategy takes into account the possible use of IT in terms of gaining competitive advantage and developing new businesses. [19,35,37,75,82,88,92,96,99,106,123,147,158,166,181,182,183,195,215, 252,260,269] However, it is not always easy to differentiate this category from the last, since there is a gradual change in relative importance of IT in the formulation of the business strategy and a certain amount of overstatement by some proponents. [e.g., 184]

The focus can be on business, or technology, allowing sectoral views, e.g., banking [216,241] and telecommunications. [76,108,129,130]

The major problem in dealing with competitive advantage is that there are only analogies, cases and classifications; there are no methodologies for this approach. Moreover, there is a dearth of cases and a shortage of intellectual justifications. Too much emphasis is put on too few cases, especially American Hospital Supplies (AHS - now Baxter Healthcare) and McKesson. [7,101]

One systematic guide to finding applications which have a competitive edge in an existing business is by Porter and Millar [212] who use Porter's value chain. This tells managers to look at links to suppliers and clients and to seek to incorporate them into the business, e.g., coupling to suppliers with electronic data interchange (EDI) for 'Just-In-Time' (JIT) ordering.

Parsons identifies three levels at which competitive factors can be discussed: industry where changes occur which are fundamental to the nature of the industry, the firm where it influences the competitive forces facing the firm, and strategy where it supports the generic strategy of the firm or SBU. [203]

IT can be used to create new areas of business, to build entry barriers, to build in switching costs for clients, and to develop new products and new services. [177] It remains unclear whether applications exist in public administration. [53,175] The only obvious applications are in defence where, for example, the Strategic Defence Initiative (alias Star·Wars) is intended to give a competitive edge to the USA, over the USSR, through the use or threatened use of high technology.

The use of IT to gain competitive advantage is clearly an important means of justifying new investments at a time when applications are increasingly difficult to justify on conventional grounds of cost savings. However, it has to be qualified in two important respects, namely whether the advantage gained is genuine and whether it is sustainable. If it does not offer both, then it is not important and may even be a self-inflicted wound. There is reason to believe that in the banking and travel sectors investment in IT has done little more than instigate ever shorter cycles of equipment replacement, encourage gigantism, push up fixed costs and push down profit margins. Newspapers are now cheap to produce but still require editorial content and advertising revenue. Failure in these respects, e.g., Today (UK), shows that low cost is an insufficient basis to bring commercial success.

Much emphasis has been put on inter-organisational systems (IOS) where the technological advances in the integration of computing and communications can be applied to the strengthening of links between businesses, with important consequences for competitive performance. [15,17,36]

Computer assistance

Computers have been recognised as being useful in the development of strategic planning for some time [10,28,51,55,112,191,202,226,265], albeit in the face of opposition. [60,62,271] The formulation of business strategy requires information that is from external sources, or inexact, or both, and requires support for decision makers through a system which allows the testing of different options. For example, strategic intelligence systems which are used to gather information about suppliers, clients and rivals. [118,138,139,187]

Keen and Scott Morton [135] showed that models rather than just information are necessary to answer the 'what if?' questions of management control; they coined the term decision support systems (DSS). The need to support decision makers in strategy formulation is even greater. [68,114,116, 141,142,145]

The Profit Impact of Marketing Strategy (PIMS) system is a combination of inter-organisational system, database and decision support system. By allowing firms to contribute information supplied anonymously to a database on marketing, and by building models in addition to the data, a formidable tool has been created for the analysis of marketing strategies. [109,156,160,259]

There is a growing market in boardroom or 'executive information systems' comprising impressive systems of graphic displays to help senior executives understand information and, through better understanding, reach better decisions.

Control

Behind the discussion of strategic information technology lies the issue of control; who should manage IT? Is IT is a technical function at the level of the corporatation, the strategic business unit or organisational unit? Can IT be transferred to general managers or should specialists have a managerial role to play? There is a growing tendency to see the future of IS departments as federal in nature. [25,150]

The growth in end user computing (EUC) is difficult to interpret. It helps reverse the historical stranglehold of the IS department by decentralising, and may help to identify opportunities for the use of IT. [94] However, it is not immediately obvious that decentralised EUC and close coordination with business strategy can be readily achieved. [267]

There have been many studies of the sociology of information systems which emphasise the importance of non-technical factors. [e.g., 48,121,137,148,167,168,246,247] There have also been specific evaluations of the role of the information systems department [169,229] and of the attitudes of end-users. [78,86,107,124,125,199,218,223]

The connection between business strategy and organisational culture has been shown [32,232] and the links with the use of IT added. [245] It is relatively easy, if expensive, to change the IT equipment and software. A business strategy can be changed, though this takes a little longer. However, slowest of all is a change of the organisational culture.

It is clear that some IT managers want to become IT directors sitting on the main board. The question is whether firms really want IT managers to have a wider role; which turns on the question of how well IT departments are run and how much IT managers know about general business activities. It could be the old politician's solution to problems at home by turning abroad for success. At the same time, Dearden has argued that the management of IT, now that it has been linked to business strategy, can safely be entrusted to Masters of Business Administration (MBAs), with technical specialists relegated to their laboratories. [63,87] How this balance will work out is difficult to predict. There will always be a battle between business specialists and technical specialists.

The issue of control requires a more extensive consideration. It will be necessary to see how far strategic IT is being used as a lever in organisational politics.

Conclusion

Strategic information technology is in danger of being categorised as hype, and is yet another example of the IT industry's remarkable ability to produce shooting stars, such as MIS [61] and IRM. [3] Moreover, the elasticity of the term is such that one must know what one means, even if one is only trying to mislead. Even greater care should be taken in trying to interprete what others might mean.

Nolan has emphasised the historical development and diffusion of applications of IT in the management and control of IT. This is best known through his 'stages of growth' model, initially with four but later extended to six stages. [98,192,193] In a similar way it would be possible to view three of the four categories identified above as a 'stages of growth' model, showing a progression from near anarchy, through internal coordination, to the use of IT as a strategic weapon. However, the number and variety of examples are still too few to allow this to be suggested in a serious way. In particular, it is not at all clear how strategic IT is being developed in Europe, and how that differs from the USA and Japan.

The research required includes more case studies over a broader range of industries and geographical scope, with regional comparisons. On this should be built a more systematic view of strategic information technology, in terms of models and methodologies, and of its effect on market segmentation and industrial location.

It is inadequate to look at the changes wrought by the adoption and use of IT, or to talk vaguely of the information economy. [45] Instead, it is necessary to provide the tools for managers, whether business managers or managers of IT departments. [151,242,275]

References

1   Abell, D F "Defining the Business" Prentice-Hall, Englewood Cliffs, NJ, USA, 1980).

2   Ackoff, Rusell L "Management Misinformation Systems" *Management Science (USA)* **14** (4) pp 147-156, December 1967.

3   Akers, J "SMR Forum - A Responsible Future - an address to the computer industry" *Sloan Management Review (USA)* **26** (1) pp 53-57, Fall 1984.

4   Allen, M G "Strategic Planning with a Competitive Focus" *McKinsey Quarterly (USA)* Autumn 1978.

5   Allen, T J "Managing the Flow of Technology" MIT Press, Cambridge, MA, USA, 1977.

6   Anderson, T A "Coordinating Strategic and Operational Planning" *Business Horizons (USA)* pp 49-55, Summer 1965.

7   Anon. "Foremost McKesson - the computer moves distribution to centre stage" *Business Week (USA)* 7 December 1981.

8   Ansoff, H Igor "Business Strategy" Penguin Books, Harmondsworth, UK, 1969.

9   Ansoff, H Igor "Implanting Strategic Management" Prentice-Hall, Englewood Cliffs, NJ, USA, 1984.

10 Ansoff, H Igor "Competitive Strategy on the Personal Computer" *Journal of Business Strategy (USA)* **6** (3) pp 28-36, 1986.

11 Ansoff, H Igor "Strategic Management of Technology" *Journal of Business Strategy (USA)* **7** (3) pp 28-39, 1987.

12 Ansoff, H Igor and Stewart, John M "Strategies for Technology-based Business" *Harvard Business Review (USA)* **45** (6) pp 71-83, November 1967.

13 Anthony, R N "Planning and Control Systems - a framework for analysis" Harvard University Press, USA, 1965.

14 Bakos, J Yannis and Treacy, Michael E "Information Technology and Corporate Strategy - a research perspective" *MIS Quarterly (USA)* **10** (2) pp 107-119, June 1986.

15   Barrett, S and Konsynski, Benn "Inter-organisation Information Sharing Systems" *MIS Quarterly (USA)* **6** (4) pp 93-104, December 1982.

16   Benjamin, Robert I "Information Technology in the 1990s - a long range planning scenario" *MIS Quarterly (USA)* **6** (2) pp 11-31, June 1982.

17   Benjamin, Robert I "When Companies Share, It's Virtually a New Game" *Information Systems News (USA)* p 24, 26 December 1983.

18   Benjamin, Robert I; Dickinson, Charles and Rockart, John F "Changing Role of the Corporate Information Systems Officer" *MIS Quarterly (USA)* **9** (3) pp 177-188, September 1985.

19   Benjamin, Robert I; Rockart, John F; Scott Morton, Michael S and Wyman, John "Information Technology - a strategic opportunity" *Sloan Management Review (USA)* **25** (3) pp 3-10, 1984.

20   Birnbaum, Philip H "Strategic Management of Industrial Technology - a review of the issues" *IEEE Transaction on Engineering Management (USA)* **EM-31** (4) pp 186-191, November 1984.

21   Bitondo, Domenic and Frohman, Alan L "Linking Technology and Business Planning" *Research Management (USA)* pp 19-23, November 1981.

22   Bogorya, Y "Communicating in the Future - managing in the information society" *Management Decision (UK)* **23** (5) pp 37-41, 1985.

23   Bowrage, John "Linking Business Strategy and Information Technology" *Arthur Young Business Review (UK)* no 11 pp 12-16, 1985.

24   Boynton, Andrew C and Zmud, Robert W "An Assessment of Critical Success Factors" *Sloan Management Review (USA)* **25** (4) pp 17-29, 1984.

25   Boynton, Andrew C and Zmud, Robert W "Information Technology Planning in the 1990s - direction for practice and research" *MIS Quarterly (USA)* **11** (1) pp 59-71, March 1987.

26   Bracker, J "The Historical Development of the Strategic Management Concept" *Academy of Management Review (USA)* **5** (2) pp 219-224, April 1980.

27   Brancheau, James C and Wetherbe, James C "Key Issues in Information Systems Management" *MIS Quarterly (USA)* **11** (1) pp 23-45, 1987.

28   Breath, Cynthia Mathis and Ives, Blake "Competitive Information Systems in Support of Pricing" *MIS Quarterly (USA)* **10** (1) pp 85-93, March 1986.

29   Brownlee, D T and Macbeth, D K "The Strategic Management of Technology - integrating technology supply and demand perspectives" *European Management Journal* **7** (1) pp 71-83.

30   Buffa, Elwood S "Meeting the Competitive Challenge" Dow Jones-Irwin, Illinois, USA, 1984.

31   Bullinger, Hans-Jörg and Niemeier, Joachim "Computer Integrated Business - corporate and information systems management in competitive environments" pp 1-14 in *Eurinfo '88; proceedings of the first European conference on information technology for organisational systems, Athens, Greece, 16-20 May, 1988,* edited by H-J Bullinger *et al.* North-Holland, Amsterdam, 1988.

32   Burgelman, Robert A "A Model of the Interaction of Strategic Behaviour, Corporate Context and the Concept of Strategy" *Academy of Management Review (USA)* **8** (1) pp 61-70, 1983.

33   Burgelman, Robert A "Managing Corporate Entrepreneurship - new structures for implementing technological innovation" in *Technology in the Modern Corporation - a strategic perspective*, edited by Mel Horwitch Pergamon Press, New York, 1986.

34   Camillus, John C and Lederer, Albert L "Corporate Strategy and the Design of Computerised Information Systems" *Sloan Management Review (USA)* **26** (3) pp 35-42, Spring 1985.

35   Canning, R "Developing Strategic Information Systems" *EDP Analyzer (USA)* **22** (5) pp 1-12, 1984.

36   Cash, James I and Konsynski, Benn R "IS Redraws Competitive Boundaries" *Harvard Business Review (USA)* **63** (2) pp 134-142, March 1985.

37   Cash, James I; Konsynski, Benn R and Mather, P W C "Emerging Strategic Use of Information Systems Technology" pp 665-678 in *Proceedings of the Seventeenth Hawaii International Conference on System Sciences, January 1984*.

38   Cecil, John L and Hall, Eugene A "When IT Really Matters to Business Strategy" *McKinsey Quarterly (USA)* Autumn 1988, pp 2-26.

39   Copeland, Duncan G and McKenney, James L "Airline Reservation Systems - lessons from history" *MIS Quarterly (USA)* **12** (3) pp 353-370, 1988.

40   Chakraborty, Samir "Strategic Planning for Telecommunications - a systems approach" *Long Range Planning (UK)* **14** (5) pp 46-55, October 1981.

41   Charalambides, Leonidas C "Designing Communication Support Systems for Strategic Planning" *Long Range Planning (UK)* **21** (6) pp 93-101, 1988.

42   Chandler, Alfred D "Strategy and Structure - Chapters in the History of American Industrial Enterprise" MIT Press, Cambridge, MA, USA, 1962.

43   Ciborra, C U "Reframing the Role of Computers in Organisations - the transactions costs approach" pp 57-69 in *Proceeding of the Sixth International Conference on Information Systems Indianapolis, 16-18 December 1985*, edited by L Gallegos.

44   Clemons, Eric K; Keen, Peter G W and Kimbrough, Steven O "Telecommunications and Business Strategy - basic variables for design" pp 707-717 in *Proceedings of the National Computer Conference,* edited by Dennis J Frailey, AFIPS, Reston, VA, USA, 1984.

45   Cleveland, Harlan "Information an a Resource" *McKinsey Quarterly (USA)* pp 37-41, Summer 1983.

46   Cooper, Randolph B and Swanson, E Burton "Management Information Requirements Assessment - the state of the art" *Data Base (USA)* **11** (2) pp 5-16, 1979.

47   Cortada, James W "Strategic Data Processing - considerations for management" (Prentice-Hall, Englewood Cliffs, NJ, USA, 1984).

48   Crandell, George M "Why EDP Projects Miscarry" *McKinsey Quarterly (USA)* pp 67-74, Summer 1978.

49   Culnan, Mary J and Swanson, E Burton "Research in Management Information Systems, 1980-1984 - points of work and reference" *MIS Quarterly (USA)* **10** (3), pp 289-301, 1986.

50   Curtice, Robert M "Strategic Value Analysis - a modern approach to systems and data planning" Prentice-Hall, Englewood Cliffs, New Jersey, USA, 1987.

51   Cymbala, R J "Good Information Can Feed the Strategic Planning Process" *International Management Europe (UK)* **39** (4) pp 62-64, April 1984.

52   Daniel, R D "Management Information Crisis" *Harvard Business Review (USA)* **39** (5) pp 111-121, September 1961.

53   Danziger, J N; Dutton, W H; Kling, R and Kraemer, K L "Computers and Politics - high technology in American Local Government" Columbia University Press, New York, USA, 1982.

54   Davenport, Thomas H; Hammer, Michael and Metsisto, Tauno J "How Executives Can Shape Their Company's Information Systems" *Harvard Business Review (USA)* **67** (2) pp 130-134, March-April 1989.

55   David, F R "Computer Assisted Strategic Planning in Small Business" *Journal of Systems Management (USA)* **36** (7) pp 24-34, July 1985.

56   Davis, David "SMR Forum - Computers and Top Management" *Sloan Management Review (USA)* **25** (3) pp 63-67, 1984.

57   Davis, G B "Comments on the Critical Success Factors Method for Obtaining Management Requirements in [an] Article by John F Rockart" *MIS Quarterly (USA)* **3** (3) pp 57-58, September 1979.

58   Davis, G B "Strategies for Information Requirements Determination" *IBM Systems Journal (USA)* **21** (1) pp 4-30, 1982.

59   Dawes, Geoffrey M "Information Systems Assessment - post implementation practice" *Journal of Applied Systems Analysis (UK)* **14** pp 53-62, April 1987.

60   Dearden, John "Myth of Real-Time Management Information" *Harvard Business Review (USA)* **44** (3) pp 123-132, May 1966.

61   Dearden, John "MIS is a Mirage" *Harvard Business Review (USA)* **50** (1) pp 90-99, January 1972.

62   Dearden, John "SMR Forum - Will the Computer Change the Job of Top Management?" *Sloan Management Review (USA)* **25** (1) pp 57-60, 1983.

63   Dearden, John "The Withering Away of the IS Organisation" *Sloan Management Review (USA)* **28** (4) pp 87-91, 1987.

64   Diebold, J "Information Resource Management - the new challenge" *Infosystems (USA)* pp 50-53, June 1979.

65   Diebold, J "IRM - New Directions in Management" *Infosystems (USA)* pp 41-42, October 1979.

66   Doll, D R "Strategic Planning" *Computerworld (USA)* **18** (15) pp 39-42, 11 April 1984.

67   Doz, Yves; Angelmar, Reinhard and Prahalad, C K "Technological Innovation and Interdependence" in *Technology in the Modern Corporation - a strategic perspective*, edited by Mel Horwitch, Pergamon Press, New York, 1986.

68   Dzubow, S R "Simulation and Strategic Planning - a case study effectiveness evaluation" *Record of Proceedings of the Seventeenth Annual Simulation Symposium, March 1984* pp 65-78. IEEE, New York, 1984.

69   Earl, Michael J (Editor) "Information Management - the strategic dimension" Oxford University Press, Oxford, 1988.

70   Earl, Michael J "IT and Strategic Advantage - a framework of frameworks" pp 33-53 in *Information Management - the strategic dimension*, edited by Michael J Earl, Oxford University Press, Oxford, 1989.

71   Earl, Michael J "Formulation of Information Systems Strategies - emerging lessons and frameworks" pp 157-175 in *Information Management - the strategic dimension*, edited by Michael J Earl, Oxford University Press, Oxford, 1989.

72   Earl, Michael J "Information Management - some strategic reflections" pp 275-291 in *Information Management - the strategic dimension*, edited by Michael J Earl, Oxford University Press, Oxford, 1989.

73   Earl, Michael J "Management Strategies for Information Technology". Prentice-Hall, Hemel Hempstead, 1989.

74   Earl, Michael J; Feeny, David; Hirschheim and Lockett, Martin "Information Technology, Strategy and Leadership" pp 242-253 in *Information Management - the strategic dimension*, edited by Michael J Earl, Oxford University Press, Oxford, 1989.

75   Earl, Michael J; Feeny, David; Lockett, Martin and Runge, David "IT, Competitive Advantage and Innovation - principles for senior managers" Research Report, OXIIM, Templeton College, Oxford, UK, 1988.

76   Earl, Michael, J and Runge, David A "Using Telecommunications-based Information Systems for Competitive Advantage" Research Report, OXIIM, Templeton College, Oxford, UK, 1987.

77   Eastlake, John Jeffrey "A Structured Approach to Computer Strategy" Ellis Horwood Ltd, Chichester, 1987.

78   Edstrom, Anders "User Influence and the Success of MIS Projects" *Human Relations (USA)* **30** (7) pp 569-608, 1977.

79   Eschenbach, T G and Geistauts, G A "Strategically Focused Engineering - design and management" *IEEE Transaction on Engineering Management (USA)* **EM-34** (2) pp 62-70, May 1987.

80   Ettlie, J E and Bridges, W P "Environmental Uncertainty and Organisational Technology Policy" *IEEE Transaction on Engineering Management (USA)* **EM-29** (1) pp 2-10, February 1982.

81   Evered, R "So What is Strategy?" *Long Range Planning (UK)* **16** (3) pp 57-72, June 1983.

82   Feeny, David "Creating and Sustaining Competitive Advantage from IT" pp 98-117 in *Information Management - the strategic dimension*, edited by Michael J Earl, Oxford University Press, Oxford, 1989.

83   Feeny, David E; Edwards, B R and Earl, Michael J "Complex Organisations and the Information Systems Function - a research study" Research Report, OXIIM, Templeton College, Oxford, UK, 1987.

84   Foster, Richard N "A Call for Vision in Managing Technology" *McKinsey Quarterly (USA)* pp 26-36, Summer 1982.

85   Foster, Richard N "Timing Technological Transitions" in *Technology in the Modern Corporation - a strategic perspective*, edited by Mel Horwitch, Pergamon Press, New York, 1986.

86   Franz, C R and Robey, D "An Investigation of User-Led System Design - rational and political perspectives" *Communications of the ACM (USA)* **27** (12) pp 1202-1209, December 1984.

87   Freedman, David H "Harvard MBAs could be Hazardous to IS Managers" *Infosystems (USA)* **33** (9) pp 26-28, September 1986.

88   Freedman, David H "Are We Expecting Too Much from Strategic IS?" *Infosystems (USA)* **34** (1) pp 22-24, January 1987.

89   Friar, John and Horwitch, Mel "The Emergence of Technology Strategy" in *Technology in the Modern Corporation - a strategic perspective*, edited by Mel Horwitch, Pergamon Press, New York, 1986.

90   Frohman, Alan L "Putting Technology into Strategy" *Journal of Business Strategy (USA)* **5** (4) pp 54-65, 1985.

91   Frohman, Alan L and Bitondo, Domenic "Coordinating Business Strategy and Technical Planning" *Long Range Planning (UK)* **14** (6) pp 58-67, December 1981.

92   Furer, D "Information as a Strategic Weapon" *Business Computer Systems (USA)* **5** (7) pp 35-37, 41, 44, 48, July 1986.

93   Gairard, M and Van Keer, G "Method of Elaborating the Information Systems Strategy" in *From Discourse to Method - Convention Informatique, 1986* **1** pp 375-76. AFCET, Paris, 1986.

94   Galliers, Robert "Information Technology Strategies Today - the UK experience" pp 179-201 in *Information Management - the strategic dimension*, edited by Michael J Earl, Oxford University Press, Oxford, 1989.

95   Gerrity, T P and Rockart, John F "End-User Computing - are you a leader or a laggard?" *Sloan Management Review (USA)* **27** (4) pp 25-34, Summer 1986.

96   Gerstein, M and Reisman, H "Creating Competitive Advantage with Computer Technology" *Journal of Business Strategy (USA)* **3** (1) pp 53-60, 1982.

97   Gibbons, T "Computer Strategy Planning" *Data Processing (UK)* **25** (7) pp 24-7, September 1983.

98   Gibson, C F and Nolan, Richard L "Managing the Four Stages of EDP Growth" *Harvard Business Review (USA)* **52** (1) pp 76-88, January 1974.

99   Giese, P "Using Information Technology to Capture Strategic Position" *Management Review (USA)* **73** (9) pp 8-11, September 1984.

100   Gluck, F W; Kaufman, S P and Walleck, A S "Strategic Management for Competitive Advantage" *Harvard Business Review (USA)* **58** (4) pp 154-161, July 1980.

101   Goligoski, Bob "Best Sellers" *Business Computer Systems (USA)* pp 24-32, May 1986.

102   Goodhue, Dale L; Quillard, Judith A and Rockart, J F "Managing the Data Resource - a contingency perspective" *MIS Quarterly (USA)* **12** (3) pp 373-391, 1988.

103   Gooding, Graham "Exploiting IT in Business Development - Ford in Europe" pp 87-97 in *Information Management - the strategic dimension*, edited by Michael J Earl, Oxford University Press, Oxford, 1989.

104   Gorry, A and Scott Morton, M "A Framework for Management Information Systems" *Sloan Management Review (USA)* **13** (1) pp 55-70, 1971.

105   Graham, Margaret B W "Corporate Research and Development - the latest transformation" in *Technology in the Modern Corporation - a strategic perspective*, edited by Mel Horwitch Pergamon Press, New York, 1986.

106   Griffiths, Catherine and Hochstrasser, Beat "Does Information Technology Slow You Down?" Research Report, Kobler Unit, Imperial College, London, November 1987.

107   Guthrie, A "Attitudes of User-Managers towards MIS" *Management Informatics* **3** (5), 1974.

108   Hall, Alix-Marie and Terren, Jean "An Effective Strategy for Information Delivery" *Journal of Business Strategy (USA)* **8** (1) pp 21-27, 1987.

109   Hambrick, D C; Macmillan, I C and Day, D L "Strategic Attributes and Performance in the BCG matrix - a PIMS-based analysis of industrial product business" *Academy of Management Journal (USA)* **25** (3) pp 510-531, 1982.

110 Hamilton, S and Charvany, N L "Evaluating Information System Effectiveness - Part 1 - comparing evaluation approaches" *MIS Quarterly (USA)* **5** (3) pp 55-69, September 1981.

111 Hamilton, S and Charvany, N L "Evaluating Information System Effectiveness - Part 2 -comparing evaluator viewpoints" *MIS Quarterly (USA)* **5** (4) pp 79-86, December 1981.

112 Hamilton, W and Moses, M "A Computer-based Corporate Planning System" *Management Science (USA)* **21** (2) pp 148-159, October 1974.

113 Hammer, Michael and Mangurin, Glenn E "The Changing Value of Communications Technology" *Sloan Management Review (USA)* **28** (2) pp 65-71, Winter 1987.

114 Henderson, John C "A Methodology for Identifying Strategic Opportunities for DSS" in *Managers, Micros and Mainframes - integrating systems for end-users*, edited by Matthias Jarke, John Wiley and Sons, Chichester, 1985.

115 Hettinger, W P "The Top Technologist Should Join The Team - the corporate office and board team that is" *Research Management (USA)* **25** (2) pp 7-10, March 1982.

116 Holloway, C and Pearce, J A "Computer Assisted Strategic Planning" *Long Range Planning (UK)* **15** (4) pp 89-93, August 1982.

117 Hubinette, Karl-Henrik "Organisation and Control of Development in Information Technology in Volvo" pp 233-234 in *Information Management - the strategic dimension*, edited by Michael J Earl, Oxford University Press, Oxford, 1989.

118 Huff, A S "Strategic Intelligence Systems" *Information and Management (Netherlands)* **2** (5) pp 187-196, November 1979.

119 Hunsicker, J Quincy "Vision, Leadership and Europe's Business Future" *McKinsey Quarterly (USA)* pp 22-39, Spring 1986.

120 IBM Corporation "Business Systems Planning - information systems planning guide" IBM, Armonk, USA July 1981.

121 Igersheim, R H "Management Response to an Information System" *Proceedings of the [US] National Computer Conference, 1976*, AFIPS, Reston, VA, 1976.

122 Ives, Blake and Hamilton, Scott and Davis, Gordon B "A Framework for Research in Computer-Based Management and Information Systems" *Management Science (USA)* **26** (9) pp 910-934, September 1980.

123 Ives, Blake and Learmonth, Gerard P "The Information System as a Competitive Weapon" *Communications of the ACM (USA)* **27** (12) pp 1193-1201, 1984.

124 Ives, Blake and Olson, Margrethe H "User Involvement and MIS Success - a review of research" *Management Science (USA)* **30** (5) pp 586-603, May 1984.

125 Ives, Blake; Olson, Margrethe H and Baroudi, Jack J "The Measurement of User Information Satisfaction" *Communications of the ACM (USA)* **26** (10) pp 785-793, October 1983.

126 James, Barrie G "SMR Forum - Strategic Planning Under Fire" *Sloan Management Review (USA)* **25** (4) pp 57-61, 1984.

127 Johnston, H Russell and Vitale, Michael R "Creating Competitive Advantage with Interorganisational Information Systems" *MIS Quarterly (USA)* **12** (2) pp 153-166, 1988.

128 Kantrow, A M "The Strategy/Technology Connection" *Harvard Business Review (USA)* **58** (4) pp 6-21, July 1980.

129 Keen, Peter G W "Competing in Time - using telecommunications for competitive advantage" John Wiley and Son, Chichester, 1987.

130 Keen, Peter G W "Communications in the 21st Century - telecommunications and business policy" *Organizational Dynamics (USA)* **10** (3) pp 54-67, 1981.

131 Keen, Peter G W "Strategic Planning for the New System" in *New Office Technology - human and organisational aspects*, edited by Harry J Otway and Malcolm Peltu, Frances Pinter, London, 1983.

132 Keen, Peter G W "Computers and Managerial Choice" *Organizational Dynamics (USA)* **14** (3) pp 35-49, 1985.

133 Keen, Peter G W "Highways and Traffic and building the telecommunications infrastructure" in *Managers, Micros and Mainframes - integrating systems for end-users,* edited by Matthias Jarke, John Wiley and Sons, Chichester, 1985.

134 Keen, Peter G W "Rebuilding the Human Resources of Information Systems" pp 254-273 in *Information Management - the strategic dimension,* edited by Michael J Earl, Oxford University Press, Oxford, 1989.

135 Keen, Peter G W and Scott Morton, M S "Decision Support Systems - an organisational perspective" Addison-Wesley, Reading, MA, USA, 1978.

136 Kerner, D V "Introduction to Business Information Control Study Methodology (BICS)" in *The Economics of Information Processing - Volume 1 - management perspectives,* edited by Robert Goldberg and Harold Lorin, John Wiley, New York, 1982.

137 Kiesler, Sara "The Hidden Messages in Computer Networks" *McKinsey Quarterly (USA)* pp 13-26, Summer 1987.

138 King, W R "Information for Strategic Planning - an analysis" *Information and Management (Netherlands)* **1** (2) pp 59-66, February 1978.

139 King, W R "Strategic Planning for Management Information Systems" *MIS Quarterly (USA)* **2** (2) pp 27-37, June 1978.

140 King, W R "Developing Strategic Business Advantage from Information Technology" in *Managing New Information Technology,* edited by Nigel Piercy, Croom Helm, London, 1986.

141 King, W R "Achieving the Potential of Decision Support Systems" *Journal of Business Strategy (USA)* **3** (3) pp 84-90, 1983.

142 King, W R "Planning for Strategic Decision Support Systems" *Long Range Planning (UK)* **16** (5) pp 73-78, October 1983.

143 King, W R "How Effective is your Information Systems Planning?" *Long Range Planning (UK)* **21** (5) pp 103-112, 1988.

144 King, W R; Hufnagel, Ellen and Grover, Varun "Using Information Technology for Competitive Advantage" pp 75-86 in *Information Management - the strategic dimension,* edited by Michael J Earl, Oxford University Press, Oxford, 1989.

145 King, W R and Rodriguez, J I "Participative Design of Strategic Decision Support Systems - an empirical assessment" *Management Science (USA)* **27** pp 717-726, 1981.

146 King, W R and Zmud, R W "Management Information Systems - policy planning, strategic planning and operational planning" pp 299-308 in *Proceedings of the Second International Conference on Information Systems, Cambridge, MA, USA, December 1982.*

147 Kislowski, R "Information Systems and Competitive Advantage" *Proceedings of the [US] National Computer Conference, 1985.* AFIPS, Reston, VA, USA, 1985.

148 Kraemer, Kenneth L and King, John Leslie "Computing and Public Organisations" *Public Administration Review (USA)* **48** pp 488-496, November 1986.

149 Kriebel, C H "The Strategic Dimension of Computer Systems Planning" *Long Range Planning (UK)* **1** (1) pp 7-12, September 1968.

150 La Belle, Antoinette and Nyce, H Edward "Whither the IT Organisation" *Sloan Management Review (USA)* **28** (4) pp 75-85, Summer 1987.

151 Leavitt, H J and Whisler, T L "Management in the 1980s" *Harvard Business Review (USA)* **36** (6) pp 41-48, November 1958.

152 Ledered, Albert L and Sethi, Vijay "The Implementation of Strategic Information Systems Planning Methodologies" *MIS Quarterly (USA)* **12** (3) pp 445-461, 1988.

153 Levitt, Theodore "Marketing Myopia" *Harvard Business Review (USA)* **48** (6) pp 76-84, November 1960.

154 Locklin, Ronald M "Choosing a Data Communications Network" *Journal of Business Strategy (USA)* **6** (3) pp 14-17, Winter 1986.

155 Lorin, Henry; Ball, Leslie D and Eloy, Gilbert "Interconnect Technology as a Management Challenge" *MIS Quarterly (USA)* **11** (4) pp 433-435, December 1987.

156 Lubatkin, Michael and Pitts, Michael "PIMS - Fact or Folklore" *Journal of Business Strategy (USA)* **3** (3) pp 38-43, 1983.

157 Lucas, H R "Alternative Structures for the Management of Information Processing" in *The Economics of Information Processing - Volume 2 - operations programming and software models,* edited by Robert Goldberg and Harold Lorin, Wiley Interscience, New York, 1982.

158 Lucas, Henry C and Turner, Jon A "A Corporate Strategy for the Control of Information Processing" *Sloan Management Review (USA)* **26** (3) pp 25-36, Spring 1982.

159 McGee, John and Thomas, Howard "Technology and Strategic Management - a research review" pp 7-32 in *Information Management - the strategic dimension,* edited by Michael J Earl, Oxford University Press, Oxford, 1989.

160 Macmillan, I C; Hambrick, D C and Day, D L "The Product Portfolio and Profitability - a PIMS-based analysis of industrial-product business" *Academy of Management Journal (USA)* **25** pp 732-755, 1982.

161 Maidique, Modesto A and Hayes, Robert H "The Art of High-Technology Management" *Sloan Management Review (USA)* **25** (2) pp 17- 32, 1984.

162 Mainelli, Michael R and Miller, David R "Strategic Planning for Information Systems at British Rail" *Long Range Planning (UK)* **21** (4) pp 65-75, 1988.

163 Malone, Thomas W; Yates, Joanne and Benjamin, Robert I "Electronic Markets and Electronic Hierarchies" *Communications of the ACM (USA)* **30** (6) pp 484-497, June 1987.

164 Malone, Thomas W; Yates, Joanne and Benjamin, Robert I "The Logic of Electronic Markets" *Harvard Business Review (USA)* **67** (3) pp 166-170, May-June 1989.

165 Mansfield, E and Wagner, S "Organisational and Strategic Factors Associated with Probabilities of Success in Industrial R&D" *Journal of Business (USA)* **48** pp 179-198, 1975.

166 Marchand, Donald and Horton, Forest "Infotrends - profiting from your information resources" John Wiley & Sons, New York, 1987.

167 Markus, M Lynne "Implementation Politics - top management support and user involvement" *Systems, Objectives, Solutions (USA)* pp 203-215, 1981.

168 Markus, M Lynne "Power, Politics and MIS implementation" *Communications of the ACM (USA)* **26** (6) pp 430-444, June 1983.

169 Markus, M Lynne and Bjørn-Andersen, Niels "Power Over Users - its exercise by systems professionals" *Communications of the ACM (USA)* **30** (6) pp 498-504, June 1987.

170 Martin, E W "Critical Success Factors of Chief MIS/DP Executives" *MIS Quarterly (USA)* **6** (2) pp 1-9, June 1982.

171 Martin, E W "Critical Success Factors of Chief MIS/DP executives - an addendum" *MIS Quarterly (USA)* **6** (4) pp 79-81, December 1982.

172 Martin, E W and Wheeler, B R "Planning, Critical Success Factors and Management Information Requirements" *MIS Quarterly (USA)* **4** (4) pp 27-38, December 1980.

173 Martin, James "Strategic Data-Planning Methodologies" Prentice-Hall, Englewood Cliffs, NJ, USA, 1982.

174 Matheson, Steve "Implementing an IT Strategy - the UK Inland Revenue" pp 202-209 in *Information Management - the strategic dimension,* edited by Michael J Earl, Oxford University Press, Oxford, 1989.

175 McCosh, Andrew "The Organisation, its Aims, and Using Information Technology to Achieve Them" *Information Technology and Public Policy (UK)* **4** (1) pp 23-35, September 1985.

176 McFarlan, F Warren "Portfolio Approach to Information Systems" *Harvard Business Review (USA)* **59** (5) pp 142-150, October 1981.

177 McFarlan, F Warren "Information Technology Changes the Way You Compete" *Harvard Business Review (USA)* **62** (3) pp 98-103, May 1984.

178 McFarlan, F Warren; McKenney, James L and Pyburn, P "The Information Archipelago - plotting the course" *Harvard Business Review (USA)* **61** (1) pp 145-156, January 1982.

179 McKenney, James L and McFarlan, F Warren "The Information Archipelago - Maps and Bridges" *Harvard Business Review (USA)* **60** (5) pp 109-119, September 1982.

180 McLean, E R and Soden, J V "Strategic Planning for MIS" John Wiley and Sons, New York, 1977.

181 McNurlin, Barbara Canning "Getting Ready for Strategic Systems" *EDP Analyzer (USA)* **24** (9) pp 1-11, September 1986.

182 McNurlin, Barbara Canning "Uncovering Strategic Systems" *EDP Analyzer (USA)* **24** (10) pp 1-11, October 1986.

183 Meyer, C B "Informatics - an element in business planning strategy" *Output (Switzerland)* **15** (9) pp 45-7, 19 September 1986.

184 Meyer, N Dean and Boone, Mary E "The Information Edge" McGraw-Hill, New York, 1987.

185 Miles, R E and Snow, C C "Organisation Strategy, Structure and Process" McGraw-Hill, New York, 1978.

186 Mitchell, Graham R "New Approaches for the Strategic Management of Technology" in *Technology in the Modern Corporation - a strategic perspective,* edited by Mel Horwitch, Pergamon Press, New York, 1986.

187 Montgomery, David B and Weinberg, Charles B "Toward Strategic Intelligence Systems" *Journal of Marketing (USA)* **43** (4) pp 41-52, Fall 1979.

188 Munro, M "An Opinion ... Comment on Critical Success Factors Work" *MIS Quarterly (USA)* **7** (3) pp 67-68, September 1983.

189 Munro, M C and Davis, G B "Determining Management Information Needs - a comparison of methods" *MIS Quarterly (USA)* **1** (2) pp 55-67, June 1977.

190 Munro, M C and Wheeler, B R "Planning Critical Success Factors and Management's Information Requirements" *MIS Quarterly (USA)* **4** (4) pp 27-38, December 1980.

191 Naylor, T "Effective Use of Strategic Planning, Forecasting and Modeling in the Executive Suite" *Managerial Planning (USA)* **30** (4) pp 4-11, January 1982.

192 Nolan, Richard L "Managing the Data Resource Function" West Publishing Co, St Paul, MN, USA, 1982.

193 Nolan, Richard L "Managing the Crises in Data Processing" *Harvard Business Review (USA)* **57** (2) pp 115-126, March 1979.

194 Nolan, Richard L and Dearden, John "How to Control the Computer Resource" *Harvard Business Review (USA)* **51** (6) pp 68-75, November 1973.

195 Notowidigdo, M H "Information Systems - weapons to gain competitive edge" *Financial Executive (USA)* **52** (2) pp 20-25, February 1984.

196 Nueno, Pedro and Oosterveld, Jan P "The Status of Technology Strategy in Europe" in *Technology in the Modern Corporation - a strategic perspective,* edited by Mel Horwitch, Pergamon Press, New York, 1986.

197 Ohmae, Kenichi "The Mind of the Strategist - business planning for competitive advantage" Penguin Books, Harmondsworth, UK, 1982.

198 Ohmae, Kenichi "The New Technologies - Japan's Strategic Thrust" *McKinsey Quarterly (USA)* pp 20-35, Winter 1984.

199 Olson, Margrethe H and Ives, Blake "User Involvement in Systems Design - an empirical test of alternative approaches" *Information and Management (Netherlands)* **4** (4) pp 183-195, 1981.

200 Orzell, F R and Ashmore, G M "Technology 'Architecture' Helps Secure Long-Range Information Resource Needs" *Data Management (USA)* **23** (3) pp 26-29, 45, March 1985.

201 Palmer, Colin "Using IT for Competitive Advantage at Thomson Holidays" *Long Range Planning (UK)* **21** (6) pp 26-29, 1988.

202 Palmer, J D and Aiken, P H "Normative Computer-Aided Strategic Planning for Large Organisations" in *Proceedings of the 1986 IEEE International Conference on Systems, Man and Cybernetics, October 1986,* IEEE, New York, 1986.

203 Parsons, Gregory L "Information Technology - a new competitive weapon" *Sloan Management Review (USA)* **25** (1) pp 3-15, 1983.

204 Peters, Thomas J "Thriving on Chaos" Free Press, New York, 1987.

205 Peters, Thomas J and Waterman, Robert H "In Search of Excellence" Harper and Row, New York, USA, 1982.

206 Peters, Thomas J and Austin, Nancy K "A Passion for Excellence and the leadership difference" William Collins Sons and Co, Glasgow, 1985.

207 Porter, Michael E "Competitive Strategy - techniques for analysing industries and competitors" Free Press, New York, 1980.

208 Porter, Michael E "Cases in Competitive Strategy" Free Press, New York, 1983.

209 Porter, Michael E "The Technological Dimension of Competitive Strategy" pp 1-33 in *Research on Technological Innovation, Management and Policy* 1, edited by R S Rosenbloom, JAI Press, Greenwich, CN, USA, 1983.

210 Porter, Michael E "Competitive Advantage - creating and sustaining superior performance" Free Press, New York, USA, 1985.

211 Porter, Michael E "Technology and Competitive Advantage" *Journal of Business Strategy (USA)* 5 (3) pp 60-79, 1985.

212 Porter, Michael E and Millar, Victor E "How Information Gives You Competitive Advantage" *Harvard Business Review (USA)* 63 (4) pp 149-160, July 1985.

213 Quinn, James Brian "Innovation and Corporate Strategy - managed chaos" in *Technology in the Modern Corporation - a strategic perspective,* edited by Mel Horwitch, Pergamon Press, New York, 1986.

214 Quinn, James Brian; Mintzberg, Henry and James, Robert M "The Strategy Process - concepts, contexts and cases" Prentice-Hall, Englewood Cliffs, NJ, USA, 1988.

215 Rackoff, Nick; Wiseman, Charles and Ullrich, Walter A "Information Systems for Competitive Advantage - implementation of a planning process" *MIS Quarterly (USA)* 9 (4) pp 285-294, December 1985.

216 Raphael, David E "Betting the Bank on Technology - technology strategic planning at Bank of America" *Long Range Planning (UK)* 19 (2) pp 23-30, 1986.

217 Rhines, Wally "Artificial Intelligence - out of the lab and into business" *Journal of Busines Strategy (USA)* 6 (1) pp 50-58, 1985.

218 Robey, D and Farrow, D L "User Involvement in Information System Development - a conflict model and empirical test" *Management Science (USA)* 28 (1) pp 73-85, 1982.

219 Rockart, John F "Chief Executives Define their Own Data Needs" *Harvard Business Review (USA)* 57 (2) pp 81-93, March 1979.

220 Rockart, John F "The Changing Role of the Information Systems Executive - a critical success factors perspective" *Sloan Management Review (USA)* 24 (1) pp 3-13, Fall 1982.

221 Rockart, John F "The Line Takes the Leadership - IS management in a wired society" *Sloan Management Review (USA)* 29 (4) pp 57-64, 1987.

222 Rockart, John F and Crescenzi, Adam C "Engaging Top Management in Information Technology" *Sloan Management Review (USA)* 25 (4) pp 3-16, 1984.

223 Rockart, John F and Flannery, L "The Management of End User Computing" *Communications of the ACM (USA)* 26 (10) pp 776-784, October 1983.

224 Rockart, John F and Scott Morton, M S "Implications of Changes in Information Technology for Corporate Strategy" *Interfaces (USA)* 14 (1) pp 84-95, January 1984.

225 Rockart, John F and Short, James E "IT in the 1990s - managing organizational interdependence" *Sloan Management Review (USA)* **30** (2) pp 7-17, Winter, 1989.

226 Rockart, John F and Treacy, M E "The CEO Goes On-line" *Harvard Business Review (USA)* **60** (1) pp 82-88, January 1982.

227 Rowe, A; Mason, R and Dickel, K "Strategic Management and Business Policy - a methodological approach" Addison-Wesley, Reading, MA, USA, 1982.

228 Runge, David and Earl, Michael J "Gaining Competitive Advantage from Telecommunications" pp 125-146 in *Information Management - the strategic dimension,* edited by Michael J Earl, Oxford University Press, Oxford, 1989.

229 Saunders, Carol S and Scamell, Richard W "Organisational Power and the Information Services Department - a re-examination" *Communications of the ACM (USA)* **29** (2) pp 142-147, February 1986.

230 Scarpello, Vida; Boulton, William R and Hofger, Charles W "Reintegrating Research and Development into Business Strategy" *Journal of Business Strategy (USA)* **6** (4) pp 49-56, Spring 1986.

231 Schoffler, S; Buzzell, R D and Heany, D F "Impact of Strategic Planning on Profit Performance" *Harvard Business Review (USA)* **52** (2) pp 137-145, March 1974.

232 Scholz, Charles "Corporate Culture and Strategy - the problem of strategic fit" *Long Range Planning (UK)* **20** (4) pp 78-87, August 1987.

233 Scott Morton, Michael "Strategy Formulation Methodologies and IT" pp 54-73 in *Information Management - the strategic dimension,* edited by Michael J Earl, Oxford University Press, Oxford, 1989.

234 Seddon, Derek "Experiences in IT Strategy Formulation - Imperial Chemical Industries PLC" pp 147-156 in *Information Management - the strategic dimension,* edited by Michael J Earl, Oxford University Press, Oxford, 1989.

235 Selig, Gad J "Approaches to Strategic Planning for Information Resource Management (IRM) in Multinational Corporations" *MIS Quarterly (USA)* **6** (2) pp 33-45, June 1982.

236 Sethi, Narendra K; Movsesian, Bert and Hickey, Kirk D "Can Technology be Managed Strategically?" *Long Range Planning (UK)* **18** (4) pp 89-99, 1985.

237 Shank, Michael E; Boynton, Andrew C and Zmud, Robert W "Critical Success Factors Analysis as a Methodology for MIS Planning" *MIS Quarterly (USA)* **9** (2) pp 121-129, June 1985.

238 Sommers, William P; Nemel, Joseph and Harris, John M "Repositioning with Technology - making it work" *Journal of Business Strategy (USA)* **7** (3) pp 16-77, 1987.

239 Steiner, G A "Strategic Planning" Free Press, New York, 1979.

240 Steiner, G A and Miner, J B "Management Policy and Strategy" Macmillan, New York, 1982.

241 Steiner, Thomas D and Teixeira, Diogo "Technology is more than Just a Strategy - the changing world of banking" *McKinsey Quarterly (USA)* pp 39-51, Winter 1988.

242 Strassmann, Paul A "Information Payoff - the transformation of work in the electronic age" Free Press, New York, 1985.

243   Sullivan, Cornelius H "Systems Planning in the Information Age" *Sloan Management Review (USA)* **26** (2) pp 3-12, 1985

244   Sullivan, Cornelius H and Smart, John R "Planning for Information Networks" *Sloan Management Review (USA)* **28** (2) pp 39-44, 1987.

245   Sutherland, Ewan and Morieux, Yves V H "Effectiveness and Competition - linking business strategy, organisational culture and the use of information technology" *Journal of Information Technology (UK)* **3** (1) pp 43-47, 1988.

246   Swanson, E B "Management Information Systems - appreciation and involvement" *Management Science (USA)* **21** (2) pp 178-188, 1974.

247   Swanson, N E "Power - a critical systems development factor" *Information and Management (Netherlands)* **9** (4) pp 209-213, 1985.

248   Synnott, W R and Gruber W H "Information Resource Management - opportunities and strategies for the 1980's", John Wiley and Sons, New York, 1982.

249   Taggart, William M and Tharp, Marvin O "A Survey of Information Requirements Analysis Techniques" *ACM Computing Surveys (USA)* **9** (4) pp 273-290, December 1977.

250   Taylor, Bernard "Strategic Planning - which style do you need?" *Long Range Planning (UK)* **17** (3) pp 51-62, April 1984.

251   Tranfield, David "Management Information Systems - an exploration of core philosophies" *Journal of Applied Systems Analysis (UK)* **10** pp 83-8, April 1983.

252   Treacy, Michael E "Toward a Cumulative Tradition of Research on Information Technology as a Strategic Business Factor" (Working Paper CISR #134, Sloan School of Management, MIT, USA, March, 1986).

253   Truath, E "Research-Oriented Perspective on Information Management" *Journal of Systems Management (USA)* **35** (7) pp 12-17, July 1984.

254   Van Gunsteren, Lex A "Planning for Technology as a Corporate Resource - a strategic classification" *Long Range Planning (UK)* **20** (2) pp 51-60, 1987.

255   Vitale, Michael R "The Growing Risks of Information Systems Success" *MIS Quarterly (USA)* **10** (4) pp 327-332, 1986.

256   Von Hippel, Eric A "Users as Innovators" *Technology Review (USA)* **80** (3) pp 3-11, January 1978.

257   Von Hippel, Eric A "Increasing Innovators' Returns from Innovation" pp 35-53 in *Research on Technological Innovation, Management and Policy* JAI Press, Greenwich, Connecticut, USA, 1983.

258   Von Hippel, Eric A "The Sources of Innovation" Oxford University Press, New York, 1988.

259   Wakerly, R G "PIMS - A Tool for Developing Competitive Strategy" *Long Range Planning (UK)* **17** (3) pp 92-97, June 1984.

260   Ward, John M "Integrating Information Systems into Business Strategies" *Long Range Planning (UK)* **20** (3) pp 19-29, June 1987.

261   Ward, John M "Information Systems and Technology Application Portfolio Management - an assessment of matrix-based analyses" *Journal of Information Technology (UK)* **3** (3) pp 205-215, 1988.

262   Warner, Timothy "Information Technology as a Competitive Burden" *Sloan Management Review (USA)* **29** (4) pp 55-61, 1987.

263   Wheelwright, S C "Strategy, Management and Strategic Planning Approaches" *Interfaces (USA)* **14** (1) pp 19-33, 1984.

264 White, N J "Telecommunications Strategy" pp 48-50 in *Conference on Telecommunications, Radio and Information Technology, May 1984*, IEE, London, 1984.

265 Whitney, G G "Business Strategy Simulation" *College Microcomputing (USA)* **1** (1) pp 39-43, 1983.

266 Wilson, Ian "The Strategic Management of Technology - corporate fad or strategic necessity" *Long Range Planning (UK)* **19** (2) pp 21-22, 1986.

267 Winski, Donald T "A Systems Strategy - in search of excellence" *Infosystems (USA)* **31** (1) pp 62-66, January 1984.

268 Wiseman, C. "Strategy and Computers" Dow Jones-Irwin, IL, USA, 1985.

269 Wiseman, C and Macmillan, I C "Creating Competitive Weapons from Information Systems" *Journal of Business Strategy (USA)* **5** (2) pp 42-49, Fall 1984.

270 Woodgate, H S "Implementing an IT Strategy in a Manufacturing Company" pp 39-45 in *Eurinfo '88; proceedings of the first European conference on information technology for organisational systems, Athens, Greece, 16-20 May, 1988*, edited by H-J Bullinger *et al.*, North-Holland, Amsterdam, 1988.

271 Wright, P "Computers, Change and Fear - an unholy trinity" *Management Decision (UK)* **22** (2) pp 31-35, 1984.

272 Wyman, John "SMR Forum - Technological Myopia - the need to think strategically about technology" *Sloan Management Review (USA)* **26** (4) pp 59-64, Summer 1985.

273 Zachman, J A "Business Systems Planning and Business Information Control Study - a comparison" *IBM Systems Journal (USA)* **21** (1) pp 31-53, 1982.

274 Zahedi, Fatemeh "Reliability of Information Systems based on the Critical Success Factors - Formulation" *MIS Quarterly (USA)* **11** (2) pp 187-203, June 1987.

275 Zmud, Robert W; Boynton, A C and Jacobs, G C "The Information Economy - a new perspective for effective information systems management" *Data Base (USA)* **18** (1) pp 17-23, 1986.

276 Zmud, Robert W and Lind, Mary R "The Use of Formal Mechanisms for Linking the Information Systems Function with End-Users" in *Managers, Micros and Mainframes and integrating systems for end-users*, edited by Matthias Jarke, John Wiley and Sons, Chichester, 1985.

Note: references 3, 19, 24, 34, 158, 220, 221, 243 and 272 are reprinted in *The Strategic Use of Information Technology*, edited by Stuart E Madnick, Oxford University Press, Oxford, 1987.

2
Strategic Analysis
and
Information Technology

Yves Morieux

The study of the relationship between business strategy and information technology is not new. In the beginning of the 1980s, the Harvard Business School first identified the logic of integrating information systems and the effect this had on industry along two main lines. [1]

- the rules of the competitive game and corporate strategies [2,3]
- the evolution of inter-organisational boundaries [4]

Parallel to this mapping of information technology onto industrial parameters, there emerged a symmetrical perspective; that of understanding the influence that business strategies should have on information systems and architectures. Investment in information technology (PCs, telecommunications and databases) were escaping from the financial assessments (ROI, NPV, etc.) as strategic perspectives were developed. These hinged on a comprehensive model of organisational data, aimed at permitting an assessment and development of information systems and architectures on the basis of business objectives. [5]

However, neither of these approaches went so far as to consider, in its full depth, the effect of the use of information technology on the most important tool of the industrial strategist, namely strategic analysis.

My purpose is to show that the fundamental clauses of strategic analysis are affected by the diffusion of information technology and to derive questions for further reflection.

Strategic analysis

Since the Second World War, the art of management can be seen as having evolved through three stages. [6]

1950s   Reconstruction and growth with priority being given to investments in production. Decentralisation and Management-By-Objectives (MBO) are the key concepts. Planning and forecasting of production capacity are viewed as equivalent.

1960s   Basic needs having been satisfied, priority is given to understanding and exploiting customers' needs and attitudes. Development of marketing and data processing allow a standardisation of means with a profit-centred differentiation.

1970s   In the face of excessive bureaucracy and the lack of a long term perspective, caused by planning which is excessively budgetary, there emerges the necessity of dividing the business into independent activity domains for planning purposes (n.b. the famous segmentation of General Electric into strategic business units). [7] So was created the first pillar of strategic analysis.

As strategic analysis evolved, it was reinforced by the concepts of experience curve and product life cycle. At the beginning of the 1980s industrial economics contributed direct investigation of the determinants of competitive intensity and competitive advantage in industrial sectors. Breadth was added by methodologies aimed at ensuring some degree of coherence between corporate goals and technological investments in terms of research and development, manufacturing, quality control, logistics and information systems. [8]

The various strategic analysis systems used by companies today draw on the same principles

- dividing a business into segments; strategic arbitrages will take place between these segments
- using relatively simple concepts that allow assessment of the strategic position of each segment and comparison of the segments
- posing a deterministic relationship between strategic position and financial performance

Strategic segmentation

The traditional terminology used by strategic analysts is varied; strategic domain, strategy centre, SBU, etc. All these terms will be treated here as synonymous, denoting a set of product lines that possess the same characteristics in terms of means to be operated (conception, fabrication, commercialisation, etc) and which, for this reason, face the same competitors. Each SBU is active on a strategic segment. A major consequence is that SBUs can be ascribed a specific strategy, independent from the strategy followed by others, in terms of pricing, quality and divestment. Strategic segmentation allows better focusing of corporate effort, the development of some form of forward-looking vision and tighter performance control.

Tools for strategic segmentation

Having defined the central function of segmentation in strategic analysis, its structure and conditions may be viewed as the basis for a model of industrial battles, including:

- the frontiers delimiting the battlefield (the strategic segment in which the SBU competes)
- a comprehensive or extensive definition of the antagonists, i.e. the various competitors (companies or domains of these), the sum of which defines the industry
- a description of the conditions of success within the battlefield

The process of formalisation of the basis for the model is both long and complex. A definition of the strategic segment that is too wide or too restictive would distort the assessment of the competitive position of the company and its rivals, thus leading to the adoption of inadequate strategies. Various indicators are used for assessing the degree of strategic interdependence between products or product lines. In addition to indicators that relate to commonalities of competitors, customers, pricing and quality, there exist a number of more complex indicators of interdependence dealing with substitutability, selective divestment and functional synergies. Documenting these indicators requires an in-depth study of markets and competitors.

Two perspectives are clearly used in this approach:

- an external perspective, relating to the nature of the demand
- an internal perspective, relating to the nature of the mechanisms used by companies to expoit the demand

It is at these levels that the effects of the diffusion of information technology are most significant.

External perspective

The main element of this perspective is that of the bases of competition, which can be defined as follows:

- characteristics of the expectations about the offer (including possible trade-offs between various characteristics), in as much as these expectations are critical for the market
- in as much as these characteristics enable those involved in purchasing to form some preferential ordering between the various offers

Industrial analysis and market research permit the identification of the bases of competition by market segment. According to a series of criteria, the market is divided into sets which, ideally, are such that the variance within a set is minimised and the variance between sets is maximised. The identification of these criteria and the division of the market into these sets or market segments draws on various approaches (technology and industrial economics, sociology, psychology and ethnology; systems and games theory, etc). In general, a single SBU deals with a number of market segments. The fit between the SBU's offer and the bases of competition that characterise each of its market segments constitute a critical element of the firm's competitiveness.

The growing role played by information in the optimisation of these processes is well-known:

- for example, the use of Minitels in France allows the acceleration and enriching of information from the field (salespersons, agents, distributors, retailers, etc) to the marketing decision-makers who can then adjust marketing strategies (see Chapter 12)
- acceleration and increased reliability of feedback information to the field, allowing rapid implementation of new marketing orientations (product mixes that maximise global profitability, modification and enhancement of selling arguments, etc.)

Internal perspective

The fundamental question raised within the framework of this perspective is 'what must be done to exploit profitably the bases of competition and to do this better than the competitors?' To answer this question requires the identification of the attributes of competitiveness specific to the strategic segment under consideration, often referred to as critical success factors.

The distinction between 'bases of competition' and 'critical success factors' may seem an artificial one, but an example helps. In the low end of the video recorder market, price is the basis of competition (i.e. this characteristic of the offer determines the final choice of consumers) while the corresponding key success factors relate to cost structure elements (development, fabrication, distribution, etc).

Each strategic segment can be related to a specific series of attributes of competitiveness which relate to research and development, marketing, sourcing, manufacturing, control, logistics, etc. In the case of lenses for professional TV cameras these attributes can be described in terms of technologies that must be mastered (e.g., optical physics) and know-how (e.g., monitoring of relationships with camera manufacturers through joint technological developments).

Whatever the strategic segment, corresponding key success factors can always be related to some generic parameters inherent in industrial mechanisms. The effect of information technology on those parameters, and therefore the influence that the technologies may have on the companies' performance *vis-à-vis* critical success factors, is already well documented. For example:

- improvement of performance control, based on the early detection of deviation from performance targets on remote sites [e.g., 9]
- improvements in cost structure, in terms of -
  conception: CAD with the help of databases that contain libraries of existing modules and components
  fabrication: connections between CAD and CAM, which limit fabrication errors
  inventory: theoretically it tends towards zero
- strengthening the links between clients and suppliers, by means of inter/trans-company networks, e.g., electronic data interchange (EDI) and inter-organisational systems (IOS) (see Chapter 11)
- enriching the offer through service integration
- developing simulations using more powerful and user-friendly spreadsheets and modelling packages

Implications

There is no doubt that IT may positively affect the performance of a firm *vis-à-vis* some key success factors. However, the effects of the use of IT within strategic segments goes beyond mere modifications of a competitive position. It affects the basis of strategic segmentation and strategic analysis.

If the military strategists are to be believed then 'the essence of strategy is the struggle for freedom of action' (General Beauffre). Taking a similar view in business, one finds a reliance on two assumptions as the basis of any analysis of business strategy:

- companies enjoy irreducible degrees of freedom
- the environment possesses irreducible levels of inertia

Considered in the light of the above analysis, these two premisses show the critical bearing of the strategic exploitation of information technology in terms of:

- reduction of information/reaction cycles, allowing an acceleration of strategy definition and implementation, whether offensive or defensive
- growing inter-dependencies
  - within the same company along and across value-added chains, thereby reducing the interdependencies between strategic segments; allocations of resources in terms of information and telecommunication technologies have effects that go beyond segment boundaries
  - between companies, thus contributing to the linking of industrial stakes

In other words there seem to be tendencies towards:

- a reduction in the levels of inertia (shortening of information cycles)
- a reduction in corporate degrees of freedom (both internal and external)

On the one hand, defining and implementing business strategies is made easier, because of enhanced information processing capabilities. On the other hand, finding independent bases for strategies is increasingly difficult because of growing linkages. While strategies are bound to be shorter-lived (since competitors can retaliate or react just as quickly). This shows that strategic degrees of freedom and industrial flexibility are not synonymous. The latter may well increase while the former decreases.

An obvious example is the situation of a manufacturer of electronic goods that has set up EDI links with a subcontractor for the supply of components. It has become easier to get a variety of specific customised circuits from the supplier, but changing the source of supply is much more difficult than in the past, because a lot of money and effort has been invested in a connection which goes beyond hardware and software. To make a comparison with mathematics, it seems that information and communication technologies have the following effects: the number of possible values that can be assumed by each variable increases (the components in the above) while the number of possible variables decreases (the suppliers). (see Chapter 15)

These types of evolution in terms of freedom and inertia can be felt at various levels. A growing number of activities show a move from the concept of product towards that of systems; service is increasingly the basis of differentiation. As a result, many companies purchase so-called platform products and then integrate a series of new functions into the platform, giving a lateral extension of the offer. For this new type of activity, i.e. the integrator, information is the key resource. Information technology and telecommunications alone allow the coordination of operations in which participants are increasingly interdependent The growing efforts that are made in the industry to reduce product development lead-time and enhance the competitiveness of new product creation processes provide another example. The key concept is design orientation towards re-utilisation and co-utilisation. A new constraint on product creation is to minimise components that will not be used elsewhere in the company. Very often this limitation is integrated into the CAD system. As a result, costs are reduced (economies of scale) but so are the degrees of freedom at the research and development level.

Conclusion

The reflections described in this paper relate to industrial contexts heavily influenced by information and telecommunication technologies. Although some of the remarks do not apply to some of the lagging sectors (e.g., fragmented industries), the main thrust cannot be neglected by strategic analysts. Not only the industrial context, but also the implicit bases of our strategic analyses along the premises of inertia and degrees of freedom, must be reconsidered in the light of the proliferation of information systems.

Does this affect the essence of strategy making? To give an adequate answer to this question, we must pay full attention to a critical distinction between strategic analysis and strategy itself. [10] This distinction, although paradoxical, is at the root of the success of any strategy. Unlike disciplines such as accounting, engineering or programming, strategy is not made up of set analytic or algorithmic principles; it is an art, used by organisations to define and pursue their objectives. As such, any strategy contains a great deal of subjectivity; the assessment of competitive intensity, of power balances and of possible ways to alter these is always the strategist's interpretation of reality (e.g., quantitative indices that measure competitive intensity within sectors are of limited validity beyond the purposes of comparison). The success of great strategists is often due to the specificity, i.e. subjectivity of their judgments; Iacocca of Chrysler or Calvet of Peugot perceived opportunities where others saw inexorable decline. In other words, a true strategy always consists of generating a process that leads to results opposed to the logic of facts. Many companies are still alive and well under the same leadership, although their business units have continuously been listed in the bottom-right cell of the various matrices that successive consultants have come up with. Which only shows that the companies' leaders were better strategists than the consultants they hired.

The objectivity of the analyses is a prerequisite for the business plan to succeed, yet the strategist's subjectivity is the only source of possible advantage against rivals. In other words, industrial changes caused by the diffusion of information systems along the dimensions of inertia and degrees of freedom are critical to the level of strategic analysis, but they do not alter the essence of business strategy.

References

1   McFarlan, F Warren; McKenney James L and Pyburn, P "The Information Archipelago - plotting the course" *Harvard Business Review* **61** (1) pp 145-156, 1982.
    McKenney, James L and McFarlan, F Warren "The Information Archipelago - Maps and Bridges" *Harvard Business Review* **60** (5) pp 109-119, September 1982.
2   McFarlan, F Warren "Information Technology Changes the Way You Compete" *Harvard Business Review* May-June 1984, **62** (3) pp 98-103.
3   Porter, Michael E and Millar, Victor E "How Information Gives you Competitive Advantage" *Harvard Business Review* July-August 1985, **63** (4) pp 149-160.

4 Cash, James I and Konsynski, Benn R "IS Redraws Competitive Boundaries" *Harvard Business Review* March-April 1985, **63** (2) pp 134-142.

5 Curtice, Robert V "Strategic Value Analysis - a modern approach to systems and data planning" Prentice Hall, Englewood Cliffs, NJ, 1987.

6 Ader, E "L'Analyse Stratégique Moderne et ses Outils" *Futuribles* Décembre 1983, pp 3-21.

7 Hax, A C and Majluf, N S "Strategic Management - an integrative perspecitve" Prentice-Hall, Englewood Cliffs, 1984.

8 Arthur D Little Inc "Strategic Management of Technology" Cambridge, MA, USA, 1981.

9 Bruns, W J and McFarlan, F Warren "Information Technology puts power in Control Systems" *Harvard Business Review* **55** (5) September-October 1987, pp 89-94.

10 Nadoulek, B "L'Intelligence Stratégique" CPE-Aditech, Paris, 1988.

3
Political Strategy
and
Information Technology

Bjarte Frøyland

While the other chapters in this book look at areas of business activity, this chapter is devoted to the effects of the use of information technology on politics. It identifies areas where political relationships are changing and where political action should be taken in accordance with the changed circumstances.

Politics and politicians have different objectives and time scales from entrepreneurs and private organisations. Moreover, the rationale of decision making and the definition of agenda within government tend to be more influenced by the need for consensus than by the efficiency requirements of private enterprise. The use of information technology in every facet of society might even change the norms by which political consensus is established.

Why politics?

Political institutions are formed to deal with community problems. The need for consensus building becomes prevalent where political decisions are concerned. The monopoly of political institutions within given areas of jurisdiction makes them especially vulnerable to embedded conflict. Consider the never ending negotiations on interest rates, where banks must have their say on policies made by the finance ministry. Similarly, government has an interest in industrial relations, where pay levels and lay-offs are recognised as a concern of governments throughout the world.

Cultural institutions, although community-based, may be challenged by alternative arrangements, while economic institutions prosper and die in the marketplace.

A political institution is global in scope. The cost-benefit calculations of any public institution go beyond the mere business rationale. The target is macro-economic efficiency for society at large. Moreover, most political institutions have regulatory responsibilities. The power of politics over market forces shows extreme durability if and when it can be established. It takes a Margaret Thatcher, once every 25 years, to change an existing equilibrium between government agencies and private enterprise.

People engage in political institutions out of necessity. Politics are required where a community interest cannot be entrusted to, or will not be performed by, any individual subject or group of subjects. [1]

Political institutions can be organised according to a variety of standards, though in most western countries the idea of participation through elected representatives has been the dominant one. Any limitation to this arrangement ought only to be based on macro-economic efficiency requirements, mainly in terms of professionalism and/or the optimal distribution of decisions.

We will get a better understanding of this hierarchy of principles for modern government if we consider the semiotic difference between politics and policies. Politics refers to the process of decision making within governmental institutions, this is defined by our requirements for participation, establishing the rules by which government decisions are made. Wheareas policies can be defined by any organisation, governmental or not. Government policies refer to goals by which macro-economic efficiency is evaluated; acceptable unemployment rates, levels of inflation, etc.

As Figure 3.1 shows, participation might be limited by the knowledge required to set policy goals and find the optimal instruments for obtaining them. The day-to-day responsibility for instrumental activities might be distributed in order to secure an efficient flow of information for decision support purposes.

Figure 3.1   Modes of decision making in different political contexts

	Policies strategic	operational
global	Participation	Distribution
Politics		
sectoral	Vested interest	Professionalism

Politics in the information age

Some features of current information technology may change our requirements for the political process. I will specifically highlight the assumptions on which modern political institutions are based.

- what is to be expected of individual subjects? What are their new assets and limitations specifically regarding the use of IT?
- which professionals do we need to guide us through the web of public decision making? May we expect the idea of professionalism to change with the coming of decision support systems and on-line databases?
- how does technology implementation influence the optimal distribution of decisions? What methods do we use to analyse such changes?

Individual capabilities

In recent years, telecommunications and data processing have been developed to make integrated information systems available to the end-users. New configurations of communications and processing tools make it possible to computerise the most vital and repetitive office routines based on:

- the intended flow of information
- the most efficient distribution of tasks
- the established structure of decision making within specific segments of the economy

Where such strategic use of information technology is targeted directly towards the needs of specific user groups it may enhance the degrees of freedom in task handling considerably for each individual participant. The strategic element of the use of information technology in this context can be found in the way computerisation automates the intended information, sharing in the process of making documented decisions. The Scandinavian concept of *saksbehandling* refers to the role of document processing in government decision making. This is a topic in itself, and will not be elaborated here. [2]

However, where public sector tasks are concerned, the information infrastructure established will not necessarily benefit the private individual; since he is not their customer and cannot act accordingly.

Government bodies are expected to administer the common pool of resources within a society. Traditionally these resources are translated into monetary terms. However, the process of governing also produces information on the state of society; its corporate and private subjects. This information is a vital part of the shared resources in any society and constitutes the basis of rational decision making in politics.

Manuals on case-handling (implementation of laws, rules and regulations) fill up considerable space in any government office. Moreover, demographic and economic data, as well as logistical systems for infrastructure development, define the rationale of public agendas.

The way this information is managed largely decides what decisions are made. The logic of a database, be it manual or automatic, influences the processing of tasks and decisions. Each piece of information will relate to a subject. The information management involved might significantly influence the outcome of inter-relationships with the government

Information technology is transforming the rules of commercial transactions. Banking, travel and trade are more at each private individual's finger-tips than ever before. Access to global accounts and merchandise multiply the alternatives available for the optimal use of scarce resources. (see Chapter 11)

In the same way private subjects will find more and easier ways to inter-relate with governmental institutions. The possibility of connecting private office systems and decision support tools to government databases will be especially important. Contrary to popular belief, 1984 might be remembered for its liberty implications. [2]

Telecommunications

Traditionally, the use of telecommunications have been the subject of tight regulation by politicians. Most countries have established public monopolies for the production and distribution of telecommunication services. Data processing on the other hand has been subject to the free market, almost since the computer was invented.

As manufacturers of data processing equipment have increasingly built telecommunications features into their computers, the user community gradually becomes less dependent on services established by the public sector monopolies.

In certain application areas, such as banking and trade document exchange, private information networks are already more important than the public services. The concepts of Electronic Data Interchange (EDI) and Valued Added Network Services (VANS) exemplify this market trend. Government agencies establish new customs procedures, revamp their investment legislation and harmonise international agreements. However, most initiative lies beyond political control. [4]

Most politicians feel uncomfortable about this. By making new financial and regulatory resources available to their PTT agencies, they try to limit the private networks' penetration of society. However, given the speed of technological development and the power in the hands of entrepreneurial user groups, politicians are gradually loosing their grip on the tools by which information is distributed within society.

The new professionals

Automation in the public sector will vary between agencies and levels of government. However, some basic similarities can be identified from a data processing point of view. Bearing in mind the bureaucratic function of all public agencies, we can identify certain basic steps of the automation process:

- information retrieval includes the systematic search for background data, case by case
- information processing will be defined by the rules of public decision making, set up by law and tradition
- information distribution is mainly a matter of the power equilibrium established at the time of systems design

These three steps of governmental information handling can and will be automated by way of information technology. State-of-the-art implementations are already widely available.

Background data can be retrieved from easy access data bases, describing 'the state of the nation'. In Scandinavia such data bases cover most of the important areas of government, including employment, finance, customs, welfare, population, law enforcement, military service, utilities and more.

Rules of public decision making can easily be put into existing office information systems, by way of defining standard documents, digitised signatures and corrections, compulsory calculations, etc.

Figure 3.2   The basic steps of government automation

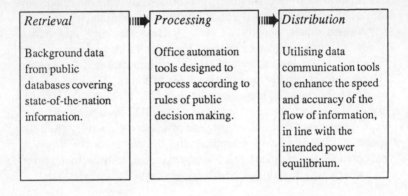

The power equilibrium defines who will have their say and in what matters. In an open society this is decided by the high level social networks established. Access to decision making means access to this flow of information in a decision making process. Information technology cements the flow of information most efficiently.

Document creation and distribution form the lifeline of communication and decision making within service sector economies. Moreover, the production of documented proposals, enquiries, decisions and answers constitute the central dataflow of government.

Electronic documents are that much easier to create and distribute. They can be standardised, changed, copied and mailed in a highly efficient manner, with no value given to the quality of their content. The information content naturally becomes more important when the amount of available information increases. Any frequent user of electronic mail will agree with this; the amount of garbage received increases with the number of people connected to your mailbox. This is why most office systems simply do not achieve organisational expectations. The system should cement the intended communication structures of the agency, deciding who should receive what sort of documents and from whom. [5]

Government agencies are highly dependent on predictability. Often the fear of something going wrong completely overrides the need for efficiency, and rightly so. Political agencies are judged by their record of treating everyone on the same terms, more so than their ability to produce services cost-efficiently.

Also the complexity of public decision making vastly exceeds that of private enterprise. A pool of interests must be considered since so many people will be affected by the outcome. A small error of recalculation can be detrimental to the established consensus. Public decisions are evaluated by their consequences for the motivation of society at large. [6]

The use of information technology constitutes a major problem in this respect, since it speeds up and neutralises information handling. Complex calculations, presented in a professional and convincing manner might hide the real conflicts of the subject matter. Common sense easily gets blurred in formats and pie-charts. The speed and precision of computer reasoning might limit our attention to simple reasoning only. However, government matters are complex by nature.

This is where our new technocrats find their *raison d'être*. The value of 'human databanks' in the shape of a lawyer or an economist (in the traditional sense) are rapidly diminishing. The need for experts on document handing (e.g., information retrieval, decision support and efficient communication patterns) in government has never been greater.

The power of calculation

The model of representative democracy was conceived in a society where information was spread extremely unevenly among its subjects. The idea of knowledge as the ticket to public decision making is still embedded in our societies, and is reflected in huge governmental bureaucracies and the extensive monitoring of elected officials.

Moreover, the theory of balance within the political system was always the main argument for limited access to decision making arenas. How would parliamentary decisions ever be made if those people most affected by their outcome were to stand up and speak for themselves? New legislation on sensitive issues like taxation or welfare might never come about. [7]

As the flow of information gradually changes with new technology we should foresee changes in the corridors of power.

Consider, for example, the complicated process of putting together a government budget. With every new state budget there will be several interest groups claiming the reverse effect of some allocation of resources or changes in taxation. Quite often they will be correct, if for no other reason than the level of sophistication in their simulations. Where banks, industrial development programmes or agricultural groups make more sophisticated use of computer simulations than the ministry of finance, then their negotiating power will be enlarged accordingly.

Above all, the ability to get hold of and utilise a web of conflicting information is highly dependent on the technology at hand. Some futurologists see a breakdown of centralised politics as a consequence, making its definite mark on the political system.

For example, some of the most sensitive decisions, currently handled exclusively by central government, might in the future be allocated either at the municipal level, to direct haggling between interested parties, or be put in the hands of the individuals whose necks are most at risk.

A system of weighting of the interests involved, giving some subjects more say in some matters and other subjects more say in other matters, has been suggested by academics. Information technology provides the tools to monitor favours given, so as to favour all equally in the long term. Possibly we will see experiments in distributed voting on special issues. That is to say, a network of input and output devices make way for instant voting, aggregation and calculations of the public interest. [8]

The optimal distribution of decision making

The search for efficient distribution of decision making has so far been most successfully performed by organisational analysts. The most appropriate level of distribution, they claim, depends on the complexity and the plurality of interests involved.

The amount of information involved in decision making, increases with complexity and pluralism. It is also believed, that the more information that is to be processed, the more freedom is needed in the actual handling of the tasks. Moreover, decisions should be distributed accordingly. [9]

Figure 3.3   The correlation between levels of complexity, pluralism and distribution

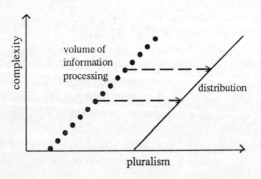

This leaves us with the problem of control. How do we establish consistency and proper timing in a highly decentralised political environment. Advances in computer aided accounting, decision support and material planning systems give new tools for handling this management problem.

We might expect to see management systems evolving within the political system by which elected politicians can audit decentralised political institutions. Then, and only then, will deregulation be a feasible instrument of government. Luckily, it is already happening.

Conclusion

Information technology might bring changes to the way our societies work, in areas that most strategic analysis leave undiscovered. The rationale of modern political institutions can be altered, much as businesses have to be reset to accommodate new technology.

I have focused some assumptions regarding stable and efficient government, introducing information technology changes to the existing consensus.

Drastic changes to political organisations might be expected in the areas of:

- individual limitations to political participation
- professional decision support
- the optimal distribution of decisions

Political institutions are confronted with new challenges caused by the introduction of information technology. Private subjects obtain new tools in their inter-relationships with government agencies. Government decisions will be made in a new environment, heavily influenced by changing standards of information handling.

References

1 Laver, Michael "Invitation to Politics" Martin Robertson and Co, Oxford, 1983.
2 "IT policies for the Government in the 90s" Norwegian Government Report NOU 1988:40.
3 Macrae, Norman "The 2024 Report" Sidgwick and Jackson, London, 1984.

4   Hendriksen, Roger "The Legal Aspects of Paperless International Trade and Transport" Juristforbundets Forlag, Copenhagen, 1982.
5   Roszak, Theodore "The Cult of Information" Butterworth Press, Cambridge, 1986.
6   Selznick, Philip "Leadership in Administration" Harper and Row, New York, 1957.
7   Olson, Mancur "The Logic of Collective Action" Harvard University Press, Cambridge, MA, USA, 1965.
8   Toffler, Alvin "The Third Wave" Pan Books, London, 1981.
9   Thompson, James D "Organisations in Action" McGraw-Hill, New York, 1967.

Part II
Selection and Planning

4

Linking Information Systems Planning to business strategy

Arjen Wassenaar

The dominant view on the use of information technology has focused exclusively on the internal functions of the business. In this conventional view the targets of information systems application are the planning and control processes of the organisation. Wiseman introduces the strategic information systems view; information systems used to support or shape an organisation's competitive strategy, its plans for gaining and/or maintaining competitive advantage. [1] To uncover these new opportunities there is a need for a new foundation for information systems planning. This should be based in the world of competitive strategy rather than in the arena of planning and control, and drawing on some of the concepts developed by Porter. [2]

Five levels of integration between strategic business planning and strategic information planning can be distinguished: [3]

- no plan; no formal planning takes place
- stand alone planning; the company may have a strategic business plan and a strategic information plan without any connection to each other
- reactive planning; the information systems plan refers only to the strategic business plan
- linked planning; strategic business planning is linked with strategic information planning, systems resources are matched against business needs
- integrated planning; strategic business and strategic information planning occur simultaneously and interactively

The central research issue is to identify forms of behaviour in information systems planning found in practice, and the key factors which determine the specific forms of the observed information planning behaviours.

The research approach is based on the case study method and interviews with information planners in selected companies. First, we consider some basic concepts and a theoretical framework for information planning. A transaction cost approach of organisations will be presented with a definition of information technology. In the framework we will identify essential characteristics of information systems planning; the case research was based on this framework. Finally, some general findings from the case research will be presented with remarks on the theoretical framework.

Basic concepts

Information technology, especially the integration of computing and telecommunications, acts as a mediating technology, i.e. a technology which links several social entities through the standardisation and extension of linkages. By lowering transaction costs, it can improve the information handling needed in transactions between companies or control transactions within the company. The effect is not contained within the existing organisational boundaries. On the contrary, shifts in transaction costs by using new information technology are affecting the existing organisational boundaries. Therefore, we believe it is necessary to rethink the concept of the organisation and the role of information technology in organisations.

As a start for our definition we go back to Barnard who defined cooperative systems as:

> 'a complex of physical, biological, personal and social components which are in a specific systematical relationship by reason of the cooperation of two or more persons for at least one definite end [4].'

Cooperative systems have to be organised. Ciborra distinguishes between two crucial factors in the matter of organising cooperative systems. [5] One factor is task uncertainty, which had already been pointed out by Galbraith. [6] The other factor is the degree to which organisational members share goals (goal congruence). Based on our transaction cost or network approach to organisations we define organisations as a complex of people, means and transactions trying to realise certain goals, based on a stable network of contractual arrangements between members who have only partly overlapping goals and perceptions governing the joint set of transactions.

In our model the future super-industrial corporation consists of a slender, semi-permanent framework from which a variety of small, temporary modules are suspended. The future firm will be a constellation of flexible, rather autonomous, small community units framed in a network of interdependencies, regulating their interfaces by continuously adapted contracts. Clear boundaries between constellations and their environment will not exist. [7]

The governance of transactions by contracts is supported by organisational information systems as systems of communicative action that create, set up, control and maintain organisational contracts and reports on their status. The coordination and control of exchange transactions depends upon contingencies which are both environmental (uncertainty and complexity of tasks and processes) and behavioural (bounded rationality and opportunism).

In our informatic view we make a distinction between the real life system of processes and transactions, and the abstract information system. We describe organisations from an informatic point of view, just as we describe an organisation in the economic model of the firm from an economic point of view. The real life system of processes and transactions are those parts or aspects of reality we want to investigate in order to know or to control them. To these ends former, present and future states of the real system of processes and transactions have to be described. The descriptions are produced by the information system in the form of data to which meanings are assigned by human beings.

Exchanging messages between people not only requires data exchange, but also a shared model for interpretation of data. Data has no value unless put into the context of the appropriate interpretation model, a process taxing human capacities to communicate, memorise and process information, thus leading to bounded rationality and limited goal congruence.

Information technology is the set of methods and capabilities for storing, processing or transporting data affecting the bounds in the rationality of organisational units and the limitations of their information related processes. There are three characteristics of information technology underlying the capability dimension: capacity, quality and cost. [8]

IT defined.

Information technology belongs to those technologies like the telephone and money, which reduce the cost of organising by making exchange transactions more efficient. The costs of organising are decreased by streamlining all parts of data processing required in carrying out an exchange. The function of computer-based systems can thus be redesignated as an exchange support system. (see Chapter 15)

The four field model

Information systems planning plays an important role in the adoption of information technology. In our definition, information systems planning has two key functions, systematically influencing the future information processing systems by specifying goals, constraints, applications and needed resources; increasing the consistency between decisions in this area in order to realise the specified future information processing system.

Information systems planning is fundamentally a decision making process resulting in agreements about the direction and structure of the future information processing system.

In our four field model we are distinguishing different levels of abstraction:

- environmental level
- substantial level
- process level
- control and managerial level
- level of integration of the specified levels

On the environmental level we specify the factors describing the context of information systems planning such as:

- the characteristics of the existing real life transaction system, information system and information management structure
- future conditions deduced from business and other functional plans
- external factors such as existing experience of information technology in the firm and the industry

The characteristics of the existing transaction system and the expected changes in this system arising from corporate strategy will affect the content of information systems planning. The characteristics of the existing information management structure and the external factors and internal constraints have an effect on the processes of information systems planning.

On the substantial level we specify the elements describing the product of information systems planning such as:

- function or aspiration level, e.g., improvements in planning and control, or support for the competitive strategy by uncovering new opportunities for the use of information technology

- the content of the information systems plan, in which we will distinguish between different planning levels (strategic, tactical and operational) different aspects (applications, development, technical infrastructure, organising and integration) and different planning horizons
- the domain of the information systems plan

On the process level we have researched the different sub-processes and can distinguish between planning processes such as:

- modelling and especially the different analysis and design levels (systelogical, infological, datalogical and technological levels of abstraction)
- choice, assessment of alternatives and allocation of financial resources
- participation and the contributions of user and consultant to the planning process
- communication, documentation and learning

On the managerial level we look at information systems planning as a project requiring control of aspects such as time, budget phasing, quality and organisation.

On the level of integration we direct attention to the interaction between the specified levels. We focus on the interaction patterns between these levels and especially the interaction between the environmental characteristics and the substantial, process and managerial levels. We suppose that there is a need for a certain fit for successful information system planning.

An electronics company

Information systems planning was conducted in the various product divisions of this company. The company is currently in a phase of reorganisation. In the new structure the product divisions will be responsible for product design, product development, logistics, manufacturing and increasingly for sales. National organisations are responsible for operational activities such as production and sales. The information systems function consists of three levels:

- central departments responsible for support in the field of technical systems, for electronic data processing and for formulating automation policy and offering professional support in the field of business information systems, CAD and CAM
- departments within product divisions and national organisations
- local departments in factories and international production centres.

Top management decided to bridge the gap between business and automation through information planning projects; the first step towards becoming a leader in the competitive application of information technology. It was decided to organise information systems planning along business lines in order to strengthen the worldwide competitive position of the product divisions. Management of product divisions was made responsible; central information systems departments and the departments within the product departments gave support. In total, seven information systems planning projects were conducted.

Short description

The managerial attitude was generally positive, although the stimulus for information systems planning in the product divisions came, in six of the seven projects, from central management. In all projects a general business strategy was available; only in three projects was there a need to formalise an existing but informal business strategy. None of the product divisions had reached stage four of the Nolan stage. [9] In all projects information systems were seen as an expense and not as an investment; information system management was assigned to the finance director. Because of technological, commercial and organisational developments there will be many changes in the existing characteristic of the real life transaction systems.

The projects are aimed at translating business strategies and possibilities for the use of IT into an information strategy, introducing a systematic approach to strategic information systems planning, and making management feel responsible for drawing up an information strategy for their unit. Product divisions were chosen as domains for strategic information systems planning. This decision was in line with general corporate strategy, giving full responsibility for strategy development to the product divisions. The content of the information strategy plan was identifying strategic issues, outlining preliminary information architecture and outlining information management concepts. All the projects were focused on strategic issues. The outcomes of the projects were:

- mission, goals, critical success factors and problems
- organisational goals in relation to the most important business functions
- business strategy points relevant to (structuring of) business information systems
- internal and external opportunities for IT applications
- assessment of IT opportunities (implementation, contribution to the realisation of business strategy and impact on the market position)
- summary of the most important IT application areas and their critical success factors

All seven projects were undertaken between November 1986 and January 1987 based on a carefully developed action plan. In almost all projects the information systems manager of the product division was project leader; members of the project team were internal and external consultants. No managers were members of the project teams; instead, management involvement was organised in different ways. The elapsed time was realised by removing activities like outlining preliminary information architecture.

Important organisational problems were:

- different perceptions about the project between management and project team
- capacity project team members
- lack of secretarial assistance

Four different approaches were used:

- a shortened version of James Martin's ISP (Information Systems Planning) method [10]
- gap analysis
- working groups consisting of managers from different business groups
- discussion groups in which experts did the investigations, and the results were discussed in reference groups consisting of managers

In general, the analysis and design was done at the systelogical level, design on the infological level of information architecture was planned but not conducted. In different projects there was a need for assessment methods to do cost-benefit analysis and for reference models especially in the field of technical (process) automation.

The participation of management was organised in different ways. In two projects management participated directly through working groups, in other projects it was difficult to interview managers. Another form of participation was the use of reference groups consisting of managers reviewing the results of the project team. At the end of the projects different managers had the feeling they were not sufficiently involved in the planning activities.

General findings

These findings are based on the described case, and cases in other companies. In practice, information systems strategy planning for linking business strategy and information technology exposed different forms. In general, information systems planning behaviour can be driven by business issues and plans or information technology issues. (see Chapter 15)

In some projects information strategy planning was driven by business strategy and issues, while in other projects the prime mover seemed to be awareness or excitement about new technology. In others, neither business strategy issues nor technology were obvious driving forces. These alternative scenarios can be depicted in a matrix. (see Figure 4.1) [11]

The information strategy planning in the electronics company was intended to be issue driven. This business issue driven model can also be characterised as a top down approach, in as much as the process really starts with delineation and prioritisation of issues at senior management level. Each issue that emerges from this process then becomes a focal point in and information resource management.

This business issue driven model was best performed in two projects. The key factor for successful use of this approach appears to be the ability to identify those issues that are the most critical to the organisation, and subsequently identifying technical solutions. This key factor is asking for specific skills from people participating in the project.

Figure 4.1 Alternative scenarios for information systems planning

	Low — information technology resource driven — High	
High top down analytical		inside out interactive
Low middle out *ad hoc* informal		bottom up adoptive

(business plan issue driven)

54

A technology driven information strategy planning behaviour is more likely to be bottom-up, and less comprehensive with respect to organisational issues. However, the technology driven approach is quite thorough with respect to awareness of potential technological opportunities and options. Information systems staff have an important role in scanning information sources. Key factors in this approach are a relatively large amount of organisational slack and flexibility within the information systems department and the ability of its managers to secure strong, high-level, sponsorship for new technology.

This model dominated our electronics company in the past. In the case of an engineering company we also found this model present. The information planning resulted in the creation of an information centre, for support of the users in the field of personal computing and office automation.

An information strategy planning process is more likely to be facility led, scanning the environment for new tools and software packages. The key success factor of this approach is probably the ability of information systems managers to secure high level sponsorship for new information technology applications.

An interactive information strategy planning behaviour model is more inside-out orientated and comprehensive, in assessing the existing and future business issues, by conducting an internal and an external analysis, in assessing existing availability of technology, and forecasting future developments in this field.

The major strength of this approach is that it is comprehensive with respect to both information technology and organisational issues; both problems and opportunities. However, the weakness is that the approach is very costly and requires the availability and participation of specialist information systems staff and senior managers. The key success factor in this approach was the ability to identify application opportunities and to identify appropriate information technology to support the potential application areas. In general there was a two way interaction between, on the one hand business strategy, and on the other, information technology and information resource management.

One of the projects in the electronics company has some characteristics of this approach. The external consultants had a boundary spanning role in this project, which seems to be especially appropriate in information-intensive businesses.

Many organisations are intentionally not comprehensive with respect to both their identification and search procedures of business issues and their information technology scanning processes. Planning is often opportunistic, and driven by personal visions. Occasionally, a match occurs between issue and information technology.

The opportunistic model is not necessarily worse than either issue driven or technology driven planning. The opportunistic, personal driven approach is the lowest of all three models in terms of costs and need for organisational slack. There is also a lower need for specialist skills, such as planners, or technical or applications gatekeepers. The key skills appear to be generalist.

Although our field studies were too limited to be conclusive, it is likely that this approach predominates in the running of small firms; it lies on the path of least resistance for organisational development.

Conclusion

In practice there are different forms of behaviour in planning strategic information systems. Effectiveness seems to depend on the characteristics of the planning environment. Figure 4.2 summarises the different planning behaviours and their most likely environments.

The critical success factors which link business strategy with information technology through strategic information systems planning are:

1   Management awareness at the different organisational levels concerning the role which IT can play in business processes. External influences such as external consultants and the behaviour of competitors play an important role in promoting awareness.

2   Organisational experience of managing information systems on the level of Nolan's stage four is needed for strategic information systems planning.

3   In projects for strategic information systems planning there is a need for an intensive interaction between IT specialists and managers, or people who know the business and have authority in carrying out plans. The mix between managers and specialists in a project team is important. Interpersonal roles by people respected by both managers and specialists are important.

4   The introduction of a new generation of methods with more business-orientation will have an important effect on management involvement in the planning of strategic information systems. In the process of strategic information systems planning the upgraded information

56

system development methods do not work. These old methods focus too much on describing existing situations in detail and do not support the understanding of the relationship between IT opportunities and business strategy. These methods require too much time for real management involvement. (see Chapter 5)

5   Fast feedback between planning and execution has to be organised especially in turbulent business environments. The danger of getting into a "planning loop" has to be avoided.

6   In large companies a decomposition of the company into planning domains is essential to reduce planning complexity.

Some recommendations

There is a need for further research in the field of information systems planning practice, in order to achieve a better fit between strategic information systems planning and the planning environment. Variables in approaches to information systems planning are:

- aspiration level of planning expressed in the intended content of the plan and the decomposition and selection of planning domains
- organisational conditions for planning: selection of the members of the project team, the internal and external integration mechanism used by the project team, mix between formalised and informal procedures and controlling implementation
- methodological conditions for modelling, assessment of alternatives, participation and communication

Relevant variables in the planning environment could be:

- current information intensity of business processes, transactions and the penetration of IT applications
- future effect of the use of IT on the real system of business processes and transactions, on the competitive position and structure of the industry
- existing experience of the management of information systems and diffusion of these responsibilities
- organisational culture, especially the management attitude towards planning in general

Figure 4.2 Modes of information systems planning behaviour

Strategic aspects	Strategic modes			
	Middle-out personal	Bottom-up adoptive	Top-down analytical	Inside-out Interactive
		Substantial Level		
Aspiration	Personal driven	Substitution resources	Complemen-tary	Competitive advantage
Domain	Personal lines	Resource lines	Business process lines	Product lines
Content	Informal commitments	Formal infrastructure plans	Formal architecture plans	Strategic information applications
		Process Level		
Analysis & design	Not formalised	Formalised methods	Formalised methods	Formal & creative methods
Choice criteria	Personal preference	Resource efficiency	Business productivity	Competitive advantage
Participants	Informal network	IS staff	User management	IS staff and users
		Management Level		
Organisation	No formal structure	IS manage-ment lines	Project teams	Project teams
Environment	Small firms not diffused	Non-diffused IT	Diffused IT	High informaton intensity

References

1   Wiseman, C "Strategy and Computers: information systems as competitive weapons" Dow Jones, Homewood, 1985.
2   Porter, Michael E "Competitive Strategy" Free Press, New York, 1980.
3   Synnott, William R "The Information Weapon" Wiley & Sons, New York, 1987.
4   Barnard, C I "The Function of the Executive" Harvard University Press, Cambridge, MA, 1938/1954.
5   Ciborra, Claudio U "Research Agenda for Transaction Costs Approach to Information Systems" pp 253-274 in *Critical issues in information systems research,* edited by R J Boland and R Hirschheim, Wiley & Sons, Chichester, 1987.
6   Galbraith, J R "Organizational Design" Addison-Wesley, Reading MA, 1973.
7   Wassenaar, D Arjen "Information Management in an Industrial Environment - an educational perspective" in *The Management Challenge,* edited by D Boddy, D A Buchanan and J McCalman, Croom Helm, London, 1988.
8   Bakopoulos, J Y "Towards a More Precise Concept of Information Technology" *Proceedings of the Conference on Information Systems, Indianapolis, 1985.*
9   Nolan, Richard L "Managing the Crisis in Data Processing" *Harvard Business Review* **57** (2) pp 115-126, March-April 1979.
10 Martin, James S "Strategic Data Planning Methodologies" Prentice-Hall, Englewood Cliffs, 1982.
11 Huff, S L and Munro, M C "Information Technology Assessment and Adoption: a field study" *MIS Quarterly* **9**, December 1985.

5

Why Systems Analysis Methodologies Fail to Respond to Strategic Change

Robyn Chandler

This chapter examines the state of systems analysis with regard to a particular type of business problem that is caused by a change in the environment which affects strategic planning. Systems analysis methodologies are assessed in terms of their usefulness in helping an organisation respond to such changes through the development of information systems. The development of proactive systems, that is those which are intended to cause change in the environment, is not discussed. These systems can be thought of as less time-critical than the systems needed to respond to the changes caused by agencies outside the control of the organisation (e.g., competitors, governments, suppliers, etc.).

The area considered is narrowed further to only those situations where such changes will have a major effect on the organisation in the short term. The organisations being considered are, at the particular point in time, vulnerable to forces in the environment which are outside their control, and the organisation's survival (in its present form) is dependent upon the implemented response. Examples of such situations are violent stock-market fluctuations, hostile company takeovers, dramatic changes in government policies, sudden disappearance of suppliers and the emergence of powerful competitors.

Decisions are usually being made to change the current state of the organisation in the short-term, whilst keeping in mind the long-term effects of such decisions on the organisation's overall strategic plan. Decisions are therefore being made which affect not only the strategic level, but also the tactical and operational levels of management, and their decision making processes.

One of the main differences between the situations considered here and the normal day-to-day decision making in an organisation is the quantity of information from the environment required to make such decisions. Each decision will require different types of information or the information in different forms. This information may not be readily available, and when it has been located may not be in an appropriate form for the decision maker to analyse. The major problem is that the information necessary for such decision making is largely unknown.

In these situations it is essential that the required information is available immediately, in order to make timely decisions. The more rapidly decisions are implemented, the quicker are the organisation's responses to the changes in the environment, and the more advantageous it is likely to be for the organisation. The development of systems to accommodate the new organisational requirements will therefore need to be done immediately. However, like all systems, changes cannot be implemented successfully without consideration of the possible effects on other areas of the organisation and other systems in operation. It is essential to consider the organisation as a whole, rather than analysing its parts, in order to get a complete picture of the situation.

Evaluation criteria

The aim of systems analysis is to determine a means of solving a given problem. This problem may be well defined or it may be unstructured and vague. Defining systems analysis as 'determining a means of solving the problem', rather than that of actually solving the problem, creates a clear divide between the task of analysis and that of design.

The systems analyst must be aware of the goals of the organisation with respect to this problem as well as the organisation's goals in general. The analyst must then set about gathering the required information from all possible sources in order to reduce uncertainty about the problem. The more structured and well-defined the problem, and the less uncertainty contained within it, the easier will be the task of the analyst.

In problems of strategic response, the situation is probably highly unstructured, there is a great deal of uncertainty and there is a high degree of interaction with the environment. The situation may also be in a constant state of change brought about by the continuous input of information from the environment which is beyond the control of the organisation's decision makers.

Such situations pose difficult problems for systems analysts, requiring that information systems be developed or modified rapidly to provide information to cope with strategic change. However, the analyst is working in an environment with a high degree of uncertainty and constant change, where timeliness of information may be measured in hours. Not only does the analyst have to determine the information requirements, the system must be developed and the information provided to decision makers within this time-frame in order for it to be useful.

The analyst's task of reducing uncertainty would be greatly aided by input from the decision makers, but these people are working in crisis mode and probably do not have much time to spend on discussions with the analyst.

The information required by the decision makers in such situations is usually of a highly sensitive nature. The consequence of this is that as few people as possible should be involved in the development process. Therefore, the analyst is likely to find himself or herself working almost alone.

There are no systems analysis methodologies that can cope with all these requirements. It would be necessary for such a methodology to handle all requirements in order that it be worthwhile even contemplating using it to respond to strategic change through information systems.

Methodologies

There are many systems analysis methodologies in existence. Rather than attempt to review all such methodologies, only a few categories of methodologies will be considered. Table 5.1 contains a list of these categories and examples of specific methodologies which fit into each category.

Table 5.1 Categories of Methodologies

Type	Examples
Structured	SSA, SSADM
Participative - Socio-Technical	Ethics
Participative - Prototyping	
Human Activity Systems	Soft Systems

Structured methodologies

Structured methodologies emerged in the mid-1970s. What differentiates these methodologies from others is their engineering-orientated approach to problem solving. Firstly the problem is defined, next the boundary (or scope) is established within which the analyst works, then the analyst has the relatively simple task of describing the current system, both physically and logically, and finally determining the changes that should take place in order that the system meets the requirements established at problem definition. This approach tends to be linear in that the system context is established, the current system is described and then the new system, etc.

Problems of strategic change are essentially unstructured, the boundaries are ill-defined and much of what is going on within the context is unknown until the very last stages of the decision making process. Hence, to define the problem initially is impossible and to establish a system boundary is unrealistic.

Given that the problem is one of strategic importance to the organisation, the solution is unlikely to be found in concentrating on the current system (even if one exists). Structured methods tends to blind the analyst's view to more radical solutions and is likely to produce a system which retains some of the problems in the current system. It is also difficult to describe the current and new systems in a situation where so much information is unknown. Structured methodologies can produce adequate systems in structured, well-bounded and well-defined situations with few unknowns to contend with. However, the highly uncertain environment in which the strategic response is required is not suited to this method of analysis.

Socio-technological methodologies

The participative socio-technical methodologies address the problem of failure of systems to fit into their organisational environment through greater user participation in the design process.

The socio-technical school of thought sees any organisational system as having a socio-psychological component as well as a technical component. As such it aims at creating a system which jointly optimises the social and technical components. The system's users and the work environment form the socio-psychological component. This system component is not formally considered by the structured methodologies in the design process, although a good analyst would certainly not ignore it, even when using a structured methodology.

In the participative socio-technical approaches, the users form a major part of the design team, possibly the entire team. The users can therefore contribute information with a greater understanding of why it is needed and how it will be used, thereby improving the analysis process. Having the users probe the problem themselves, a richer picture should emerge on which to base the new system. The new system should therefore embrace the problem situation more closely and also fit the work environment satisfactorily.

The participative socio-technical approaches tend to be time consuming for the users and analysts involved. To the users, participation in such a design team is probably a new experience and one that will take them time to settle into before the team can produce any substantial results. The methodologies are very thorough and, judging by case studies, the systems they produce are highly successful in meeting users' requirements. The price to pay for this success is the time taken in development.

In the type of system being considered here, the system's users are high-level managers and decision makers who care much more about obtaining the required information quickly than whether or not the system suits their working environment. The amount of time which needs to be invested by users in such an approach to systems development would most likely not be justified under these circumstances. The time-frame required for development of the system would also not be tolerated in such circumstances. Hence, these approaches, although highly suited to the development of systems that have a high amount of user involvement in operation, simply do not suit the time-imperative nature of the type of problem under consideration.

Prototyping

Prototyping covers the analysis, design and programming phases of systems development, but instead of using a linear approach as in the life cycle approach, these tasks are done in synchrony. The developer and user work closely together in development of a model or prototype of the required system. As an analysis tool, the prototype helps the analyst extract information from the users and helps the users to clarify their own view of what they require of the system. The model being developed is used as a means of aiding communication between the analyst and user. Prototyping involves the user and the analyst who is developing an early version of the system and then refining the model until it satisfies the users' requirements.

Prototyping does not demand that the full details of system requirements are known from the outset, but only that a broad understanding of the requirements are known. With each iteration of the model, more detail is incorporated as it becomes known. This approach is therefore suited to situations in which there is considerable uncertainty. The iterative approach allows the user to watch the system evolve. Research indicates that this enables the user to identify more closely with the final system and enables the system itself to fulfil more adequately the requirements of the user. The prototyping approach appears to produce more successful information systems compared with more traditional methodologies.

However, there is one major drawback to using prototyping methodologies in the development of systems for strategic response. It requires a high level of user involvement in the development process. In many situations the system users do not have this time available. This is a very important consideration since the success of the prototyping methodology depends upon the extent of user involvement. Therefore, reluctantly, it must be concluded that prototyping is not the answer in such cases.

Human activity systems

The human activity systems approach is primarily related to the Soft Systems Methodology of Peter Checkland. Checkland's methodology aims at understanding the environment of the problem in order to define possible problems and hence develop solutions. It considers the problem as a whole, and from as many different perspectives as possible. The analyst builds up a rich picture of the situation and develops root definitions of the situation from these many different perspectives. Theoretical models which aim at describing the problem are then derived from the root definitions and used as a basis for discussion of possible changes, with the system users. Changes can be of four types - procedural, structural, attitudinal or 'hard' (i.e., development of a system). Methods of implementing changes differ depending on the type of change required. The first three (soft) changes require a person with the appropriate authority to implement them. Hard changes can be implemented using the other methods of systems development that have been described above.

Checkland's methodology is concerned with ill-defined and unstructured problems and with defining existing problems. It views the system in a holistic way, incorporating analysis of the system's environment as well as of the internal workings of the system. However, it requires a great deal of user participation in most of the methodology's phases, and results in a problem definition rather than a solution. This of course makes solving that problem a relatively simple task, but nevertheless a time consuming one. The methodology also appears to be rather too time consuming for problems of this type. It appears that the richer the analyst's picture of the problem, the better will be the quality of the results. The more people considered in building the picture, the better the picture will be. Hence, Checkland's methodology, whilst containing elements which appear well-suited to this type of problem, contains the same drawbacks as the other methodologies; those of a long time-frame required to produce a good analysis and extent of user involvement.

The current situation

It can be concluded from this study that systems analysis in the forms available today is ill-suited to the problem of systems development in situations where time is of the essence and a large amount of uncertainty exists in the problem. Systems analysis, as defined, is the task of reducing uncertainty in the problem. No tools currently exist to help the analyst reduce this uncertainty and develop the rich picture required of the problem.

It appears that, given a good systems analyst, the quality of his or her analysis is directly related to both the amount of time available in which to complete it, and the extent of user involvement in the analysis process. Therefore, in order to reduce the time required for analysis, the amount of user involvement must increase accordingly. Conversely, to reduce the amount of user involvement, the time available must increase.

In analysis of systems for strategic response, the requirement is to reduce both time and the amount of user involvement required.

Such situations are not just isolated, one-off events for organisations. In the future there will be a huge increase in organisational problems of this type. It is therefore most important that we address the problem of developing information systems to respond to strategic change.

Organisations and their environments

Traditional organisation theory has viewed organisations as closed systems in that it concentrates on the internal workings of the organisation in isolation from its environment. In the past this may have been a reasonable simplification of the real world, given that the extent of interaction with the environment was minimal and the time-frame considered for this interaction was somewhat longer than is acceptable in the 1980s. Organisation theory concentrated instead on maintaining a stable internal state for the organisation. It was possible in the past for organisations to survive in this way. So long as the organisation could maintain a steady state, with gradual changes to procedures and products in line with the slowly evolving market for these products and gradual developments in technology, then the organisation could survive and grow steadily.

However, today we are living in a more complex environment. Advances in areas of production technology, marketing techniques, information technology and telecommunications have had a great effect on many areas of the organisation's environment. Advances in communications technology have widened the geographical scope for the marketing of products and introduced international competition into local markets. Production in some industries has been automated, providing the ability for organisations either to exploit further efficiencies of scale, or to enable production of a variety of goods, thereby allowing companies to diversify their production without the associated overheads. This means that technology is lowering entry barriers to different markets, making existing producers vulnerable to competition from previously unknown forces. (see Chapter 2)

Along with this increased complexity of the local and 'known' market place, the entry of organisations into international markets brings added complications of government regulations, local customs to which the envisaged market may adhere, currency problems and, of course, communication problems. This increase in complexity is multiplied by the number of different localities the organisation wishes to enter.

The organisation and its relationship with the environment has changed considerably. It is therefore no longer appropriate to view organisations as closed systems. Organisations are inextricably tied to their environments, and must be studied from the view of the larger environmental system as well as from the organisational level.

The amount of information entering organisations has increased exponentially because of the increased amount of information generated by the environment, the organisation's ability to process information, the increased use of knowledge workers in organisations who generate information and, of course, the more complex and dynamic nature of the environment.

This proliferation of information does little to reduce uncertainty in organisations which cannot assimilate it in such quantities. Instead, more uncertainty may be introduced because the information providers act on that information, assuming that because an organisation has it, it is aware of its contents. What is needed by organisations is a means of filtering information to provide it in a concise, accurate and relevant form to decision makers and within an appropriate time-frame to suit the problem situation.

Organisations today, and in the future, face more complex environments than ever before. The amount of uncertainty the decision makers have to cope with increases with this complexity. With the rapid advances in technology, organisations cannot plan as far ahead as in the past. Production technology installed today may well be out of date within three years. Governments who have allowed an organisation to enter its market could be overthrown at any time, or may erect trade barriers. Competitors rise and fall, as do suppliers. Consumers' preferences change more frequently with the diverse array of products available on the market and, of course, investors' preferences change.

Change is occurring in the environment at a much faster rate than in the past. Organisations are more vulnerable to changes in the environment because of the greater complexity of the relationship between the organisation and its environment. Therefore, the organisation is facing more frequent and complex changes and is having to react to them in a shorter time-frame than has been previously required.

The development of appropriate information systems may be the only way that organisations will be able to cope with the amount of information required for decision making in the future. However, without an appropriate methodology for analysis of such systems, it is doubtful whether such development can be successful.

Coping with strategic change

The systems analyst needs to be able to reduce uncertainty in order to determine a means of solving the problem. In these situations the analyst is restricted by the short time-frame in which to work, the lack of user interaction possible, and the necessity of working with as few people as possible for security reasons. Added problems for the analyst are the unstructured nature of the problem and the high degree of uncertainty.

The analyst needs to be in close contact with the decision making process. He or she provides information on which the decision makers base their decisions, and also needs to know the information requirements of the decision makers at as early a stage as possible in order to supply the processed information quickly. The analyst is concerned with reducing uncertainty in the decision makers' problematic environment and therefore must probe that environment, gathering information relevant to the decision making process.

It seems that placing of the analyst within the decision making team would serve a number of useful purposes. The analyst would be constantly aware of the decision makers' actions and may be able to anticipate their information requirements. The analyst's task of reducing uncertainty would be aided by the communication of information from the decision makers, without requiring these decision makers to spend their valuable time in direct consultation with the analyst.

The decision makers should also benefit from this approach. The analyst should be able advise the decision makers about the ability of the organisation's information systems to provide the information needed, and also on the ability of the organisation to obtain information from various parts of the environment. Such advice may help in reducing the time needed to obtain such information, or enhancing the quality of information on which the decision makers can base their decisions.

This is not a solution to the problem by any means, it is simply a way of enhancing communication between the decision making process and the information system development process. There is obviously more work to be done on development of a systems analysis methodology to address such problems.

Bibliography

Ackoff, R L "Towards a System of Systems Concepts" *Management Science* **17** Theory (11) pp 661-671, 1971

Ackoff, R L "From Information to Control" North Holland, Amsterdam, 1980.

Alavi, M "An Assessment of the Prototyping Approach to Information Systems Development." *Communications of the ACM* **27** (6) pp 556-563, June 1984.

Benyon, D & Skidmore, S "Towards a Tool Kit for the Systems Analyst" *The Computer Journal* **30** (1) pp 2-7, 1987.

Boulding, K E "General Systems Theory - the skeleton of science" *Management Science* **2** (3) pp 197-208, 1956.

Brittan, J H G "Design for a Changing Environment" *The Computer Journal* **23** (1) pp 13-19, 1981.

Checkland, P "Systems Thinking, Systems Practice" John Wiley, Great Britain, 1981.

Dawson, S "Analysing Organisations" Macmillan, Hampshire, 1986.

Dearnley, P A & Mayhew, P J "In Favour of System Prototypes and their Integration into the Systems Development Cycle" *The Computer Journal* **26** (1) pp 36-42, 1983.

DeMarco, T "Structured Analysis and System Specification" Yourdon, New York, 1978.

Earl, M J "Information Systems Strategy Formulation" Oxford Institute of Information Management Research and Discussion Paper, 1986.

Earl, M J "Formulating Information Technology Strategies" Oxford Institute of Information Management Research and Discussion Paper, 1986.

Emery, F E (ed.) "Systems Thinking" Penguin Books, Middlesex, 1981.

Episkopou, D & Wood-Harper, A. "Towards a Framework to Choose Appropriate IS Approaches" *The Computer Journal* **29** (3) pp 222-228, 1986.

Fitzgerald, G; Stokes, N & Wood, J "Feature Analysis of Contemporary Information Systems Methodologies" *The Computer Journal* **28** (3) pp 223-230 1985.

Galbraith, J "Designing Complex Organizations" Addison-Wesley, USA, 1973.

Gerloff, E A "Organizational Theory and Design" McGraw-Hill, USA, 1985.

Jagodzinski, A P & Clarke, D D "A Review of Methods for Measuring and Describing Users' Attitudes as an Essential Constituent of Systems Analysis and Design" *The Computer Journal* 29 (2) pp 97-102 1986.

Kast, F E & Rosenweig, J E "The Modern View: A Systems Approach" in *Organization and Management: A Systems Approach,* edited by Kast, F E & Rosenweig, J E. McGraw-Hill, New York, 1970.

Lucas, H C; Land, F F; Lincoln, T J and Supper, K (eds) 'The Information Systems Environment', Proceedings of the IFIP TC 8.2 Working Conference on The Information Systems Environment, Bonn West Germany, 11-13 June, 1979.

McNurlin, B C "What Information Do Managers Need?" *EDP Analyzer* June 1979.

Markus, M L & Bjørn-Andersen, N "Power Over Users: its exercise by systems professionals" *Communications of the ACM* **30** (6) June 1987.

Mayhew, P J & Dearnley, P A "An Alternative Prototyping Classification" *The Computer Journal* **30** (6) pp 481-484, 1987.

Mumford, E "Defining System Requirements to Meet Business Needs: a case study example" *The Computer Journal* **28** (2) pp 97-104, 1985.

Nygaard, K "The Impact of Social Movements" *The Computer Journal* **23** (1) pp 19-22, 1981.

Olle, T W *et al* "Information Systems Methodologies; a framework for understanding" Addison-Wesley, Wokingham, England, 1988.

Podger, D N "High Level Languages - a basis for participative design" Manchester Business School.

Robb, F F "Operational Research and General Systems Thinking" *European Management Journal* **4** (1) pp 55-62, 1986.

Sharp, J A & Price, D H "Systems Dynamics and Operational Research: an appraisal" *European Journal of Operational Research* **16**, 1984.

Shemer, I "Systems Analysis: a systemic analysis of a conceptual model" *Communications of the ACM* **30** (6) pp 506-512 June 1987.

Somogyi, E K & Galliers R D (eds) "Towards Strategic Information Systems" Abacus Press, Tunbridge Wells, 1987.

Srinivasan, A & Kaiser, K "Relationships Between Selected Organizational Factors and Systems Development" *Communications of the ACM* **30** (6) pp 556-562, June 1987.

Verrijn-Stuart, A A "Themes and Trends in Information Systems" *The Computer Journal* **30** (2) pp 97-109, 1987.

6

The Role of Information Systems in Marketing Success

Jo van Engelen

The management of a company has to be aware of the need to analyse and understand the continually changing environment, for which advancing information technology offers both possibilities and challenges. The realisation of an information system tuned to a marketing strategy could lead to the acquisition of a new competitive advantage, which for most companies is the key to growth. The development of information systems is based on the increase in the applicability of information technology. Meaningful developments in allied technologies such as computers, telecommunication, the storage and accessibility of data, drawing equipment and software have created a number of new possibilities for management. (see Chapter 2)

The driving forces behind information technology, which can be decisive for a marketing strategy, can be considered as being divided into two categories; on the one hand is the development and software, while on the other hand is the challenging commercial environment in the shape of increasing, and in some sectors world-wide, competition. This is the economic imperative of information technology; if no advantage is seen in it then it is perceived as a disadvantage. Nevertheless, a growing gap can be observed between the possibilities for applying information technology and its genuinely effective use. Understanding of, and insight into, the existence of this gap is essential for the successful exploitation of the hidden possibilities of information technology and marketing strategy.

In the research reported here the chosen task was to investigate the properties of an information system which deliver better results in an arbitrary product-market combination. A product-market combination constitutes the bringing of one product onto one market; a product-market combination is systematically managed and the underlying plan is called a marketing strategy. The information needed to make a product-market combination successful will vary from plan to plan, in other words, each marketing strategy will require a (slightly) different information system. The intention of this research has been to define what types of marketing strategy can be discerned, how the properties of the information systems related to each strategy differ and, if possible, whether they contribute to the success of the product-market combination.

For this research it was necessary to have a marketing model that gives a clear picture with regard to market trading. Based on the principles of systems theory a model has been developed for this research that has been introduced under the name 'double unity cell'.

It is necessary for various marketing strategies to be distinguished from each other; this distinction can be based on the double unity cell and leads to a marketing strategy classification. Subsequently, various information systems have to be separated from each other by identifying all the important information relationships for marketing activities in the model of the double unity cell, and describing each of these relationships by a number of qualities. Finally, we describe the field research that tests the statement of the problem.

What is the purpose of this research? Or, what does this research mean? The results of the study give the manager a good insight into the importance of information use and the contribution that this use of information has in the profitability of the product-market combination. It has been determined that the setting up of an adequate information system makes a certain contribution to the results of the company. It has also been determined what the characteristics of such an information system should be; this gives managers and system developers a first handhold.

There has been renewed and radical pleading for a synthetic approach instead of the purely analytical approach. A view is taken of market trading that is more integrated than the usual approach. The conviction of this new approach, made tangible by the use of the double unity cell model, offers new possibilities. Further, this study makes it possible to distinguish strategies in a completely independent way. The marketing strategy classification presented, distinguishes strategies from each other in an unequivocal way, and does not get stuck on what the manager himself thinks of it.

A marketing model: the double unity cell

Today the majority of managers begin from a two-part marketing model when they draw up their marketing strategy; on the one side is a supplier and on the other a buyer. The supplier plies the buyer with a so-called marketing mix that consists of the four P's: Product, Price, Place and

Promotion. In this presentation of business no account is taken of the response of the customer, of the relation between the purchasing and sales functions of the supplier, and the difference between control and operational activities. With the rapid improvements in the communication infrastructure and the intensification of competition, this model will sooner or later fail. Those who first adopt a more integrated view of marketing, in accordance with system thinking, will have an advantage.

An organisation buys goods or services, adds value to them and then sells them. To be able to manage this process the organisation has to know its own capabilities and have contacts with suppliers and buyers. Not only is the interaction with the buyers important for managing marketing activities, but the internal information, logistic and financial flows of an organisation are also important, as is the interaction between the organisation and the supplier. A model is introduced under the name 'double unity cell'. (see Figure 6.1)

Figure 6.1 The double unity cell as a marketing model

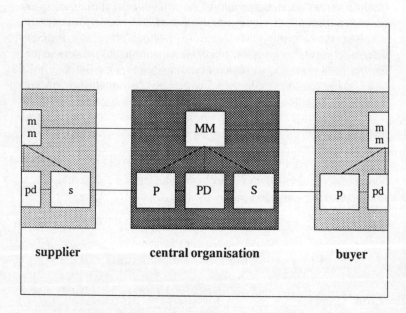

mm = marketing management	p = purchasing
pd = product development	s = sales

This model owes its name to the fact that although three organisations are represented, only two complete organisations could be made with the parts of it. In addition to the central organisation, which it is all about, half is identified as the supplier and half as the buyer. More is unnecessary and less would be insufficient. In every organisation four functions are distinguished: marketing management, purchasing, sales and product development. These objects may be represented by departments, but they need not be organisationally distinct. They are, in principle, abstract concepts just as in the classical two-layer marketing model in which, for example, all strategic and operational items are also collected under the four P's.

From left to right in the bottom of the double unity cell in Figure 6.1 is shown a value chain. From top to bottom is shown the compound of managerial strategic activities and current operational activities. The double unity cell is therefore a cross between a value chain and a management structure (control situation). Naturally, the central organisation is absolutely essential. However, the supplier and the buyer are primarily concerned with the relation between sales and purchasing, as well as a number of general affairs related to product development and management considerations. In this respect the model does not need to be a complete representation of supplier and buyer.

The marketing management components of the model are mainly occupied with strategic matters, with the medium-term and with the distribution of means over the parts of the organisation. However, purchasing and sales concentrate on operational matters, on the short-term and on the composition of the four P's for a specific product-market combination. Product development is meant here as the creative link between purchasing and sales and concerns the continuous development, i.e. the increase in value of the product.

Once again it should be said that this concerns an abstract picture of business. In larger organisations the various functions will appear as similarly named departments, while in smaller companies more than one function will often be represented by the same person. It is important that one remains aware of the possibility that various functions can be united in the same person. Separate attention with separate objectives is necessary for each of the functions.

A classification of marketing strategies

To be able to test the definition of the problem the various marketing strategies should be distinguishable from each other. The search is for a single marketing strategy classification. The double unity cell, the result of system thinking, offers the possibility of giving form to the marketing strategy classification. In the double unity cell three parties are distinguished that contribute to the character of a marketing transaction: the supplier, the buyer and the central organisation.

As the purchasing market (all suppliers), the sales market (all buyers) and the central organisation develop themselves further with regards to one particular product, the experience relating to that product in the markets and with the central organisation will increase. In the suppliers' market other relationships and possibilities will arise as the suppliers acquire more experience in producing and supplying a particular product. Therefore the (information) relationship between the purchasing market and the central organisation will have to change.

In accordance with the situation in the purchasing market, the central organisation's sales market will be subject to a learning effect. After a while the buyers will have more knowledge and experience of the product to be bought. They will, as that experience increases, need different information about the product and appreciate other qualities. To establish an optimal tuning to the sales market the central organisation will have to adjust its marketing strategy and also its information system to meet these changes.

Next to this, the central organisation in its strategy cannot avoid the fact that, after a certain period of time, they too will gain more experience. They will be able to produce more effectively and supply at a higher quality. This internal experience can also be recognised in the knowledge that the central organisation has of its buyers and suppliers.

In order to arrive at a classification of marketing strategies the learning effect of the three organisations can be introduced into the double unity cell. In the double unity cell two major strategic points can be seen. Firstly, there is the creation of a scheme on the purchasing side that is indicated here as purchasing strategy. Secondly, there is the creation of a scheme on the sales side that is indicated here as sales strategy. Naturally, it is not possible to arrive at an all embracing marketing strategy for a product-market combination, because a purchased product can be used for more than one saleable product and vice versa.

The next step is to describe the learning effect of the sales market, the purchasing market and the central organisation. For the purchasing market and the sales market this is relatively straightforward. The product life cycle can be used for this. A product has a life that consists of the following consecutive stages: development, introduction, growth, maturity and decline. In each of these stages the market knows various qualities, its own opportunities and threats. For an optimal result the marketing strategy will have to be tuned to this.

The level of experience of the central organisation can be expressed by a comparable internal product life cycle that is called here an experience curve. This experience curve describes the different stages that the central organisation goes through as its knowledge of a specific product-market combination increases. In principle two separate experience curves have to be distinguished in accordance with the two strategic points of view in the double unity cell; one in which the development of the central organisation is expressed with regards to a specific product on the purchasing market, and one in which the development of the central organisation is expressed with regard to a specific product on the sales market. The central organisation goes through an experience curve for every product-market combination consisting of the following stages: development, adoption, diffusion, maturity and withdrawal. In each of these stages the central organisation has several qualities, namely its own strengths and weaknesses. For an optimal result the marketing strategy has to be tuned to this.

With the stages of the product life cycle of the purchasing and sales market and the experience curve of the central organisation the target is nearly reached. The position of the product-market combination in both sets of stages determines the contents of the marketing strategy. What must now be done is to combine the various stages, which can be done very neatly, in two matrices; one for the purchasing side and one for the sales side. The stages of the product life cycle and the experience curve are the axes. In the matrix cells a summary of the characteristics of the market, as well as of the central organisation, can be given. Indications can be devised based on these summaries that best describe the strategy of each matrix cell. (see Figure 6.2)

These classifications actually came about very naturally. On the horizontal axis a description of the market has been given, which proceeds from an external analysis of opportunities and threats in that market. On the vertical axis a description of the central organisation has been given, which proceeds from an internal analysis and gives a description of the strengths and weaknesses of the company. A marketing strategy is, after all, nothing more than a joining of the external analysis with the internal analysis; the opportunities and threats with the strengths and weaknesses.

Figure 6.2 Classification of sales and purchasing strategies

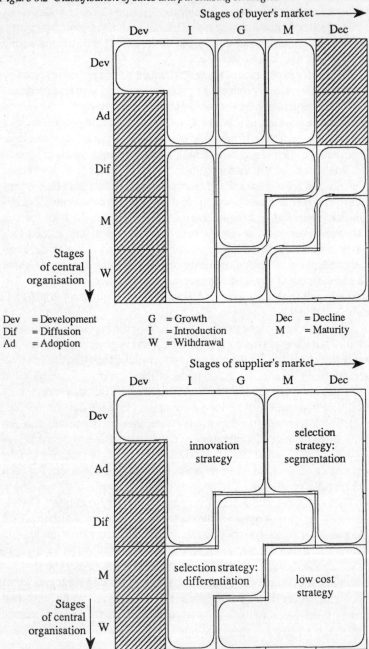

Stages of buyer's market ⟶

| | Dev | I | G | M | Dec |

Stages
of central
organisation ↓

Dev	= Development	G	= Growth	Dec	= Decline
Dif	= Diffusion	I	= Introduction	M	= Maturity
Ad	= Adoption	W	= Withdrawal		

Stages of supplier's market ⟶

| | Dev | I | G | M | Dec |

innovation strategy

selection strategy: segmentation

selection strategy: differentiation

low cost strategy

Stages
of central
organisation ↓

Figure 6.3 Characteristic trajectory of a product market combination

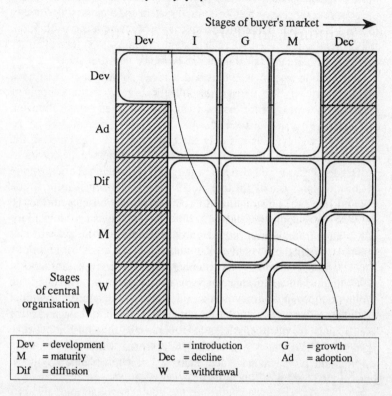

Dev	= development	I	= introduction	G	= growth
M	= maturity	Dec	= decline	Ad	= adoption
Dif	= diffusion	W	= withdrawal		

The matrix makes it clear that a strategy once chosen and described is not valid for ever. As the market and the central organisation improve, a different balance between external and internal factors will develop which therefore demands a different strategy. So a kind of lifeline for a product-market combination can be indicated in the matrix, and from this one can decide what strategies should follow each other to obtain an optimal result. An example of a so-called strategic trajectory for a sales strategy is given in Figure 6.3.

Qualities of information systems

In addition to the classification of marketing strategy, insight into the qualities of information systems is necessary. Only if both are known can one trace, in field research, the qualities which information systems possess that can lead to success. Since little research has been done into the connection between an information system and a marketing strategy in terms of the contribution to the result of a product-market combination, it will be sufficient when, for each strategy, a number of system qualities can be indicated that contribute to the profit for that strategy.

'Information system' is understood to mean all the people, facilities, methods and activities aimed at the collection, processing and supply of information to provide for the information needs of an organisation and the external parties concerned. An information system has to be interpreted widely; it is not only the computer network, but also the informal information that is exchanged between people in the corridor.

The double unity cell also offers assistance in arriving at a description of information systems. In this model a great number of information relationships can be distinguished. Each of these relationships can then be described by a number of qualities. If for each relationship the score for one or more information systems is now determined on the basis of these qualities, the total can be given in a matrix.

Within the double unity cell a number of information relationships can be distinguished for further analyses. (see Figure 6.4) There are ten different information relationships indicated in the diagram.

In Figure 6.4 all the relationships which are important for marketing transactions are distinguished. For example, the relationship between marketing management and sales (5) is essential, where job definition information of the management starts as strategic planning and the

Figure 6.4 Double unity cell with relevant information relations

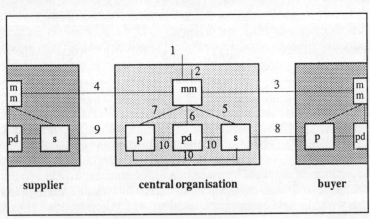

distribution of means. Further the relationship between sales and the buyer (8) is determined for the marketing transaction; formally, it is here that the contents of the marketing mix is communicated to the customer. Relationships 1 and 2 represent the influences of respectively the external surroundings (e.g., environment, legislation and competition) and of the higher management of the organisation. Relationship 10 is also special and includes the mutual tuning of activities at operational level. In industrial environments especially, frequent consultation between purchasing, sales and product development will be necessary.

Each of these relationships now has to be described in terms of a number of information system qualities. To arrive at a list of qualities an extended literature search has been carried out in which as many system qualities as possible were collected. From this list a final choice has been made of nine qualities that best describe the information relationship. The level of formality in the exchange of information will be examined and the degree to which making a decision takes place from the top-down or from the bottom-up (bottom-up/top-down). Does the exchanged information come from a central or local database (centralisation level)? How often is the information exchanged (frequency) and does that happen automatically or only on request (degree of automation)? Is the information exchanged of immediate importance for decision making (importance of content) and the level at which the necessary information is given (utility)? Finally, there is the time that passes between asking the question and getting the answer (response time) and whether the level on which information is used is personal or public?

Naturally the selection of the nine qualities was not random. The following demands are made of every selected quality: the quality is related to an information relation, has an unequivocal, relevant meaning and is measurable. The total set of qualities selected has to provide a reasonable contribution to effective control. In the case of information exchange between two objects one assumes that the aim is goal-directed influence, so that one can talk of a control situation. The literature provides conceptual conditions for effective control.

The information system can now be characterised by judging all the selected system qualities for the selected information relationships of the double unity cell. For example, this could be done by giving a number or a plus and minus scale. An overview of this is given in Figure 6.5.

Figure 6.5 Information system qualities of an organisation in a matrix

Relations Dimensions	1	2	3	4	5	6	7	8	9	10
Formality										
Bottom-up/top-down										
Centralisation level										
Frequency										
Degree of automation										
Importance of content										
Reaction speed										
Utility of Information										
Personal/Public										

Relations
1 = marketing management - external environment
2 = marketing management - internal environment
3 = marketing management - buyer
4 = marketing management - supplier
5 = marketing management - sales
6 = marketing management - product development
7 = marketing management - purchasing
8 = sales - buyer
9 = purchasing - supplier
10 = purchasing - product development - sales

Field research and the results

By tracing the strategy used by a great number of product-market combinations, judging the information system on its qualities and determining the level of success, one can establish by comparison what the relation between marketing strategy and information system is like.

This practical test happens quite simply through an inquiry sent to a number of companies. The covering letter explains what is understood by a product-market combination and the respondent is requested to pick one for his/her company. For this product-market combination the respondent answers three groups of questions. Firstly, there are four multiple-choice questions. Each alternative answer describes a situation of the market or of their company. The respondent has to make four choices from five situations that best fit his/her own product-market combination. From this the marketing strategy is unambiguously determined. (see Figure 6.2) Secondly, questions were asked about the information system, that is assisting the product-market combination. This is achieved by naming the ten relationships from the double unity cell one by one and asking how important the nine qualities are for each of these relations, judged on a scale of seven. By processing the results, all these scores can be placed in a matrix. (see Figure 6.5) Finally, the third group of questions refers to the results of the product-market combination. It was simply asked what the profits of the product group are. Out of interest it was also asked how satisfied the respondent was with the information system.

With the use of non-parametric statistics, profiles can be drawn up of: the information system that on average appears most often for each strategy, the information system described by product managers for each strategy and the most profitable information system for each strategy. It is interesting to compare what a manager would like to do, with what turns a strategy into a success. Phrased differently, how does the information system a manager wants compare with the information system which would contribute most to the profit of the product-market combination? If only result-orientated managers appeared then the score on the satisfaction analyses and the profit analyses, as described above, should be almost equal. However, this is not the case at all. There appears to be a big difference between what the manager aims for and what would be best for the profit of the product group. What is more, the existing information system strongly deviates from both situations. There are at least three gaps in the information supply, shown in Figure 6.6.

Figure 6.6 Gaps in the information supply

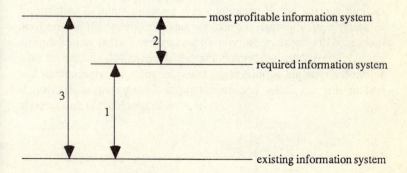

83

As a result of the research, it can be stated that there is indeed a connection between the information system and the marketing strategy. It can be accepted that a carefully designed information system delivers a demonstrable contribution to the profit of a product-market combination. However, one has to be careful since what managers in general aim for in a system design, does not always improve the profitability. For example, it is striking to note that managers would like to see automation in all strategies. However, it is clear that automation is not necessary in all strategies. Even strategies where automation does not expressly contribute to success, still tend to have managers wanting to automate. Automation seems to be a fashion from which unspecified miracles are expected.

This also applies to other characteristics of the information system. However, the research shows that the manager is not familiar with the situation necessary for success. The closure of the gaps in Figure 6.6 will demand a lot of dedication as much from researchers as from managers. However, this research has shown that this dedication is worth the effort.

Bibliography

van Engelen, J M L "The Tuning of Information Systems To Marketing Strategies - a systematic perspective" (Dutch) Uitgeverij Keikes Diepenheim, ISBN 9052310033.

7

IT Investment Decisions - a UK perspective

Juliet Sheppard

Whilst Alan Marsden defines information technology as an enabling tool 'whose whole purpose is to enable the company to improve the bottom line' other authors have more grandiose definitions. [1] Synnott discusses the information age that has covered three eras: the Computer Era, involving centralised computing and a focus on hardware, the Information Era, in which decentralised computing led to a focus on software and information, and now what he defines as the New Vision, which is the exploitation of IT as a competitive weapon. [2] Porter emphasises the effects on competition of rapid technological change in information systems, due to the pervasive nature of information in the 'value chain'. [3] The potential for IT to contribute to an organisations' competitive advantage is as yet unfulfilled according to a report by A T Kearney. [4]

Several clients of Logica, a leading UK consultancy and software house, who are relaunching a business or entering a new one, view the investment in IT as essential to provide the underlying administrative infrastructure rather than a competitive weapon in their overall corporate strategy. (Mike Watkins, Logica 1988) There are are also some authors, who would wish to sound a note of caution, notably Edwards and Ward. [5] They seek to redress the balance concerning today's claims for information technology; not all IT investments are successful. Edwards and Ward argue that the successful use of information technology as a strategic weapon requires an external focus for its use, technical excellence, value added justification and a sharing of benefits between organisations. Their *caveat* argues that organisations who forgo this 'advantage' might have ensured their organisations' survival.

However, judging from the quantity of literature on the subject there is no doubt that companies are being exhorted to consider their use of information technology as a strategic issue. Competition *per se* and client

85

expectations are major pressures on companies to adopt information technology as part of their strategic objectives (Ian Buckingham, Coopers & Lybrand 1985).

The initiative for expanding the use of information technology within organisations is increasingly outside the DP department. In the average UK company 34% of the expected IT expenditure will be made by end-users within the organisation [6]; end-user computing is 'set to grow like wild fire over the next five years'. [7] The trend towards greater end-user computing raises issues as to the management of these changes and a positive requirement for new organisational structures to encourage innovative use of IT. A key question for an organisation to consider is who takes the decision as to the level of IT investment? (Logica 1988).

This chapter presents the results of empirical research in the UK completed in 1988. Nine in-depth interviews were conducted with the following companies: ICI, Rank Xerox, Shell, IBM, British Airways, Coopers & Lybrand, Bank of Ireland, Van den Berghs and Logica. There was no attempt to select a random sample to be representative of any industry, the desire was more for commitment to share their experiences of IT investment decisions. The interviews were conducted with key managers within the organisation; they involved seven open question which sought their perceptions of

- the strategic management of IT investments
- evidence of organisational structure to manage IT development
- the size of the organisation's current expenditure on IT
- the stimulus for IT investment, expected 'benefits' and the measures used for investment appraisal
- future issues which will be relevant for their organisation's IT investment decision

The interviews were taped and have been transcribed. This has afforded a rich set of qualitative experiential data. Included below are several examples of the responses together with a review of the literature.

It is argued that the change associated with the growing size of IT investments stimulated by several different areas within the organisation requires explicit management. A realistic approach to the assessment of the performance of IT investment includes distinguishing between those which supported the *status quo* of the organisation and the investments which will potentially contribute a sustainable competitive advantage. The literature unanimously prescribes the need for IT and corporate strategies to be aligned for the successful management of investments and the ensuing change, and also to realise the potential of the IT investment.

86

However, the evidence from the interviewed companies was not convincing. The specific use of IT to yield a competitive edge highlights a basic dilemma for organisations, namely that the most innovative uses of IT defied rationalisation using the organisation's traditional investment appraisal procedures (at the time of the decision). This was due to their highly uncertain nature. Yet the size of the investments demands a great act of faith without some such analysis.

The expenditure on information technology for an average UK company has increased to £2.67 million in 1989, including user expenditure and hardware maintenance, representing 1.4% of corporate turnover [8]. There are, however, significant differences between spending within different industry sectors. For example, the average spend as a percentage of turnover is shown in Table 7.1. [9]

Table 7.1   *Sectoral expenditure on information technology*

Public Utilities	1.6%
Process	1.4%
Manufacturing	1.7%
Finance	3.0%
Government	2.0%
Education/Research	4.8%
Services	2.3%

Whilst the differences for the education sector have been explained in terms of the large numbers of users (students), the size of investment in the financial sector has been characterised by a choice; 'computerisation or die'. [10] The total UK investment in currently operational IT systems is approximately £40 billion. [11] The specific effect of the stock market crash in October 1987 was surveyed by IBM; the crisis had little or no effect on investment intentions, the majority of chief executives were planning higher levels of investment for 1988. [12] Not all of this expenditure has been invested wisely. A survey by A T Kearney indicated that some £80 million or 20% of the annual expenditure was wasted by inappropriate investment in IT, typically due to missed benefits, expensive hardware or over-engineered designs. [13]

The expenditure on information technology then is already large; comparison with the United States of America may indicate what we can expect in the future. In 1985 the information industry made up 3.3% of the GNP and is predicted to be 6% in 1995; data-processing and communications accounts for some $300 billion, which is expected to rise to one trillion dollars in 1990. [14] The increasing size of spending on IT requires organisations to exercise some investment appraisal of proposed IT projects in accordance with their usual procedures and to manage the ensuing organisational changes (often across traditional functional boundaries). Although year-on-year cost comparisons and an observation of their competitors can indicate how their expenditure on information technology compares, it does nothing to help firms identify those new applications which might allow the organisation to take the lead from their competitors. Meanwhile the existing organisational structure may inhibit the management of such multi-disciplinary projects.

The identification of the proportion of IT investment that relates to maintaining the *status quo* and the amount that is going to contribute to overheads and profits is important. Previously it might have been believed that the total IT investment was a contribution towards profit. (Peter Begley, Bank of Ireland 1988) An estimate of the Bank of Ireland DP budget was £35 million, of which £25 million was required to maintain the current operation and £10 million was available as an opportunity to contribute to profit. It was important to establish as an investment software expenditure as much of the costs of systems development as possible (typically staff costs) which could then be annualised. Begley argues that software, and staff associated with it, should be treated as a capital item. Within banking he estimated that a current industry standard was between 2.5% and 3% of revenue.

In 1989 Rank Xerox spent about £12 million on IT compared to £444 million revenue. (Derek Hornby, 1988) Logica were often asked for industry standards in terms of IT expenditure, but they do not use them and try to avoid talking about them. For Shell UK, the revenue cost of IT was running at about £80 million, which is less than 2% of turnover. However, Shell do not feel that this is an appropriate statistic to determine the level of IT expenditure. In 1988 British Airways spent £50 million in capital and a further £50 million in operating costs for IT. In terms of an industry standard the range is from slightly less than 2% to slightly over 6% of revenue. European airlines tend to be clustered around 2-3%, whereas the American airlines, which have decided to make IT a business in its own right, are currently spending 5-6% of revenue. British Airways is currently at 4% of revenue which has increased in the last two years from just under 3%.

In discussing the use of industry standards with IBM's customers, IBM more typically talk of a growth in their capability of processing power, measured in MIPS (millions of instructions per second). For example, with some customers they are likely to use measures which are 30-40% compound growth rate in MIPS. Also, whilst IBM UK compare their performance within other IBM organisations, they do not currently compare with their competitors. The National Office Support System (NOSS), which cost in excess of £70 million, has been a major investment. (Andy Thorn, IBM 1988)

Last year ICI spent £220 million on IT, which is about 1.7% of revenue. Derek Seddon did not believe industry average percentage expenditures gave a useful measure. He had more sympathy with a stage theory of IT which is described by an S-curve that reflects a slow uptake of IT in its innovative stages and then very rapid expansion as the technologies begin to be assimilated within an organisation, with the S-curve flattening out in the control phase. In his view, IT in ICI and many other major companies was now going to move into the control phase; the growth between 1982 and 1987 had been something like 30-40% capacity growth, corresponding to about 15% per annum real expenditure. In his view, companies were now putting constraints on total expenditure.

[margin note: S curve effect]

Coopers & Lybrand spent £5 million in 1988, which was 3% of their turnover. Ian Buckingham thought companies were spending between 0.5% and 2% of turnover on IT and about 5-15% of their operating costs. There are specific companies (in banking) that have spent as much as 18% of operating costs and some building societies which have spent as much as 20% of operating costs. The industrial companies spend a much lower percentage of turnover. Examples were given of 0.7% of turnover and of a bank spending 16% of operating costs in 1988 having only spent 13% in 1987. The Post Office was spending between 2 and 3% of turnover on IT. The financial sector's ranges are between 0.5% and 15%, service industries between 2% and 6%, manufacturing 2%, while government departments are between 0.5% and 8%. The Manpower Services Commission (now the Training Agency) spent 7% of operating costs of £2000 million. Operating costs seem to be a much better measure than revenue against which to measure IT expenditure.

The IT industry

Companies involved in the provision of both computing hardware and software see their future as increasingly competitive. The life cycle of their products is typically 2-3 years, in order to have innovative products in the market, they invest a high percentage of their revenue on R&D (e.g., 6.5% of revenue for Rank Xerox). Competition is seen to come from the Japanese, whose financing institutions take a longer view of investments, such that their expectations of return on investment differ markedly from those in the UK. Shorter term financing requires companies to view a three-year payback period as a maximum. Further, smaller companies appear to be more effective in the development of software. (Hornby, Rank Xerox 1988)

As software costs are an increasing proportion of the IT investment within an organisation, this is an important issue for larger service companies. Not all organisations are aware of the significance of software within their successful IT application. (Watkins, Logica 1988) However, increasing emphasis on quality is likely to focus attention on its significance.

The development of networks between organisations will stimulate the industry further as organisations wish to be part of these working relations. For example, retailers can now be connected to their wholesalers and their suppliers, so that companies wishing to do business with retail companies of this kind will need to contact their business electronically. The London Market Network connects banks and insurance companies together; organisations in these industries will require systems that can be linked to the network, both for operating business and for the information. (Buckingham, Coopers & Lybrand 1988) (see Chapter 11)

The lowering of trade barriers in 1992 is expected to affect IT investments in the industry. Companies would have to react if it became apparent that there existed different user expectations in the different countries. (Watkins, Logica 1988) For companies like Rank Xerox, that have substantial stand-alone operations in Europe, any reduction in the bureaucracy associated with cross-border transfer and shipping of spares, would reduce their distribution costs (1-2% margins). There is also likely to be an opportunity to establish standards. (Hornby, Rank Xerox 1988) For British companies, who do not currently have networks across Europe, the establishment of a market that has no barriers will present both exciting opportunities and more severe competition.

The size of future IT investments means that they have to compete with other funding requests of a very different nature within the organisation. For example, British Airways' purchase of British Caledonian reduced the number of potential IT investments. Future developments for British Airways will include the continued purchase of other IT companies. During 1988 they bought a 10% stake in Covia, United Airlines' reservation system, and they purchased Bedford Associates, an American software consultancy. (Teather, British Airways 1988)

One view of the future of information technology is that, whilst some applications are new, many successful applications of IT are associated with the rewriting of an existing system. The advantages of IT come from being able to achieve the same objectives in a better way and more immediately. For example, it is the goal of IBM that everything, except delivering their hardware to their clients, can be done electronically. (Thorn, IBM 1988) IBM see one of the major future issues to be standardisation of the business process within organisations requiring an increase in the number of corporate projects to be reviewed.

Derek Seddon (ICI 1988) has a very different view of the role of information technology in the future. He predicts it will be that of a utility, namely that the company itself will not be involved with running their own networks, this would be a service they would purchase. He predicts the future focus will be on how to exploit knowledge in business. Currently the existence of a Director of IT is seen to be evidence of a company's culture which is pro-active in the use of IT, the role in the future will require a 'Director of Knowledge Engineering', whose key objective will be to enable the business to access large amounts of knowledge and be able to exploit that knowledge.

The IT skills of managers was raised as an issue by several of the companies interviewed. For consultancies (e.g., Coopers & Lybrand) new staff would have an expectation of the level of IT available in the organisation. In a more general sense, the awareness and training of business managers was seen to be critical. The technology-driven stimulus for IT investments is likely to be replaced by business or demand-driven need. For strategic process, IT was needed to provide data, abstract information from that data that the business wants and establish the structure to support the information. (Begley, Bank of Ireland 1988)

The management of change

Initial disappointments with IT investment proposals have encouraged senior management to be clearer about the requirements and implications of future investments.

In Shell's experience some of the proposals for larger IT investments have been too ambitious and have had to be aborted. Further, IT projects are required to produce attractive earning powers, the emphasis needs to be the enhancement of current and future business, rather than merely cost-savings. Such investments should not distract the company from its focus; they need to have specific business deliverables associated with them.

In the future the company will operate very differently and will of necessity comprise of a more flexible computer-numerate workforce consequently the establishment of an appropriate appraisal and organisational structure will be important issues. (Reid, Shell 1988)

Many companies see changes in their IT strategy as imminent. Although organisations find it difficult to manage their large IT investments; specifically they do not know what are the appropriate measures to estimate return on investment? Nevertheless they appear to be convinced (notwithstanding the *caveat* issued by Edwards and Ward [15] that more IT investment is the key to a successful business culture.

The measurement of IT performance

Given the size of IT expenditure, an increasing number of companies are asking how these investments should be appraised. They wish to treat IT expenditure as a normal capital investment which has to show definite profits. Thus the size of IT investments requires that they conform to the companies' usual rates of return on capital and yet, at the same time, the more adventurous applications of IT make such quantifications difficult.

A recent survey investigated the return on capital employed associated with IT investments. [16] 36% responded that the return on capital for IT investments was above average, 45% replied that the return was average and 18% that the return was below average. Two out of three of the companies surveyed treated IT expenditure as investment, but only one in three considered the return on capital expended (ROCE) as above average, whereas one in five saw it as below average. It appears that the emphasis placed on IT investments as being equivalent to capital investments is not totally coherent. Companies adopt other measures to indicate a return on their IT investment. 35% of the companies could not provide a short answer on how they knew the ROCE. Some justified it by reduction in staff and salaries saved. Others established it by detailed cost-benefit analysis, some defended it by gaining a competitive edge, whilst other investments were intuitively justified as an act of faith or as being dictated by requests from departments. Companies in the early stages of introducing IT justified the investment in terms of saving salaries, later on in terms of some cost-benefit analysis and, when more mature in the investment of IT, in terms of gaining competitive advantage. Interestingly, the amount invested in IT bore no relation to the company's business performance. Large-scale investments were even seen to hamper profits by slowing a company down.

Marsden is quite explicit about the requirements that investments have to be cost-justified; further he argues that attention has to be given to good initial specifications to prevent over-engineered design. [17]

Price Waterhouse indicate that the cost-containment focus has been replaced by 'what are we getting in return?' and by capacity management and unit cost per transaction measures. The controls advocated as a minimum were year-on-year cost comparisons. The following method for measuring year-on-year computer performance was proposed; the company needs to take a thumb-print of computer resources and identify the applications that are the most expensive to support, there will be one or a group of transactions, which vary with each application's workload in terms of seconds of CPU time or memory, etc. These measures need to be tracked to see if they are constant. The resource requirements need to be evaluated and a best resource located.

There is no doubt that organisations find it very difficult to derive a realistic level of IT expenditure and rate of return to be expected from them. The Coopers & Lybrand survey describes some of the yardsticks that had been adopted namely, cash, staff-savings, subjectively evaluated quality improvements, and image with the client. [18] Some companies derived a realistic IT expenditure and rate of return based on their clients' expectations. By far the most prevalent measure observed was a percentage of the organisations' revenue. Many different benefits have been cited as justification that it will improve the efficiency of existing business areas, open up a number of new business services, improve internal administrative control and the availability of information. The Kobler survey indicated the following management advantages of IT in decreasing order of importance and frequency: [19]

- increased speed of communication of more accurate data
- better quality of communication
- speeding up of the business cycle
- increased business flexibility
- improved decision making gaining a competitive edge
- savings (mainly to staff)
- increased direct control
- awareness of outstanding duties to be completed

The top three benefits in business generally were indicated by the Coopers & Lybrand Survey to be: the provision of management information (88%), reduction of costs (45%) and easy retrieval of information (41%). Whereas the top three benefits for accounting firms indicated in the same survey were: provision of a new or better service for clients (76%), improvement of professional performance (70%) and provision of management information (48%).

Edwards and Ward indicate that there can also be 'disbenefits' for failures. These include the creation of a system that does not fully function, a system that has been implemented half-heartedly and IT investments that allow changes in power against the organisation that implemented the development. [20]

Clients of Coopers & Lybrand are divided in terms of proceeding with investments if there are only tangible benefits, while other clients are prepared to take into account intangible benefits (e.g., quality improvement). In terms of major intangibles the person responsible for achieving it has to be identified and consideration given to its measurement as staff or stock savings. There was a view within Coopers & Lybrand that all intangibles can be translated into tangible benefits if you are prepared to spend enough time experimenting and getting data, etc. (Buckingham, Coopers & Lybrand 1988)

At ICI Derek Seddon viewed quantitative information as a starter for the qualitative discussion. He argued that all return on investments have a risk factor which nobody can really assess.

Conrad Brigden (IBM 1988) gave electronic mail as one example where only a very few companies had established a business case for the investment. The majority of companies felt there was an obvious need for it, which had been stimulated by senior management. It was felt to be too expensive to establish a business case. In the banking and insurance industries productivity seemed to be the major benefit.

Mike Watkins (Logica 1988) gave two measures of worth for the benefit of a particular IT investment. One might be a potential headcount saving, in the sense that if a business is increasing they might calculate the nominal number of staff that would be required, and then argue the proposed IT investment could contribute substantially by reducing this potential headcount. The other measure would be that a particular IT investment could lead to tighter financial control, for example, arguing that invoices could be sent to clients faster and therefore cash received sooner. (Mike Watkins, Logica 1988)

The measures of performance that an organisation uses is one aspect of the IT investment decision. The strategic issues underlying IT investments are of a growing concern to management.

The relationship between IT and corporate strategies

The integration of information systems (as a support service) and business strategy has been accepted as an important goal for many years. [21] The current emphasis (following successful IT applications) is directed towards reviewing the opportunities that IT affords to 'do the business differently'. Many reports address the difficulties of aligning a company's IT investment with its business strategy. This integration is necessary for IT investments to reach their full potential. The Kearney survey identified few companies who at that time had taken full advantage of IT, and who had so aligned their business and IT strategies. IT had been relegated to providing a reactive service for middle-management. The survey indicated that few companies were aware of their competitors' action in the field of IT. Companies lagging in the use of IT were six times more likely to have a poor financial performance within their sectors than the companies leading in the use of IT, and the gap between leading and lagging companies was seen to be widening. [22]

The report of the Kobler Unit confirms these conclusions; market leaders were seen to have a sound IT investment policy based on their business strategy. Although many companies in their survey employed IT to cut costs, leading companies were moving away from this towards longer-term effectiveness, even though such IT investments were harder to justify quantifiably. Aleksander argues that IT investments ought to be judged in terms of defending a company's vulnerability from attack by competitors. [23,24] The Kobler Unit's survey indicated that leading companies exploited their IT investments, whereas lagging companies tended to have a reactive attitude. Whilst integration between the two strategies is argued to be essential, it requires that IT investments undergo the rigours of corporate control as well as the involvement of the DP department in the corporate planning exercises.

There is much in the literature to argue that the ethos or environment of a company most likely to generate new applications for IT is one where there is a 'techno-boss'. A 'techno-boss' is someone who sits above function specialisms and looks at the company from an IT point of view, "someone who has an understanding of the politics or organisational change, span of control and responsibility, work organisation and job design ... who has a good understanding of the technology, but is able to understand 75% of business internal politics.' [25] The need for a person at board level who has business acumen and a good appreciation of IT (but not necessarily a technical specialist) is recognised variously in the literature. Leading companies have a champion for IT as a member of the board.

The role of IT in the organisation

Peter Begley (then Group Coordinator of IT at the Bank of Ireland) defined his role as strategic planning for technology. His job was to understand the company's current business strategy and to identify the ideal technology strategy that would be required for target companies within that strategy. Then, once the target companies had been acquired, to identify the gap between their current technology and the ideal, so that the technology strategy matched the business strategy. (Begley, Bank of Ireland 1988)

Derek Seddon (Director of Information Technology, ICI) identified three distinctive roles as Director of IT. The principal role is to formulate an IT strategy for ICI worldwide and to assist individual autonomous units of ICI to formulate their own IT strategies. Secondly, as Head of the IT/IS function for the group he is concerned with human resource issues of skills balance and career development. Thirdly, he has line management responsibility for the operations of computing and telecommunication networks within Europe and for ensuring that the management of these networks is co-ordinated across the ICI group worldwide. Additionally, Seddon acts as a missionary, to encourage senior management to understand how IT can aid their business; this requires a different management approach from data processing.

His appointment in 1982 reflected ICI's view that IT should be managed more strategically. The first strategy approved by the main Board of ICI was to separate the design, implementation and operation of computing and telecommunication (network) from applications, and to centralise the management of the IT infrastructure. The responsibility for the application of the technology was devolved within ICI's businesses.

This contrasts with Shell's view (Reid, Shell 1988) who sees strategic decision-making as the key role of the Chief Executive office, whereas IT and its management as an essentially line-management operation; the role of Chief Executive is to ensure that line management takes as much positive advantage of IT as they can.

In 1976-77 when Rank Xerox decided to evaluate the IT market as an arena for expansion, they found that their organisation was ill-equipped to deal with initiatives generated from a group of Xerox companies based at Palo Alto, California. The group had been given a very open, non-specific brief. It was considered with hindsight that the exercise would have been more successful had their terms of references been a working remit that involved where the business was going, and what contribution their ideas could have had to that direction. Palo Alto invented a design for a PC mouse but Rank Xerox could not produce it at a saleable price at that time. Instead, it came onto the market 10 years later. (Hornby, Rank Xerox 1988)

At British Airways, applications responsibilities are devolved out into the airline businesses, leaving the corporate IT function with three distinct responsibilities: the overall architecture, technical policy and the infrastructure to support the technical policies that the airlines follow. Below certain levels of investment the decision-making authority exists within the devolved groups, but resides with the Investment Review Group and the Director of Information Management to agree contracts over a certain size. (Teather, British Airways 1988)

[handwritten: 3 areas in BA]

Of the companies interviewed, there seem to be differences in opinion as to how the IT investment decisions were managed and how information technology sits with relation to the company's overall strategy. There were differences in opinion as to how the decision-making should be managed centrally or devolved; and as to the alignment (or not) of IT and business strategies.

[handwritten: differences in views]

The structure of an organisation determines where the IT decisions are taken. Results from the Coopers & Lybrand survey indicate that 20% of these decisions are under the control of finance, 36% were separate from finance, and 24% of the companies had designated an individual manager to make these decisions. [26] The Kobler Unit survey indicated that an increasing number of companies were employing a special IT manager to co-ordinate their IT investments and that there was an increasing trend to remove finance directors from the responsibility of making the companies' IT investment decisions. One of the respondents, who was more successful than most in introducing IT in the Kearney survey, felt that more improvements could be made if organisational boundaries were changed. [27]

*[handwritten: depends on dept's * Today IT man's decide.]*

Organisational structures to manage change

The increasing trend for user departments to be pro-active with respect to the service they request of the DP department (acting as supplier) means that it is often the end-users who insist on priorities. Several of Logica's clients have a structure whereby IT development and IT departments report to a non-technical manager. (Watkins, Logica 1988) Shell's organisation structure is a much more centralised and traditional one; the Information and Computer Services manager is responsible for a centralised service centre. However, each managing director of an operation (for example, EXPO the exploration and production organisation) has members of this centre within their business unit, with a dotted line relationship to the Manager of Information and Computer Service. (Reid, Shell 1988) As we saw earlier, British Airways devolved levels of investment below a certain level into the end-user application areas and retained central

decision-making for larger investments. At ICI, the organisational structure has moved away from decentralisation for IT infrastructure decision
making. Each business unit has responsibility for ensuring that part of
their business strategy included an IT strategy for applications (which
would have been agreed with the Director of IT), but the responsibility for
the technology is centralised so that a coherent infrastructure could be
achieved, thereby ensuring compatibility across the whole of ICI.

Coopers & Lybrand's clients have many different ways of dealing with
the responsibility for IT. Different companies have different styles but
there seems to be a general tendency away from committee decision-
making towards individual responsibilities for the strategy and for the
means of delivering it. In the private sector the whole board may meet to
discuss strategy, whilst some companies operate a sub-committee of the
board. Government department deal with the decision via a committee or
steering committee for IT. Whether it be a private or public sector client,
Coopers & Lybrand are often invited in to deal, in the first instance, with
an IT steering group for the client organisation. (Buckingham, Coopers &
Lybrand 1988)

The Bank of Ireland identified a new organisational structure and
person to promote their technology strategy. The structure involved a
holding company with approximately ten members at the top and below
it sat the business units, each of which have to prepare an individual
strategic statement. The holding company then looks at a group strategy.
It was emphasised that it was a 'top-down, bottom-up' kind of approach,
namely that it was iterative and sought information from the business
units. (Begley, Bank of Ireland 1988)

Alignment of IT and corporate strategies

As an example of the relationship between IT strategy and corporate
strategy within ICI, Derek Seddon gave the implementation of their
corporate accounting system. This example has been written up elsewhere. [29] It illustrates the difficulty that a matrix organisation has in
handling an investment of this nature. A central requirement was to be able
to measure in a consistent manner the performances of individual businesses within the ICI worldwide company; after a major piece of work to
define precisely the accounting language that would be used inside ICI,
the specification required a whole new software system. It was the introduction of this software system and its impact on IT strategies that has
been the major problem.

Derek Seddon highlighted 1982 as a crossover year in which the demand for computing outstripped the price performance of the technology. As a consequence senior management saw a dramatic increase in the total cost of IT. The size of IT investments now required companies to evaluate the total growth in costs more explicitly. Derek Seddon identified about 80% of their current investment as maintaining what they do already, an integral part of the business. Not more than 1-2% of investment was going into things which may or may not yield a competitive advantage. He emphasised that one criterion of success in identifying areas of competitive advantage is that the ideas were evaluated by the customers and perceived to be valuable. His role within the company identified a corporate view with respect to IT strategy which was articulated in terms of two stages, one identifying where the IT resources were deployed today, and the other where they might be deployed tomorrow. The former question accounted for 80% of a company's resources. To redirect resources a clear mechanism linked to business goals is needed. In identifying the use of IT for the future, the key seemed to be to develop a partnership in a business between the IT specialist and business functions in order to identify how IT could help the businessman think differently about his business. (Seddon, ICI 1988)

Andy Thorn at IBM echoed the emphasis of IT strategy in terms of what the company is currently doing and what it may do in the future. The IS director will manage the day-to-day running of information systems in the company; the investment associated with maintaining the base operation was differentiated from investments, which are taken at a higher level, because they would have to compete with other investment opportunities within the company (for example, different office locations, larger sales force teams, etc). The strategic planning conference is a once a year event, which concentrates on the investment associated with the base year, and sets specific targets for performance (e.g., that 98% of the batch jobs are delivered on time). IBM's NOSS was given as an illustration of an investment which gave a competitive edge, primarily in terms of reinforcing IBM's image as an advanced user of its own technology within the market place. NOSS was a decision taken by Tony Cleaver, IBM UK Chief Executive, as a new investment opportunity rather than a maintenance investment decision taken by the IS director. (Thorn, IBM 1988)

At British Airways the organisation structure reinforces the integration of information systems strategy with the business strategy. It is at the level of the investment review group, where the investments to support updated applications is reviewed in line with the corporate strategy. The information for this group comes from the top-down, in the form of corporate imperative missions, and from the bottom-up with requirements from the business centres. One of its tasks is to ensure that corporate imperatives are met in order to support corporate missions and goals. (Teather, British Airways 1988)

Reid agreed that currently there is not a relationship between the IT and business strategies at Shell UK; business strategy is developed in isolation from the IT strategy. He argued that there is an IT strategy whose objective is to support the operation. He saw IT as an integral part of the operation of the business but not of the corporate strategy. (Reid, Shell 1988)

Rank Xerox was described as a 'total systems company'. Their IT developments have focused on what they need to do and for the last three years have progressed along the same direction. (Hornby, Rank Xerox 1988)

Peter Begley (Bank of Ireland 1988) sees businesses strategy sitting above technology strategy, and that the latter would be defined as implications of the business strategy.

One of the most important questions for a company to answer may be 'Who in our organisation will take the decision as to the level of IT expenditure?' In a way the answer to this question identifies explicitly the relationship between IT and business strategy within an organisation. For IT to be closely related to the business strategy of a company, the position of this person would have to be close to the corporate decision-making of the organisation.

IT and competitive advantage

The analyses from the Kearney survey indicate that leading companies have a better financial performance than lagging companies; the implication being that leading companies are using IT to give them a clear competitive advantage. Porter argues that technology (and in this he includes all technologies in his value-chain, not just IT) affects competitive advantage if it has a significant role in determining relative cost position or differentiation and is sustainable. A firm that can discover a 'better' technology for performing an activity than its competition thus gains competitive advantage. This may be either for the value activity itself, or for other drivers of cost or drivers of uniqueness. Such technological developments can raise or lower economies of scale, establish new inter-relationships and create opportunities for advantages in timing. He argues that organisations need to ensure that competitive advantage, rather than scientific interest, is the prime consideration for technological investment. [30]

Companies that are more experienced in large IT investments see the use of IT as a weapon in their strategic plans. The literature includes many examples of exciting applications of information technology that have gained a new position in the market, or new businesses for the companies. (see Chapters 1 and 8)

Arthur Andersen & Co indicate some interesting trends in IT and give many examples of the variety of its uses. They define information for competitive advantage (IFCA) and consider a methodology developed by Porter and Arthur Andersen, which is seen to be an extension of Porter's work. In telecommunications, IFCA allows organisations to reach their outcome anywhere; the benefits include improving relation times and broadening the market. Expenditure on telecommunications has increased by 30%-100%. [31]

Artificial intelligence has been developed by hardware manufacturers seeking to satisfy front office needs. The ability of this technology to emulate the experience of limited human resource, in a technology that is re-usable and easier to maintain, has been hindered by the time taken to develop the appropriate software. (see Chapter 14)

Computer-aided software engineering (CASE) has been developed as a recognition that large mission-critical projects differentiate organisations from their competition, and that the development of such systems is often lengthy with unpredictable costs that often exceed budgets, and require high intensity of labour. The benefits of CASE are that it is the production facility of software which is argued to be the life-blood of an organisation. The survey argues that CASE returns a higher value per dollar spent than more traditional non-integrated methods.

Computer-integrated manufacturing (CIM) has been developed as a reaction to competition which requires manufacturers to maximise customer service efficiency/productivity/quality, whilst simultaneously shortening product life-cycles by simplifying systems and then automating them and integrating across departments and functions. CIM is proposed to considerably lower costs it has been argued that in a typical American manufacturing cost-breakdown, CIM saving will be in the order of 15%-30% in engineering, 30-60% in work-in-progress inventories, but 500% in engineering productivity and 300% in capital equipment operating time. (see Chapter 9)

Business led IT investment

Peter Begley emphasises the need for the following question to be asked 'how can we identify areas where technology can be an generator rather than a spender of resources?' A business led application was the oil stock product at Shell. The main stimulus was to be able to identify the location and quantity of oil stock. This was also a technically driven application because the existing systems had been in place for a long time and were becoming very difficult to maintain. A comparison was not made across alternative IT investments; the investment was a request within a business area. Some of Logica's clients are motivated to replace older systems with newer technology and sometimes by a needs-driven requirement (e.g., the establishment of a new business).

British Airways' investment in Galileo would seem to be expanding the services that the airline could offer. They wish to be seen as a total service business in the travel industry, one end of it is identifying all the business needs through to the supply of a flight. Identifying business needs is important so that British Airways controls the channel through distribution. Secondly, the technology itself was seen to dictate that there would only be a few of these systems and hence British Airways wished to be involved. The illustration at ICI of the corporate accounting system was also seen to be an application, rather than technology driven stimulus, for IT investment.

Coopers & Lybrand illustrated a business led application by one of their clients, the Department of Transport. They were invited to formulate an IT strategy as a reaction to an accumulated loss of funds due to the lack of recovery of licence fees, etc. The investment of £56 million was cost justified. However, in looking at the IT strategy it became apparent that the organisation's structure could not support it and so recommendations were made for changes, which were subsequently implemented.

IT for competitive advantage

Coopers & Lybrand express the view that there is no doubt that the large IT investments for a bank (approximately two thirds of their capital investment) is directed toward gaining competitive advantage. For example, Barclays' Connect Card was originally opposed by retailers, but such is the influence of the Bank that not only do retailers now accept it but other banks have had to follow suit. Hence Barclays was able to steal a march on the competition. Electronic Point of Sale (EPoS) systems was given another example of IT used to gain competitive advantage. As well as increasing the throughput at checkout points, with much better information, Sainsbury's are able to stock their shelves more efficiently, reducing the risk of stock outs. Customers will seek this level of service and get frustrated by other supermarkets which do not offer it.

The examples were used to illustrate the view that there appeared to be a life-cycle associated with the use of IT as a competitive weapon, namely that in the early stages the company was differentiated from its competition by its innovative use of IT. Later as the industry adopts the innovation, (for example EPOS) the organisation is no longer differentiated from its competition, the whole industry now has to offer an improved service. (Buckingham, Coopers & Lybrand 1988)

Models for IT investment decisions

Porter advises organisations to make the conscious decision to be a leader or a follower of technology. He argues this decision should not be taken by default. His model includes the following steps:

- identify all the technologies in the value-chain to include all of the operations and not just product or process
- identify the potentially relevant technologies in other industries and those under development
- determine the likely path of change of key technologies
- identify which technologies are significant, i.e. those that create a sustainable competitive advantage themselves, shift the cost or differentiation in the firm's favour, yield 'first mover' advantages, or improve the overall industry structure by providing additional barriers to entry
- assess the company's relative capabilities and cost improvements
- select an IT strategy to reinforce the firm's overall competitive advantage, which should include a ranking of projects, which are described below in terms of effect on cost and/or differentiation;
  * the leader or follower decision
  * licensing policies
  * the means of obtaining the technologies (internally or externally)

Marsden indicates that the company needs to identify their critical success factors (CSFs), audit their current operating practices, search for cost savings, and review existing and proposed systems. [32] They are advised to define the management control information that they require, outline a functional specification and indicate priority. The model advocates a survey of competitors' IT application and a review of technical issues. Thus the development strategy can be formulated, the system management issues identified and implementation plans drawn up.

Lindsay identifies a model for public sector agencies that reflects the influence of Porter, but also interestingly includes the necessity for a 'techno-boss'. [33] The strategic objectives and CSFs need to be developed. He further requires the decision processes, information used and the people involved to be established. The Porter value-chain and cost-drivers have to be constructed and an approximate cost per unit established from the organisation chart and annual budget. An information map of the activities is constructed, indicating the movement of information and the activity cost-shifts modeled. Alternative information strategies should be evaluated across the value-chain, with relation to the business strategy and appropriate hardware/software design prototypes and applications selected. Finally, the person who designs the strategy needs to be identified and the author evaluates the case for an external agent, namely someone who can stand outside the internal politics of the organisation to give an impartial view. Hence, the concept of 'techno-boss' would require such a person to be aware of the internal politics, to be able to relate to both the technical and business objectives of the organisation.

Butler believes that the three models of Rosenberg, Abernathy and Utterbach and Sahal can be used together to establish an IT strategy. [34,35,36,37] He amalgamates the meta-learning projections of Sahal with the product-process model of Abernathy and Utterbach. Butler's explanation considers a product in the segmental stage of development. At $t = 0$ when the product is being considered, it may be technologically advanced and highly differentiated, which at $t = 1$, when it is manufactured and marketed, the expectation may be that it lags technically or, at least, be difficult to differentiate. Rosenberg's 'learning by using' suggests that between $t = 1$ and $t = 2$ further improvements should be incorporated into the product, so that it may be differentiated again. The period between $t = 2$ and $t = 3$ is the technologically differentiated shelf-life of the product. 'The period over which the product maintains its competitive advantage, is directly related to its stage of development.' Product success is more likely if the product is being introduced in the later stages of development of the production processes of the customers.

Max Hand describes Kearney's approach to developing an IT strategy. in three steps. [38]

1 The Company has to identify its CSFs and must succeed in doing these better than their competitors. For each CSF there will be a number of dependant accountabilities within the business for which performance objectives can be set. For example, if the CSF is delivery time, the accountability would include inventory and control, demand forecasting and production scheduling, etc. The

associated objectives will be an inventory control system, forecasting accuracy within a lead time, and a lead time associated with a production schedule, where higher priority items have different inventory controls, forecasting and production schedules, etc. IT is then focussed on providing the management control information needed to monitor the performance against these objectives and to improve the effectiveness of activities, which contribute to the performance objectives set.

2 The IT development plan has to be based on clear cost-benefit justification. He argues that the organisation is split into activity units (AU) and that information is available on each of these AUs as: organisation, tasks, objectives and level of service, the 8-12 main activity headings, a breakdown of people costs against activities, a breakdown of other costs against activities and the volumes of flows of information for each activity. This provides a horizontal view of how people spend their time instead of the vertical view of companies' costs. High cost activities, duplications and cost displacement opportunities will be identified by this type of analysis. Inefficiencies will be indicated in the form of backlogs, long processing time and errors. Each development project is individually subject to cost-benefit analysis and the data already collected on activity cost can be used to establish cost displacement benefits, so that projects may be ranked in descending order of cost-benefit. The list now shows increasing development costs and increasing cumulative benefit. It is at this point that senior management can agree priority sequences, not only in terms of the cost-benefit, but also in terms of the potential opportunity benefits of the IT proposal.

3 The final step is to define the technical framework (TF) expressed in business rather than technical terms. Hardware and software should be chosen and technical architecture established to meet business needs and maximise opportunities; to have an appropriate architecture for data, computers and telecommunications and to provide a logical development path from the existing IT usage. Hand argues that it is very important to have an IT strategy that is thoroughly examined during development. Companies should have a clear view of what they expect from IT in relation to their business strategy.

Synnott uses established strategic models to indicate how IT can be incorporated. [39] He adopts portfolio analysis methodology to indicate a five-step procedure:

1 Strategic business units (SBU) are located on a matrix that indicates their relative position with respect to sales versus profits. For example, some SBUs will occupy positions in the upper left quadrant, which produce both high sales and high profit (Zone 1), whereas Zone 4 SBUs are low sales/low profit activities.
2 SBUs are coded against return on capital
3 SBUs' position on the Boston Consulting Group (BCG) matrix are identified and missions signed as indicated by whether their position is 'star' which would indicate a 'lead mission'
4 Information resources are matched to mission, so that lead and niche SBUs get most of the support
5 Information and business strategies are matched. The three basic business strategies (c.f. Porter) are
  • cost leadership - where IT is focused on product activity
  • product differentiation - where IT is focused on technological innovation
  • market focus (to find a niche) - where IT might be a mix of productivity/technological innovation or just support.

Hence Synott's model an amalgamation of portfolio analysis, the BCG Matrix and Porter's work. He does not argue that it is a particularly innovative model, rather that whichever model is adopted integration between IT and business strategies is required.

Conclusions

The in-depth interviews added some interesting insights and context to the literature review and allow the following summary and recommendations.

Some major uses of IT remain in the area of doing what was done better but quicker and better. Applications of IT range from administrative infrastructures to new ways of doing different things, the latter in some cases affording the organisation a 'competitive advantage'.

Notwithstanding that there are quite wide industry differences in the percentages of revenue invested in IT the expenditure is still increasing, currently some £40 billion (although Derek Seddon thought this growth will slow down). Software will account for an increasing proportion of the investment.

An important distinction has been made between IT investment associated with maintaining the organisation's *status quo* and proposals which, by allowing the business to offer a new service, will directly contribute to profits and overheads. There is the additional concept that expenditure associated with this (staff, software, etc) is capital which can be annualised over time. The evaluation of this maintenance IT support requires a year-on-year monitoring of the most expensive applications in terms of CPU or memory and search for the most effective resource to provide the support.

IT investment for 'new business' will require money and non-monetary assessments. Organisations use industry 'standards' (e.g., percentage of revenue or operating costs) as one measure for their relative performance. ROCE and payback period cannot be used in isolation because of the high uncertainty associated with the potential for competitive advantage.

The literature advocates that an organisation's IT strategy needs to be aligned with its corporate goals; further that IT provides the opportunity to view the business differently. A champion for IT at the corporate level decision making contributes to the achievement of integrated policies. The identification of who in the organisation is responsible for the levels of IT expenditure is an indicator of the relationship of the two policies. Integration also requires IT investments to be justified using the usual organisational investment appraisal procedures.

There is no model that generates an innovative use of IT. What is important is that the innovation be evaluated as to the likelihood of it providing a sustainable competitive advantage for a long enough period to be profitable. Porter's work can be used as a checklist to estimate each alternative's potential.

The author is of the view that the use of any one of the formal approaches outlined has major benefits for an organisation. The increase in end-user applications and IT proposals from many different functions within an organisation has led to the adoption of IT investments which have not been evaluated with respect to the organisation's mission statements nor compared across IT alternatives. Porter's model requires the organisation to make a conscious decision to lead or lag, the model is applicable to technology as a generic term and it outlines pertinent questions to place the IT strategy within the context of the organisation's corporate policy.

References

1   Marsden, Alan "Getting the Right Return of IT" *Management Services* January 1988.

2   Synnott, William R "The Information Weapon - winning customers and markets with technology" John Wiley & Sons, Chichester, 1987.

3   Porter, Michael E "Competitive Advantage - creating and sustaining superior performance" Free Press, New York, 1985.

4   Hand, Max "Developing a Business Needs Strategy for Information Technology Development"
5   Edwards, Chris and Ward, John "Beware of the Hype" *The Guardian* 1988.
6   Price Waterhouse "Information Technology Review 1988/89" Price Waterhouse, London, 1988.
7   National Computing Centre "Members' Survey" NCC, Manchester, 1987.
8   Price Waterhouse, op cit.
9   NCC, op cit.
10 *Which Computer?*, 1987.
11 Alvey Research Programme, 1987.
12 Brigden, Conrad "A Survey on Investment in Information Technology" Internal Report, IBM Market Research Group, February 1988.
13 Kearney, A T "The Barriers and The Opportunities of Information" A T Kearney & DTI, London, 1984.
14 Synnott, op. cit.
15 Edwards and Ward, op cit.
16 Griffiths, Catherine and Hochstrasser, Beat "Does Information Technology Slow You Down?" Kobler Unit, Imperial College, London, 1987.
17 Marsden, op cit.
18 Coopers & Lybrand Associates "The Chartered Accountant in the Information Age" 1985.
19 Griffiths and Hochstrasser, op. cit.
20 Edwards and Ward, op. cit.
21 Feeny, David and Brownlee, C G "Competition in the Era of Interactive Network Services" Oxford Institute for Information Management, Templeton College, 1986.
22 Kearney, op. cit.
23 Aleksander, Igor "The Measure of Success" *Business Computing & Communications*, October 1986.
24 Aleksander, Igor "A Remedy for Vulnerability" *Business Computing & Communications,* May 1987.
25 *Which Computer?*, 1987.
26 Coopers & Lybrand, op. cit.
27 Griffiths and Hochstrasser, op. cit.
28 Kearney, op. cit.
29 Grindley, Andrew, North Western University Case Review, 1987.
30 Porter, op. cit.
31 Arthur Andersen, op. cit.
32 Marsden, op. cit.
33 Lindsay, John "Designing and Implementing Information Systems Strategies" Kingston Polytechnic, School of Information Systems, Working Paper for Second Kawasaki City Conference 1987.
34 Butler, John "Theories of Technological innovation as useful tools for corporate strategy" *Strategic Management Journal* 9 pp 15-19, 1988.
35 Rosenberg in Butler.
36 Abernathy and Utterbach in Butler.
37 Sahal in Butler.
38 Hand, op. cit.
39 Synnott, op. cit.

Part III
Implementation

8

Examples and Implications of Strategic Information Systems

John Fripp

There are many well-documented cases of companies which have used information technology (IT) and information systems (IS) to give competitive advantage. These include American Hospital Supply (AHS, now Baxter Healthcare), Otis Lifts, American Airlines, McKesson Corporation and others. AHS set up communications links with it's major customers, allowing them to place orders direct. The result was that over a five year period AHS revenues grew by 17% per annum when the rest of the business sector was declining. They also achieved a return on sales which was four times higher than the industry average.

In what follows the term strategic information system (SIS) will be used where companies have developed systems that have either given competitive advantage, as in the above cases, or have developed systems which have significantly affected the overall conduct and success of their organisations. Most commonly quoted examples originate in the US, two exceptions being Thomson Holidays and Benetton. [1,2] The work described below began as an attempt to discover other examples of UK or European organisations using strategic information system. Information has been compiled on nearly 200 such cases, and detailed research has been conducted into a smaller number of these.

Some writers (e.g., the Index Group) have suggested that accounts of SIS are somewhat exaggerated or oversimplified. [3] In what follows the results actually achieved in each case will be detailed. A further problem with most of the published accounts is that they focus on the technology and its benefits and say very little about how the systems were introduced. Managers are becoming increasingly concerned with means as well as with ends. It is not very helpful to quote examples of the results that have been achieved, impressive as these are; the crucial question is how can they be achieved? What managerial processes and methods were involved? Who in the management or technical team is best able to develop these systems? The cases described here have therefore been studied more deeply than is usually reported, focusing on the following major concerns:

- how was the system introduced? Was it the result of a deliberate corporate planning process, conceived by the top management and carried out according to plan? Was it introduced as a reaction to external events or was it conceived by technologists?
- what planning process was used? Were the traditional project management methods involved, or were the usual methods inadequate for what are often far-reaching systems? Was it an evolutionary or a revolutionary process?

A related issue is the extent to which the companies made use of external consultants, either to help them rethink the whole of their business objectives, and the integration of information systems within those objectives, to create new opportunities for strategic information systems, or to provide technical input at appropriate times. Also, what use did the companies make of any of the well publicised conceptual models to develop these ideas? How close is the planning of strategic information systems to central business planning? What was the role of top management?

It has been stated that there needs to be a solid 'base' of experience in the traditional transaction-orientated data processing activities, from which strategic applications develop and grow over a period of time. [4,5] The opposite hypothesis has also been advanced, namely that firms deeply entrenched in traditional DP applications will be blind to new opportunities. Being good at internal efficiency or transaction processing orientated systems does not necessarily make the firm able to respond to strategic applications, which may require a fundamentally different way of conceiving the business and of information systems within it. [6]

- what was the contribution of data processing? Did the DP department change in order to facilititate the new applications of information systems? How does DP report to the rest of the organisation? To what extent did the company have a good 'track record' of more traditional data processing applications, or was this type of expertise irrelevent for the types of systems described here?

The 'Product Champion' is often advanced as the key figure in the development of strategic information systems. [7,8] This is a powerful individual who plays a major role in developing the initial idea, or in driving it through to fruition. Conventional wisdom is that the champion must come from outside the information systems department, often from among the ranks of users. The product champion notion finds widespread support in technological innovation and in other major change activities: [9]

- what evidence was there of the product champion? What part of the organisation did he or she come from, and what role did he play?

Extending the argument for a product champion, since technology-induced change is a subset of organisational change, and since it is often a profound process, even the product champion is not sufficiently powerful to make the change happen. What is needed is an organisation that has proved to be good at carrying out important change programmes:

- to what extent were the companies good at managing change generally? Did they have a 'New Venture' mentality which made the introduction of the system easier?

Contrary to many claims made by the first references, some recent findings have shown that investment in IT is no guarantee of success, indeed the misplaced investment in IT can do more harm than good. [10,11] So the final issue is:

- what was the effect on the 'bottom line' for the company?

Methodology

Two companies were chosen from each of several business sectors, including light manufacturing, retail banking, insurance, and retail and distribution. Interviews were carried out with senior managers and directors of each firm, and additional documentary evidence was gathered. Interviewees included systems managers and directors, other directors and chief executives. Interview times averaged about two hours per company. Interviews were semi-structured, concentrating on the above major issues, and were tape recorded. Summaries of the main points arising were sent to the companies for comment. The methodology did not involve any formal statistical testing as the sample was too small and this approach was not thought appropriate at this stage of the research. We now give a brief account of each case.

Implementation

ABC International

ABC International are part of the Reed International group and produce a range of travel guides, the best known of which is the ABC World Airways Guide. The Guide is circulated mainly to travel agents, airlines and corporate users, and is considered the 'bible' of air travel.

The Guide had several unique advantages. It was an accurate account of virtually all the scheduled air flights throughout the world, and it also included details of transfer connections between airports. The data for the production of the guide was sent by airlines each month on paper and on media suitable for direct computer input. Each month ABC's mainframe computers produced data on tape ready for computer typesetting. The volume of data was a severe problem and in 1983 the computers were showing signs that they needed to be updated.

In the same year a new Chief Executive of ABC Travel Guides was appointed, also having responsibility for data processing. He took a close look at the company's computer equipment and found it was incompatible with that of the airlines. The fact that the department was situated 80 miles away from ABC International was also a severe limitation. Competitors (especially Dun and Bradstreet) were beginning to introduce on-line services which were becoming a major threat to ABC.

The new chief executive recognised that it was vital for ABC Travel Guides to be available on-line to customers. If ABC's systems could be made compatible with those of the airlines it would be possible to offer a range of added services with the Guide. Shortly afterwards the business was reorganised into Reed Telepublishing and, after detailed negotiations with SOGAT 82, new staff were hired, the computer department relocated, new mainframe computers were purchased and all the relevant software re-written. Responsibility for the latter was given to a newly appointed director of IT.

The result was that the Guide was produced electronically in 1985 and a range of additional services were made available. Travel agents can now view the Guide through viewdata terminals. Unfortunately many agents feel they need access to both the printed and the on-line versions of the Guide, and the terminals are also heavily used for other purposes, e.g., Thomson's TOP system. However since 1985 the sales and profits of Reed Telepublishing have increased rapidly. In 1987 the Chief Executive of Reed International said that 'ABC International had an exceptional year in spite of difficulties in the travel market.'

Clydesdale Bank

The Clydesdale Bank's Counterplus system was developed in 1982, jointly by British Petroleum (BP) and by Clydesdale, one of Scotland's major banks. It is a unique electronic payments (EFTPOS) system which operates at over 60 BP filling stations. The system will accept 13 different types of cards.

The system was introduced on a trial basis in two filling stations in Aberdeen and the results of the trial were sufficiently encouraging for the scheme to be expanded. Garage proprietors found that EFTPOS encouraged customer loyalty and both customers and proprietors were impressed with the speed of the transaction. The system works in the usual way; after purchase details are entered by staff, the customer enters his or her PIN number, or authorises the transaction by signature. Authorisation takes five or six seconds, and the total transaction time is similar to that of a cash transaction. Actual funds are not transferred into the retailer's account until after close of business. At the discretion of the proprietor, cash may be withdrawn, thus giving convenient banking facilities.

Advantages for both parties include the reduction in cheque processing. The customer still has credit if required, as credit cards are also accepted. The system uses terminals which are either linked to communications equipment at the nearest Clydesdale Bank branch, or to the Bank's central computing facilities in Glasgow.

Clydesdale plan to link their system to the national EFTPOS system once it becomes possible. The national scheme will give the further advantage of accepting all cards and providing a single nationwide settlement system.

Counterplus was the pioneering EFTPOS system which many others have followed. The Midland Bank has started its own Speedline system, which was opened in Milton Keynes in February 1986. This accepts all Access cards and Midland Bank Group Mastercards, and will allow customers to pay for up to £200 worth of goods or services per week. Charges for Speedline are £1,000 per terminal and 6p per transaction, about the same as the Counterplus charge.

An example of the effect of EFTPOS is shown by the fact that in an Aberdeen food shop the average value of Counterplus transactions is 50% higher than for other methods of payment. A retailer using EFTPOS comments that 'EFTPOS gives us that extra dimension of service, added value and efficiency'.

W H Smith

One of the UK's strongest retailers, W H Smith are sustaining their performance by new store designs and an ambitious refurbishment programme. Central to this is the installation of electronic point of sale (EPOS) technology in 200 of their High Street stores and a unique computer aided design (CAD) service to aid their architects and store planners.

EPOS is particularly valuable in stores which can sell 60,000 lines of merchandise. Before introducing EPOS one London store made use of no less than 70 books to monitor stocks on a three week cycle. This was a tedious and error-prone business. The system gave no idea what was selling well, since items could be sold out within the first day and be out of stock for three weeks. EPOS gives better stock control leading to better contribution to profits, better use of staff with no more need to do manual stock checks and a higher stock turnover. Smith's plan to spend over £20m on point of sale technology.

The CAD software, called RUCAPS (Really Useful Computer Aided Planning System), contains a detailed file of information about the store being redesigned and about all the many fixtures and fittings that could go inside it. W H Smith see it as the answer to their problem of how to redesign 20 existing stores each year and design 20 new ones. It saves time at the stage of making changes to layout, and in printing out plans for use at stores.

The system allows W H Smith's own interior designers to see on screen a 'three dimensional' image of each of their stores. They can then alter the layout at will, within the constraints of the overall site, to find the best positions for displays, bookshelves, etc. It shows how the new arrangement looks from the perspective of a customer, whether child or adult.

The greatest benefits are expected when the information from the EPOS system is linked to the RUCAPS database. The link will allow Smith's to extend Direct Product Profitability, by attaching a value to each of it's product lines, thus maximising the selling value of each metre of shelf space. W H Smith are already among the leaders in both point of sale systems and computer aided design. By bringing these together, they will create a retailing advantage that other retailers may find hard to match.

Examples and implications

Interflora

Interflora is the world's largest independent association of florists, having some 2,700 florists in the UK, with 44,000 members worldwide in 140 countries. In 1986 they dealt with 4.5 million orders, 10% of which were international. They depend very much on the confidence that members have in the quality of their service.

To place an order, the customer visits or telephones a local florist and asks for flowers to be sent anywhere in the world. The customer pays the local shop but another shop delivers the flowers. Instead of one florist dealing directly with another to ask for payment, Interflora works out who owes what at the end of the month. Each shop claims the cost of delivery that month from Interflora, which is deducted from the amount claimed against it from other florists. Profits are shared between shops and Interflora. In the past, accounts were settled by post or direct debit and a batch computer system was used at Interflora HQ for clearing and banking operations.

In the mid-1980s the existing batch system needed redesigning and the company took the opportunity to expand their system. By the end of 1987 Interflora had installed 1900 terminals in its shops, all linked to a central mainframe computer. The terminals were provided by British Telecom and are basically expanded microcomputers with printers. They transmit orders directly between Interflora members and they also collect and store accounting information, dialling up HQ periodically to transmit the information to the central mainframe.

Interflora own the terminals and the florists pay whenever they use the system. Data can also be sent to florists from the central computer, for example, to prevent orders being sent to any florist which is unable to cope for any reason. Interflora can also use the system to monitor how florists are performing.

The automation of its business has allowed the 2,700 members to operate more efficiently. Advantages for the florists include reduced ordering costs, compared with a normal telephone call, and automatic dialling and printing of orders. Accounting is also done automatically, thus relieving the florist of the need to add up orders and keep a check on what is owed.

International orders can also be handled in most overseas countries. Interflora uses leased lines to communicate with other countries. Interflora have recently expanded to Russia; Mrs Thatcher used this service recently to send Mrs Gorbachev a bunch of flowers.

Benetton

Benetton is one of the best documented European examples of companies which have used information systems as an integral part of their operations. Information systems have certainly played an important part in Benetton's success, but less so than many accounts suggest.

The company was founded in Italy in 1965, and has grown to be the biggest producer of clothing in Europe, three times the size of the next biggest firm. Benetton were the first to introduce bright colours and new materials into the Italian fashion market. They have recently diversified into other types of fashion goods and into new businesses, including financial services and IT consultancy. The company has maintained low production costs and is highly flexible, using information systems to ensure production is able to respond rapidly to customer demand.

Benetton is a good example of industrial "networking", in order to make use of far more resources than they actually control. They handle the supply side of their business through a large number of subcontractors, who produce 80% of their products, and sell through a network of 4,000 shops worldwide, which are franchised.

The clothes are designed on video screens linked to computers which can translate a new design into patterns very quickly. In principle a new design could be transferred into production in a matter of hours. They also operate a fully computerised warehouse that can handle up to 36,000 boxes of barcoded goods per day.

Another component of the Benetton information system is their use of data communications networks. In this way their agents, or representatives who control a group of shops, can transmit orders and other information to the control centre in Italy, thus letting the company know how customer preferences are developing. Benetton also have a simple shop management system for use in their shops. The goods are all bar coded and the system allows shop owners to collate information on sales every day, thus providing up-to-date reports on sales by product line or sales assistant.

Benetton have succeeded in a notoriously difficult market. Although geographically dispersed, their integrated production, distribution and sales communications systems have removed much of the risk from the fashion business, and allowed the company to maintain its feel, and quick response to, the market place.

Friends' Provident

Friends' Provident has grown from a small mutual society set up in 1832 to cater for the Quakers, to one of the major mutual life assurance offices in the UK. The company have used computer systems for the last fifteen years as a means of delivering faster customer service and to cope with vastly increased levels of business. The company relies heavily on giving a personal service to customers, and have developed systems which bring the power of the central mainframe computer into every office.

To cope with this need the GLADIS system was introduced between 1974 and 1978 and was one of the earliest examples of the "paperless office". Every Friends' Provident location was connected to the head office, and GLADIS spans the entire range of business functions required to set up and look after a policy - including instant quotations, once given information on the proposer and type of insurance required. GLADIS can also produce the final policy, given the completed proposal form. System development took 120 man-years.

The next step in the development of strategic information systems took place when FRENTEL was introduced. This became possible when British Telecom introduced their Gateway system, thus giving the opportunity for anyone, with an adapted TV set linked to Prestel, to send and receive messages. Friends' Provident were thus able to extend their service to brokers and other agents, giving them the full range of support services. FRENTEL was a natural evolution of GLADIS, and only involved redesigning the "front end" of the GLADIS system; so the cost was only about 10% that of GLADIS. (see Chapter 12)

FRENTEL has become a huge public relations success and a byword in the industry, although as Friends' Provident admit, some brokers have remained sceptical and only about one third actually use the system. In 1985 PA voted Friends' Provident "the world's most innovative insurance retail group".

Friends' Provident achieved a major strategic alliance when they entered into a marketing agreement with Abbey National Building Society. After January 1988 Abbey National branches sold Friends' Provident life policies exclusively. Abbey National has 700 offices and 7 million customers, thus giving Friends' Provident a vast increase in current and potential business. The company attribute this development mainly to the FRENTEL system.

System introduction

The cases described above seem to be of two opposite types. The ABC case is an example of a company whose markets were being attacked by competitors which had already adopted a technology more appropriate to the needs of their business. This allowed them to collect information worldwide, process it and make the final product available rapidly in a number of ways. ABC found themselves left behind and in order to survive were forced into adopting a 'revolutionary' course of action; one which reorganised their business and its technology in a short time. Hence the need for a top level product chanpion.

In the other cases there was no such threat to survival and they show a much more evolutionary development of systems, inspired usually by a particular individual, or by comparison with other organisations which were not threatening their survival. The companies were thus largely able to develop the systems in their own way, free of the pressure placed upon ABC. In these cases the individuals concerned often played a role equal in importance to the product champion, but at a lower level in their organisations. However, without their contribution the systems may never have succeeded.

One suggestion is that because of the revolutionary nature of strategic information systems, conventional project approval and control techniques are not adequate for the task. [12] The view is that traditional methods must be cast aside, and this is best done by a product champion who is in a powerful enough position to insist on the necessary changes.

This was certainly true in ABC International, but not in the other cases. At ABC the Chief Executive carried out an analysis of strengths and weaknesses of the company and its DP department and realised that major changes were needed. Nevertheless the new system could not be cost justified before hand, and was introduced largely as an act of faith. In Friends' Provident, FRENTEL was introduced with the minimum of formality but was most carefully monitored once under way. Indeed so professional are the company's carefully selected data processing staff that Friends' Provident have to devote less than 10% of IT department resources to program maintenance. In Interflora, there was also a very deliberate process of equipment selection, pilot trials, gradual implementation and training, but a less deliberate project management process once the Messenger project was underway.

A number of models have been devised to help managers develop ideas for strategic information systems. [13,14] These highlight the various forces acting upon a company in a particular industry and point out the variety of ways in which a company can respond to those forces. Paramount among these strategies are those of differentiation, cost, innovation, growth, or alliance. Strategic information systems are considered as ways of supporting each strategy. But, of course, ideas for such systems only arise after of a great deal of knowledge and study of the company, its products or services, and of customers needs.

In order to conceive and develop possible applications companies are sometimes encouraged to hire the services of an outside consultant. This view is of course put forward most strongly by the consultants themselves. In none of the case studies we have studied was this the case. In fact in some cases the companies had tried to do so, but found it very hard to gather genuinely objective advice, or to cope with overt attempts to sell equipment which proved to be inappropriate.

The planning process

Galliers found that in 50% of cases information systems planning was either totally divorced from business planning or was only remotely connected to it [15]. He also found that comparatively few British companies had been successful in exploiting information systems to the full. Yet in the case of strategic systems, how can they be divorced from top managements' attention? (see Chapters 4 & 5)

In all cases reported here, other than that of ABC, the strategic information systems were subject to cost-benefit analysis before introduction. Once the decision had been taken to go ahead, most systems were deliberately planned and comprehensive project control procedures were applied. This covered equipment selection, software development, pilot testing and extensive training.

Friends' Provident is a case where the planning took place at the highest possible level; the Chief Executive himself chaired the computer steering committee. The executive who saw the potential of viewdata technology communicated directly with him and agreement was quickly given. IS managers appear on fortnightly planning meetings, and it is this frequent exposure to top management thinking that ensures that systems are always strategically relevent. The computer steering committee is responsible for approving and progressing major projects and is now chaired by the deputy Managing Director. This underlines the crucial importance of systems being developed which fit in with overall corporate purposes. To achieve this, top management must be closely involved in the conception and implementation of strategic IS.

W H Smith carried out a very deliberate piloting process, costing over £20m. Then a team was set up and the system was gradually introduced into the shops on a phased basis. Line managers then assumed responsibility. Clydesdale Bank also used a deliberately phased process to gradually introduce Counterplus. In all these cases formal project approval and planning methods were employed.

In W H Smith the directors started the process of introducing EPOS, and handed the subsequent work to teams of managers, while keeping a watching brief. At the Cydesdale Bank, at the time of the initial introduction of EFTPOS, a research manager in Clydesdale developed the idea, initially without a great deal of encouragement, as the strategic implications were not recognised.

At ABC there were regular briefings, newsletters and training sessions. There were also protracted negotiations with SOGAT, and the whole process of introducing the new systems and the consequent organisational changes was a difficult experience for some of the managers involved.

The contribution of data processing

There are a number of alternative views on how data processing or information systems departments can be represented at the top level within the firm. One possibility is to have a main board IT director and another is that the chief executive himself becomes sufficiently aware of the potential of information systems. Further options are to have a top level adviser or steering committee reporting to the chief executive.

Surveys have shown how the proportion of IT directors on company boards have changed. [16] Five years ago 18% of IT directors were on the board, compared with 23% now. In five years time, chief executive's believe that 63% will be in that position, while IT executives believe the figure will be 37%. Most chief executives feel they have the expertise to guide their companies in information systems, but Galliers states that they still use inappropriate yardsticks to measure achievement, including cost comparisons and savings achieved. [17] The chief executives were broadly satisfied with their operational IT systems, but they considered the use of IT for strategic purposes was not well developed. The survey also showed the declining importance of the data processing manager, the role often being replaced by a main board member with responsibility for information systems. Only in the most technologically complex areas like communications were data processing managers still in control.

In Friends' Provident the role of DP was crucial, not only in doing all the systems design work, but also in keeping in close and continual touch with top management, through the computer steering committee and the top level general managers committee. W H Smith's data processing staff bought off-the-shelf software which they developed in conjunction with the suppliers.

At Clydesdale Bank the contribution was also central. Software was developed entirely in-house and funded by Clydesdale and by BP. As a result of previous experiences the IT division has recently been reorganised. Two individuals had in the past succeeded in working well together, apparently had the right 'chemistry' and developed a new system, without strong support from the business side or the IT side of the bank. Senior management saw that this formula worked well and decided to capitalise on it. A number of staff from both the business and the IT sides of the Bank were brought together and worked side by side for eighteen months. The result was a number of 'hybrid' individuals, who now form a new organisational unit which is the sole interface between IT and the rest of the Bank.

Benetton's data processing department consisted of around 70 people in 1987, was well-funded and they themselves decided which systems to develop. In Friends' Provident and in Clydesdale Bank the DP departments had a long and successful track record at producing effective business-orientated systems.

The chief executive of ABC appointed a new IT director and staff, able to deal with the new online systems. The data processing department was serving several different divisions of the company, and had become removed from the real needs of the business. Computer hardware had become incompatible and too much time was being devoted to system maintenance.

The product champion

The above cases contain several examples of a product champion, but also show that it is not necessary for the 'champion' to be at a senior level. At the Clydesdale Bank, for example, a fairly junior member of the IT department conceived and first developed Counterplus, and in Friends' Provident a similar individual first connected the business need with the newly available technology.

ABC International's case shows that the champion was at the top level. The Chief Executive saw the opportunity, got the parent company to fund the project and saw it through to the implementation stage. The immediate scale and strategic impact of the ABC case was of course greater than in the other cases.

Interflora have a very unusual management structure. They have a small team of permanent officers in the UK headquarters, but the organisation is run by an elected Council who are all owners of florists shops. Each of the main Interflora departments is supervised by one of the Council members, and the one responsible for computing matters took on the job of selling the idea to the membership and providing support to the data processing manager when necessary. He acted as a very visible product champion among the membership at large.

Managing change

Friends' Provident gained a lead on other financial service companies in using viewdata because they had the technology to exploit it, while competitors were still using batch systems. Also, they were generally able to react quickly to new opportunities. 'We had a sort of ambiance in the company, that enabled us to go for things; this was quite foreign to most insurance companies who tend to be run by rather conservative people'. Friends' Provident admit they go to inordinate lengths to involve end users in systems design, particularly in assessing broker requirements during the development of FRENTEL. They believe that systems that do not meet the style and needs of the user will not succeed. Friends' Provident also see systems as agents for organisational change, not just as a means of mechanising current methods.

Interflora offered a new service designed to support a traditional product. The main difficulty was in convincing the population of users of the advantages of the new system, not in managing the internal changes that resulted.

Benetton's senior managers spend a great deal of time talking to shop owners and consumers. Technology is also high on the agenda and there are more programmers on the payroll than cutters and stitchers. Every office in the company's 17th century Head Office has a terminal.

In W H Smith the disruption to store staff was considerable, particularly in the early stages of EPOS. For example, staff had to barcode items by hand and enter all information into the computer system manually. Managers spent a lot of time rewriting manuals in terms that they felt would be appropriate to their own staff and specially selected managers also became staff trainers. The overall result was that a 'sense of excitement' was created among staff whose shop was about to have point of sale equipment installed.

The effect on the bottom line

So successful were FRENTEL and Counterplus that these two systems have become generic in their industries. In Friends' Provident, GLADIS gave a tenfold growth in a static market and cut unit costs dramatically. FRENTEL was instrumental in moving the company from around twelfth or thirteenth to fourth or fifth in the insurance business. Friends' Provident are confident that it was their pre-eminence with Viewdata which was the single biggest factor in this improvement. Market share of traditional life assurance products increased from 2% to over 7% in the ten years to 1988. In the same period the number of new policies issued rose tenfold, and in a period when the retail price index increased 250%, Friends' unit costs rose by only 45%.

W H Smith assessed the EPOS project on normal return on investment grounds and achieved around two percent increase in gross profits. One initially surprising result is that stock levels rose after the system was implemented, reflecting the increased availability of many items. So successful has the system been that the company now has difficulty providing enough unsold stock for end of season sales. Suppliers have gained better information on sales and future order requirements and are now able to deliver to one central point, giving grounds for further savings. Information provided from EPOS systems is being used to allocate shelf space in shops. When Smith's are able to fully capitalise on the twin advances of EPOS and CAD they will have created a unique competitive advantage.

Counterplus, although a much reported early UK example of competitive advantage, has remained a small project, but one which has given Clydesdale an enviable reputation in EFTPOS circles and valuable experience among retailers. One of the earliest users of the system was Norco, the Northern Cooperative Society. Their Chief Executive has gone on record by stating that customer loyalty has been improved, and that average transaction values have increased by 50% in the shops and 100% in the filling stations. In 1987 he stressed that technology was not an end in itself but a 'key opportunity to give that extra dimension of service, added value and efficiency which was either previously unavailable or highly labour intensive'.

Reed Telepublishing is now the most profitable division of Reed Publishing UK. After the business had stood still for several years, both sales and profits are now growing at an impressive rate. The new system has been instrumental in putting a previous competitor, OAG, out of business. OAG were recently sold by their parent company, Dun and Bradstreet.

In the case of Benetton, it is doubtful whether the company would have grown the way it has without the use of technology in several phases of its operations, but the company's success is undoubtedly also due to fashion flair and other key ingredients. Income increased over 300% from 1982 to 1987 while profits grew by 800% in the same period.

One way of viewing the types of information systems is the development of internal operations support systems (OSS), management support systems (MSS), and customer support systems (CSS). [18] The research described above has shown that any of these types of system can become strategic in impact. Examples of OSS are to be found in Friends' Provident and Benetton, and they offer increased productivity and reduced production costs of goods or services. Information systems can therefore help companies become low cost producers by automation of labour intensive operations. MSS can provide information which is itself of use as a competitive weapon, as in the case of W H Smith, or for market research or customer analysis to find an appropriate niche. CSS is the traditional domain of competitive systems, used as a means of differentiating the service or product offered, often to bring the supplier much closer to the customer; examples are ABC, Interflora, Benetton, and Clydesdale Bank.

Not all the above examples are as dramatic as the US examples quoted at the start of this paper, but they are all successful and show that information systems can be strategic in several ways. In addition to providing the type of competitive advantage described above, they can provide the 'organisational independence' in which the various functions of an organisation can be linked and integrated more closely, thus compressing stages in the value chain. [19] Also where organisational units are geographically dispersed, as in the case of Benetton, increasingly global businesses can be linked together using communications networks.

The Friends' Provident case is a good example where systems, developed originally as internal efficiency-orientated purposes (OSS) were extended to become customer-orientated systems (CSS systems), linking different company outlets together. The same systems are now being further developed to provide additional internal cost savings. These savings allow the company to persue the generic strategy of cost minimisation, in addition to that of differentiation via its network services.

Implications for managers

Successful innovation can be defined as a combination of invention and exploitation. Technological innovation is a multi-stage process, involving the recognition of an opportunity, generation of technology or systems to fulfil the opportunity, the development and testing of a prototype and then a full-scale product, and then ensuring the technology is fully used.

The incentive for innovation can come from two sources: from the development of new technical capability (internal technological push), or from close interaction with the external market place and customer needs (market pull). Utterbach and Gerstenfeld have shown that most successful innovations come about by the organisation being continually aware of customer needs and competitor activity, and the ABC International case is an obvious example of market pull. [20] The other cases are either examples of internal developments, or where external non-competing organisations have provided examples of what could be achieved and a stimulus for new developments.

The vital elements in successful implementation are the availability of the right people at each stage of the innovation process, and this is where managers of all levels can play a part. [21] At the idea generation stage, it is important that there is an individual or a group who are able to get involved in conceptual and creative work, and that they have the necessary freedom to be creative. Managers can also play an important part in keeping a watching brief on other organisations, so that ideas for new or improved systems can be evaluated for their own use. At the later stage, when the project ideas have been full developed, the championing (or entrepreneuring) role becomes important. Here the qualities needed are a strong interest in practicalities, selling ability, possession of a wide range of interests and contacts, energy and determination.

When a more formal project leadership role emerges, the best individual will be someone who is sensitive to the needs of others, who has good knowledge of the organisational structure and knows how to get things done. The project leader should also have the ability to motivate, lead and coordinate the team.

Another role is that of sponsor or coach; someone who has experience in developing new ideas, often a senior person who can 'pull a few strings'. He or she acts as a sounding board for new ideas, provides access to important power centres in the organisation and shelters the project team from unnecessary outside influences and disturbances. Each of these roles can be carried out by one or several different people.

As to the process of developing systems, in many cases the standard management techniques and disciplines are still required. The projects described above involved a wide range of activities, from assessing and purchasing equipment, developing and testing software, establishing customer neeeds, relocating parts of the company, and hiring and training additional personnel. In none of these were there activities which are unique or even unusual, and in many of the cases, normal if rigorous project approval and planning techniques were used.

The presence of powerful top level product champions, and the need for a new venture mentality lead to a strong 'top down' view of strategic IS; one initiated and led from the top of organisations. If this view is correct, what is the place of the middle manager? The research shows there are many roles a manager can play. The middle manager is often best equipped to get to know the market place, and seek opportunities for information systems. A crucial skill is being willing and able to work closely with information systems people. Managers also have a crucial role in explaining the system, its purpose and mode of operation, and in helping to train end-users.

Above, we discussed the attempts of external consultants to advise companies on how to develop strategic information systems, and to sell them equipment which did not do the job. There was often an innate 'cynicism' of external suppliers and technical experts, and a determination to deal in the type of language appropriate to their business. It was the company managers themselves who created and implemented the systems, achieving this not by acquiring the technical expertise themselves, but by insisting that new ideas for systems and for technology were expressed in ways that could be understood by business managers.

It may also be vital for managers to give continual attention to tasks that might not seem too important, like the rewriting of manuals, and personal involvement in training. A major issue is the development of appropriate planning and implementation methods in each company, and the fulfilling of the various key roles in each organisation. What is certain is that managers need a broad perspective to understand the processes involved in strategic IS, and be able to communicate in business terms with those who provide such systems. Technologically driven systems must be managed by business driven managers.

Implications for researchers

None of the companies we studied used any of the conceptual frameworks to help them develop ideas. This raises the question as to whether these models are of any practical use. The question of what would be useful ways to raise managers' awareness of the potential of strategic information systems in their own firms therefore arises. In teaching, we have often found it more useful to highlight a variety of examples of strategic information systems which managers can relate to their own organisations.

This area of research provides particularly difficult methodological problems. Often considerations of commercial secrecy make it difficult to discover examples of company's developing strategic IS. Typically, several years' work are involved to develop such systems and the advantage so gained might be lost if news was leaked to competitors. Hence the concern for commercial secrecy. On several occasions we have approached a company only to be politely declined access, being left with a tantalising insight into a forthcoming project.

Often the results are that it is only possible to gain access to a company when the work is finished and the strategic information system is fully operational. Even then, there is no guarantee of access, as not every project succeeds and no company wants its mistakes publicised. Only when it is a proven success might permission be given. Even in the case of successful projects, memories can fail.

What are the possible remedies? These include alerting senior managers in potential firms that researchers would be interested as soon as permission is given, and confidentiality assured. Early warning of this type could help to prolong memories. There would seem to be a role here for a 'network' of European researchers and management teachers. They could share in the detection of suitable research sites, provision of case study material, in the research work and in the development of useful concepts. The purpose of this is to develop a better understanding of the processes involved in the introduction, development and implementation of strategic information systems.

Bibliography

1   Keen, P G W "Competing in Time - using telecommunications for competitive advantage" Ballinger, 1986.
2   Bruce, L "The Bright New Worlds of Benetton" *International Management* November 1987.

3   Index Group "A Hard Look at Strategic Systems" *Indications* **6** (1) 1989.
4   Keen, op cit.
5   Bakoupolis, J A Y and Treacy, M E "Information Technology and Corporate Strategy - a research perspective" CISR Paper 1639-85, 1985.
6   Wiseman, C "Strategy and Computers - information systems as competitive weapons" Dow Jones-Irwin, 1985.
7   Runge, D "Using Telecommunications for Competitive Advantage" Templeton College, University of Oxford, DPhil Dissertation, 1985.
8   Wightman, D W L "Competitive Advantage through Information Technology" *Journal of General Management* Summer 1987.
9   Roberts, E B "Generating Technological Innovation" OUP, Oxford, 1987.
10 Index Group, op cit.
11 Griffiths, Catherine and Hochstrasser, Beat "Does IT Slow you Down?" Kobler Unit, Imperial College, London, November 1987.
12 Synnott, W R "Information Weapons" *Information Strategy* Fall 1987.
13 Wiseman, op cit
14 Porter, Michael E "Competitive Advantage" Free Press, New York, 1985.
    Porter, Michael E and Millar, V E "How Information Technology gives you Competitive Advantage" *Harvard Business Review* **63** (4) pp 149-160, July-August 1985.
15 Galliers, R "A Failure of Direction" *Business Computing and Communications* July/August 1986.
16 Price Waterhouse/Financial Times Survey 1989.
17 Galliers, op cit.
18 Synnott, op cit.
19 Rockart, J F and Short, J E "IT in the 1990s: managing organisational interdependence" *Sloan Management Review* **30** (2) pp 7-18, Winter 1989.
20 Utterbach, J M "Innovation and the Diffusion of Technology" *Science* Feb 15th 1974.
21 Roberts, E B and Fusfield, A R "Title Staffing the Innovative Technology-Based Organisation" *Sloan Management Review* **22** (3) pp 19-34, Spring 1981.

9

Strategic Applications of Integrated Information Systems

Mark Ebers and Hans-Dieter Ganter

Information technology today plays an important role in the formulation and realisation of business strategies. Visions of computer aided industry (CAI), the computer controlled company (CCC) or computer integrated manufacturing (CIM) enter into the strategic considerations of many managers. It is widely held that information technology is a powerful means of gaining competitive advantage.

Indeed the potential of rationalisation opened up by integrated information systems is tempting. The utilisation of information technology increases the availability and quality of information and thus allows better planning and control. Integrated information systems accelerate the processing of information thus providing a crucial prerequisite to faster response to demands both from the market and from organisational sub-units. Information technology also enables new and more beneficial ways of managing and organising. Integration of information systems accelerates organisational processes and improves the coordination of operations and their efficiency. For example, it is possible to reduce redundant work and economise on labour costs by automating manual information processing, to reduce stocks, and to improve the flow of material and utilisation of capacity. [1,2,3,4]

Such general consideration of the strategic potential of integrated information systems provides justification for including information technology on the agenda for business strategy. Yet many barriers have to be overcome before the envisaged potential can be realised.

We point out some critical contingencies that should be borne in mind when applying integrated information systems. On the basis of relevant research we shall identify problem areas as well as some prerequisites and strategies for the successful application of integrated information systems. However, since a comprehensive theory of information technology application does not exist and as there is only limited empirical research evidence we can only address part of the problem and merely provide limited answers to the issues in question.

Integrated information systems

Integrated information systems may comprise different levels, stages and functional areas of company operations, from top-level long-term strategic planning to short-term operations management, from product development to product dispatch systems, or from marketing to finance, etc.

Figure 9.1 The structure of integrated information systems

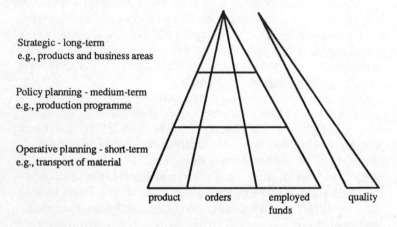

Strategic - long-term
e.g., products and business areas

Policy planning - medium-term
e.g., production programme

Operative planning - short-term
e.g., transport of material

product   orders   employed   quality
funds

Different degrees of integration may be achieved and integration patterns may vary among industries and regions. [5] A survey of 1,285 companies in the German capital goods industry revealed that 9% of the companies had integrated two or more functional areas, while another 14% were planning to do so during 1988. [6] In the US automobile, electronics and machine industries 44% of the companies had computerised manufacturing facilities in 1982, of which 60% had at least partially integrated their managerial information systems with production technology. [7]

To date few applications of fully integrated information systems have been realised, though considerable progress towards such systems is under way, especially within manufacturing. CIM appears to have been accepted as a cornerstone of manufacturing strategies in the 1990s. Application of computer integrated manufacturing aims at controlling the company on the basis of current manufacturing data that is optimised in a holistic way. It thus influences the design of manufacturing and of information systems.

CIM includes both technologically orientated functions such as CAD (Computer Aided Design), CAP (Computer Aided Planning), CAM (Computer Aided Manufacturing), CAQ (Computer Aided Quality Control), and administrative functions such as order processing, inventory management, production planning and control referring to quantities, time limits and capacities. Figure 9.2 illustrates the integration of information technology achieved in CIM.

Figure 9.2   Information system integration in CIM

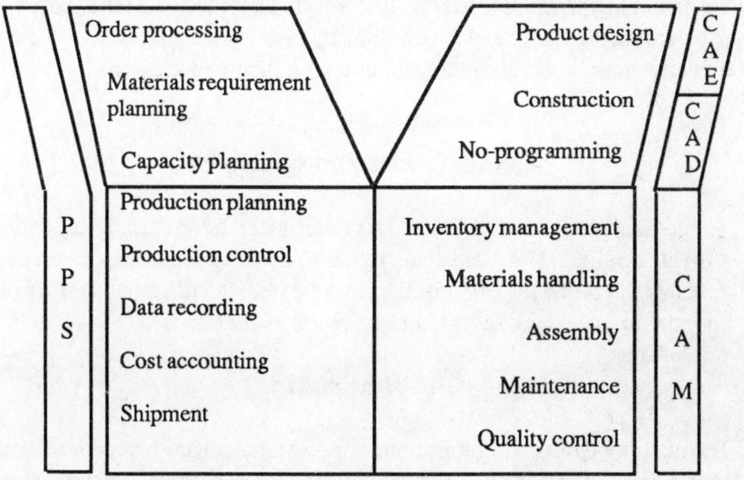

[Adapted from A W Scheer]

Applying integrated information systems

A common way of acknowledging the process of technological innovation is to define different phases which then provide the theoretical framework for investigation. Gerwin, following Hage, assumes the innovation process to be composed of an adoption phase (Hage calls this evaluation), a preparation phase (which Hage calls initiation), and an implementation phase. [8,9] Each phase poses specific challenges with regard to the successful application of technological innovations.

During the adoption phase actors within the organisation for a variety of reasons recognise the need for change and take a decision on the new technology. Uncertainty in this phase of the innovation process is fairly high since all decisions must be taken on the basis of vague knowledge of the technology, the required infrastructure, etc.

In the preparation phase the necessary infrastructure to support the new technology is developed and the implementation strategy decided. Technological innovation must be supported by new skills, tasks, roles, and perhaps new organisational structures in order to work effectively. However, design of the required infrastructure turns out to be difficult due to the prevailing uncertainty about what is needed.

Implementation is the phase in which the new technology is tried out for the first time. Only then can it be evaluated on a real basis. Compared with the preceding phases uncertainty is lower since, for the first time, participants from both inside and outside the organisation are provided with data on performance and can contrast these with their expectations.

Contingencies and strategies

The general problem of applying integrated information systems is coping with uncertainty. The main challenge is to devise conditions and procedures which allow the organisation to cope with the different sources of uncertainty for which several strategies are available.

Adoption phase

The likelihood that an organisation adopts a technical innovation is related to features of its structure. Companies which have an organic organisation structure tend to be more innovative than mechanistically structured firms. [10] Centralised decision-making, extensive formalisation, and lowered complexity seem to impede the adoption of innovations. [11]

One could assume that economic reasoning is an important influence on a company's decision to adopt an innovation. Yet the adoption decision for an integrated information system is associated with considerable financial uncertainty. The return on investment (ROI) is difficult to estimate for such complex technology, which affects many functional domains of a company. Expected ROI therefore seldom determines the investment decision. Instead, expectations of long-term strategic advantages predominate. Whether the expected advantages can be realised depends in part on the technical properties of the information system to be purchased. Technical criteria are therefore important in providing information for the adoption decision. Expectations of relative economic advantage, innovativeness, compatibility with existing needs, and complexity of the technology exert the strongest influence on the adoption decision. [12,13,14,15]

The preponderance of technical criteria is important for management's role in the decision making process as well as for the way the new technology is implemented and applied. The more complex the technology under consideration and the more sophisticated the technology already in use within the company, the less decisive will management's role become in the decision-making process, as management often lacks technical expertise.

Management has at least two strategies to cope with this situation. It may either try to regain control by insisting on financial criteria. That is, it may resort to its proper field of expertise which is the financial evaluation of investments. Alternatively, management may share its decision-making power with technical experts, usually a task force of the company and the vendor of the system.

The two strategies have different consequences. It is likely that the first will more often result in a rejection of the technological innovation than the second. This is due to the fact that acquisition and implementation costs are often high, while returns are difficult to estimate. [16,17] Indeed Hayes and Abernathy with Rosenthal have shown that predominance of financial decision criteria was a major reason why technological innovations were turned down. [18,19] With respect to integrated information systems this result is more likely to occur if management is interested in short-term performance improvements at the operational level rather than in gaining long-term competitive advantage. [20]

If management chooses to follow the second strategy and shares its decision-making power with technical experts, a positive adoption decision is more likely. However, the technical experts' interests and design strategies will then help shape not only the adoption decision but will also help set the course for future modes in which the integrated information system is applied. Due to its lack of technical expertise, management in this case has less chance of realising its long-term strategic preferences. Moreover, predominance of technical issues in the preparation and implementation phase may undermine the successful application of integrated information systems, because the role of organisational design and personnel issues is unduly diminished.

Management's choice of strategy is contingent upon a number of factors, for example, on the business strategy it follows, risk preference, time orientation, its willingness to decentralise decision-making and its confidence in the abilities of the system vendor and in-house technical staff.

Preparation phase

The predominantly technical orientation towards the application of integrated information systems carries over to the preparation phase. Accordingly, this phase has been discussed in the literature mainly as a problem of technological design. For example, some researchers analyse problems of interfaces and the efficient design of the hierarchy of functions and computers. Others deal with technological problems in various fields of integrated information system application, e.g., they discuss the design of flexible manufacturing systems, the transport of goods, or quality control.

There is no doubt that these are important topics, crucial to the successful application of integrated information systems. However, there is growing evidence that problems of designing integrated information systems cannot be restricted to technological problems, since adequate design of information and manufacturing systems does not guarantee efficient solutions. A number of empirical studies show that dominant technological aspects in designing, implementing and applying integrated information systems in manufacturing bear the risk of friction. The reason is that quite a number of problems of implementation and application of integrated information systems cannot be solved totally by means of technology but require organisational and personnel measures. [21,22,23, 24,25]

However, we know little about the critical contingencies that lead to eventual successful application. Certainly, there is no one best way of organising the application of integrated information systems. As there is no technological determinism of organisation, particular organisational and personnel solutions which apply to one type of innovation may not apply to others.

A number of relevant contingencies have been identified in organisational research on technology. These include organisational size and structure, the occupational and professional structure, and the power structure within organisations.

Notwithstanding these and other possible contingencies, a key success factor of the preparation phase seems to be that management devises organisational and personnel measures which allow for the absorption of uncertainty.

According to Thompson, organisations are open systems which are challenged by uncertainty from their environment but need certainty for their technical core in order to function efficiently. [26] It is management's task to reduce the uncertainties affecting the technical core. Integrated information systems are believed to be conducive to this end, as they are said to increase information processing capacity and organisational flexibility, as well as the controllability of operational processes. [27]

However, although integrated information systems may reduce uncertainty, they also provide temporary new uncertainties for the technical core of the organisation. For example, Gerwin stresses the technical uncertainty (difficulty in determining the precision, reliability, and capacity of new processes) and social uncertainty (nature of the required support system, possibility of conflict during implementation) associated with integrated information systems. [28]

Moreover, Ebers and Lieb highlight problems of organisational uncertainty [29]. They note that integrated information systems may make organisations more susceptible to disruptions if the setting in which the technology is applied is not sufficiently buffered from uncertainty. This consequence is due to the greater integration as well as acceleration of information processing and to the reduction of organisational slack (i.e. excess capacity, inventory, backlogs) achieved by integrated information systems. Because of the tighter coupling of different organisational domains any error or disruption has much graver consequences than in less integrated settings. The reduction of organisational slack decreases the organisation's capacity to deal with uncertainty, as organisational slack is a means of coping with uncertainty. [30,31]

Several measures may be taken to reduce the possibly adverse effects of technical, organisational and social uncertainty. On the technical side it seems advisable to cooperate intensively with system vendors and to benefit from their technical know how before system implementation, especially if the system is complex and the users have little experience with the technology. [32]

It is very difficult to reduce organisational uncertainty, as integrated information systems affect company structures and processes widely. Changes in information flow, power and authority relations, forms of supervision, performance appraisal, functional area strategies, and patterns of resource allocation accompany the application of integrated information systems. During preparation it therefore seems important to examine, for example, the utility of the information the system provides, its effects upon job content and on the distribution of influence and autonomy within the company. [33] Yet, the more complex the technology, the less divisible it becomes and the more innovative the solutions envisaged, the less it seems possible to design an adequate infrastructure before the integrated information system is actually implemented.

A way of dealing with organisational uncertainty is to devise a strategy of incremental change. Managers should pay careful attention to the process in which a specific design is developed and implemented and should not push the design of the development and implementation process into the background by questions of technology and configurations. Integrated information systems cannot be installed in a turn-key fashion. Careful planning and management of the implementation process is required. [34] Furthermore, organisational designers should be aware that they only have an incomplete understanding of those factors which are crucial for process capabilities. They should therefore avoid premature rigidity of the process configuration, as this may lead to serious operational friction. [35] Management should also develop emergency plans in case of system breakdown and serious operational friction.

It may also seem worthwhile to consider the potential role of labour in the application of integrated information systems. It might be profitable to acknowledge the ability of human labour to absorb uncertainty rather than simply view labour as a source of uncertainty and plan to substitute it by technology. Labour should not only be regarded as the object of, but also as the indispensable subject for, rationalisation. The capacity of labour to resolve problems should be estimated as high because it is indispensable. It therefore seems reasonable, if the organisation's technical task force and operators participate in the decisions of the preparation phase. In this way information on the consequences of the technological innovation for staff, tasks, and organisation can be obtained. [36]

Implementation phase

The experience of change agents indicates the implementation process to be a major problem. [37,38,39] Empirical studies provide evidence for the design of the implementation process to influence type and success of the application of information technology. Critical issues include the composition and influence of the task force implementing the innovation, the scope of problem definition with regard to the innovation, the mode of change and the development pattern that is chosen.

Several studies have indicated that specific characteristics of the innovation task force significantly influence the process and result of integrated information system implementation. Integration of system vendors into the task force seems to be beneficial, especially when the information technology is complex, not fully matured and if considerable software adjustment or organisational change is necessary.

However, the more management believes it depends on vendor know-how, because in-house staff is not sufficiently qualified or lacks experience, the more likely it is that responsibility for system design and implementation is entirely with the vendor. Then there is little opportunity for in-house staff to gain experience, expertise and confidence into the innovation, because suppliers are inclined to realize turn-key projects. Due to insufficient preparation and problems of motivating future users, such turn-key projects bear considerable risk of failure.

Management can reduce this risk by helping its staff obtain the necessary skills during the preparation phase and by integrating targeted users into the innovation task force. Indeed many researchers have observed that involvement of targeted users is an effective implementation tactic. Top management support of the innovation project, leadership and motivation for change in any case is an essential prerequisite of successful implementation.

Implementation of integrated information systems runs the risk of friction if the design problem is defined too narrowly. [40] Disregard of organisational and social issues, i.e. when integrated information system implementation is viewed as a technical rather than as a socio-technical problem, is likely to lead to protracted implementation and inefficient conduct. Discrepancies with the organisational infrastructure or mismatch of performance criteria may likewise occasion serious performance gaps. [41]

In order to overcome such difficulties mutual adjustment of both the integrated information system and organisational structures and processes seems necessary. A heterogeneous composition of the innovation task force is conducive to detecting the necessary adjustments and to reconciling possible solutions, because different groups in the organisation are likely to hold different beliefs about the innovation and its consequences. [42] Possibly, a large degree of relevant problem areas will be considered during implementation, if management representatives, organisation development experts, information systems staff, and future system applicants participate in the implementation process. [43] Yet the size and composition of the project team depends on various factors, e.g., on whether the innovation concerns many organisational sub-units, on the complexity and degree of decentralisation of task performance, or on the extent of necessary organisational change. [44,45]

As each of the participating groups emphasise different aspects of the innovation and of its consequences, conflict over solutions may occur. The extent of conflict will be the greater, the more organisational and personnel changes are made and the more the expectations and interests of the participating groups and individuals diverge. The implementation process may therefore often be characterised by power struggles and it may result in solutions which diverge considerably from any single group's original objectives. In part, such discrepancies are unavoidable, due to the technical, organisational and social uncertainty associated with any innovation; nevertheless, in part it also speaks of insufficient preparation. [46,47]

Management may choose different modes of change when implementing integrated information systems. Complete turn-key installations only seem feasible when management can fully anticipate and realise the necessary prerequisites for integrated information systems application. This will only be the case if:

- management has great experience and is pressed to take immediate action
- the workforce is motivated to accept the innovation
- the innovation is of limited complexity and has proven feasibility
- its functioning can easily be communicated to future users
- only minor organisational adjustments are required

In most cases information systems have been gradually integrated and implemented step-by-step. This strategy allows trial adoption and piecemeal adjustment. Incremental implementation avoids the hazards of having to plan and design comprehensive technical and organisational solutions under conditions of uncertainty. System designers and users receive feedback on performance. They may thereby learn to cope with specific application problems. An incremental approach towards implementation realises synergies, if innovators are encouraged to share their experience with subsequent users. Piecemeal implementation also reduces the risk of major disruptions as only a few functional areas are affected at a time. Moreover it allows for less disruptive and more flexible adjustments of structures and processes. Such a strategy is only feasible if the application of the integrated information system can be divided into stages of application. In addition, system application must deliver some benefits from each step of implementation. [48,49,50]

The choice of the pattern of system development, i.e. of locus and of consecutive stages of implementation, is a crucial issue in the application process. In his survey of 172 large European manufacturing companies De Meyer found the following pattern of steps towards the realisation of integrated information systems. [51] Most companies had opted for the creation of a number of integration islands. These islands of integration clustered around internally oriented administrative systems (e.g., inventory management, accounting), market orientated administrative systems (e.g., sales planning, order entry, distribution), and technical control systems (e.g., CAE, CAD, CAM). Most frequently the companies planned to integrate their sales planning systems with master production scheduling. Other frequently mentioned integration steps were process controls with quality reporting, inventory status with master production scheduling, and design engineering with manufacturing engineering. In most cases master production scheduling and material requirements planning were the pivotal database through which greater integration was to be achieved. The central role of master production scheduling could be due to the fact that, as Rosenthal's survey showed, these systems are already highly automated and standardised.

However, this development pattern of integrated information systems should not be regarded as the only one advisable. An international survey of 560 manufacturing companies revealed significant regional differences in application patterns. [52] European firms seem to favour a top-down approach towards the development of integrated information systems, while a bottom-up approach is more common in the USA and Japan. When integrating their information systems European manufacturers start with strategic planning and sales related subsystems, whereas US and Japanese firms tend to start integrating their informations systems at the shop floor level (inventory management, cost accounting and production planning). [53]

Hence, it can be assumed that there is not a single best strategy of implementation. A number of contingencies of implementation strategy have been identified in the literature.

On the basis of fourteen case studies, Leonard-Barton suggests three implementation characteristics of an innovation which shape the tactics that successful managers use to disseminate an innovation, namely transferability, implementation complexity and divisibility. [54] Transferability is composed of two dimensions: preparedness, denoting the extent to which a technology has shown proof of feasibility, and communicability of application know how, which indicates the degree to which documentation and training is available to users. Implementation complexity refers to the number of people affected by the innovation and to the number of organisational sub-units that must alter their input or output in order to accommodate to the innovation. Divisibility, finally, denotes the degree to which an innovation can be partitioned to allow partial adoption.

Leonard-Barton suggests that a higher degree of implementation success may be achieved under conditions of low to moderate transferability, moderate to high implementation complexity, and some degree of divisibility, if users are involved in the development process, if leaders or change champions assume responsibility for the innovation, and if the technology and organisation structures and processes are mutually adapted.

Wildemann showed that the implementation strategy for information systems depends upon the competitive strategy of the company and on the type of information system.[55] With regard to office automation Wainwright and Francis propose that when approaching the problem of choosing a design approach management should consider issues such as the complexity of the tasks to be reorganised, the degree of task (de)centralisation, the pervasiveness of tasks with regard to organisational domains, as well as the qualification of current and future personnel. [56] Gerwin adds that the chances of successful implementation also depend upon the degree of intra-organisational conflict and upon the discrepancy between the expectations for the innovation and its consequences. [57]

Conclusion

A comprehensive understanding of integrated information system application requires to develop a multi-phase process view. An adoption phase, preparation phase and implementation phase may be differentiated. Each stage poses specific challenges and is exposed to specific contingencies which influence its course and results. Moreover, the phases are contingent upon each other so that in each phase design possibilities and outcomes are constrained by past and present decisions as well as by expectations of future challenges and opportunities. Therefore, each phase is likely to be modified in its course due to specific feedback loops from previous phases.

In both theory and practice it thus seems important to develop a process view of integrated information system application. As Hedberg *et al.* note, 'understanding of processes is designers' most precious skill.' [58]

We see the success of integrated information system application to be the result of a complex process by different contingencies of actions of constrained choice. (see Figure 9.3)

Although our knowledge of the relevant contingencies, alternative strategies and their possible outcome is still very limited, there seems to be agreement on a few central propositions. For successful implementation it seems necessary that management takes a wide range of financial, technical, organisational and social application problems into consideration, encourages participation of everyone concerned with the innovation, devises motivation strategies, follows an incremental implementation strategy, allows for organisational learning and encourages communication of pertinent experiences, and mutually adjusts the technology, organsation structures and processes.

Figure 9.3 Basic parameters of successful application of integrated IS

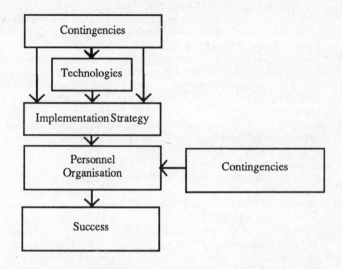

The application of integrated information systems is a very complex matter. However, the strategic potential opened up by integrated information systems makes the effort worthwhile to try and improve our understanding of the dynamics of systems application.

References

1   Czeguhn, K and Franzen, H "Die rechnergestützte Integration Betrieblicher Informationssysteme auf der Basis der Betriebsdatenerfassung" in *Zeitschrift für betriebswirtschaftliche Forschung* **39** (2) pp 169-181, 1987.

2   Wildemann, H "Auftragsabwicklung in einer computergestützten Fertigung" *Zeitschrift für Betriebswirtschaft* **57** (1) pp 6-31, 1987.

3   Zahn, E "Produktionstechnologien als Element internationaler Wettbewerbsstrategien" pp 475-496 in *Innovation und Wettbewerbsfähigkeit* Edited by E Dichtl, W Gerke, A Kieser. Gabler, Wiesbaden, 1987.

4   Meredith, J; Hyer, N L; Gerwin, D; Rosenthal, S R and Wemmerlöv, U "Research Needs in Managing Factory Automation" *Journal of Operations Management* **6** (2) pp 203-218, 1986.

5   De Meyer, A and Ferdows, K "The Integration of Information Systems in Manufacturing" *International Journal of Production and Operations Management* 5 (2) 1985, pp 5-13.

6   Nuber, C; Schultz-Wild, R; Fischer-Krippendorf, R and Rehberg, F "EDV-Einsatz und computergestützte Integration in Fertigung und Verwaltung von Industriebetrieben" Working Report Institut für sozialwissenschaftliche Forschung e.V. (ISF), München, 1987.

7   Majchrzak, A; Nieva, V F and Newman, P D "A National Probability Survey of Contemporary CAD/CAM Adoption" in *Managing Technological Innovation. Organisational Strategies for Implementing Advanced Manufacturing Technologies,* edited by D D Davis and Associates, Jossey Bass, San Francisco, 1986.

8   Gerwin, D "A Theory of Innovation Processes for Computer-aided Manufacturing Technology" *IEEE Transactions on Engineering Management* 35 (2) pp 90-100, 1988.

9   Hage, J "Theories of Organisations" Wiley, New York, 1980.

10 Burns, T and Stalker, G M "The Management of Innovation" Tavistock, London, 1961.

11 Zaltman, G; Duncan, R and Holbek, J "Innovations and Organisations" Wiley, New York, 1973.

12 Walleck, S A "Cim und Wirtschaftlichkeit - Widerspruch, Chance oder Realität?" Dokumentation IBM Anwenderkongreß '87 "Industrie und Technik", Garmisch 21.-23.10.1987, ed. by IBM Deutschland GmbH, 1987.

13 Rosenthal, S R "Progress Toward the Factory of the Future" *Journal of Operations Management* 4 (3) pp 203-230, 1984.

14 Voss, C A "Implementing Manufacturing Technology: a manufacturing strategy approach" *International Journal of Operations and Production Management* 6 (4) pp 17-26, 1986.

15 Tornatzky, L G and Klein, K J "Innovation Characteristics and Innovation Adoption-Implementation: a meta-analysis of findings" *IEEE Transactions on Engineering Management* 1982 **EM-29** (1) pp 28-45.

16 Gerwin, D and Tarondeau, J C "Uncertainty and the Innovation Process for Computer-Integrated Manufacturing Systems: four case studies" pp 384-399 in *Implementing New Technologies*, edited by E Rhodes and D Wield. Blackwell, Oxford, 1985.

17 Kaplan, R S "Must CIM be Justified by Faith Alone?" *Harvard Business Review* **65** pp 87-97, 1986.

18 Hayes, R H and Abernathy, W J "Managing our way to Economic Decline" *Harvard Business Review* **58** 1980, pp 67-77.

19 Rosenthal, op. cit.

10 Gerwin, op. cit.

21 Ebers, M and Lieb, M "Computer Integrated Manufacturing as a Two-edged Sword" *International Journal of Operations and Production Management* 9 (2) 1989.

22 Bjørn-Andersen, N; Eason, K and Robey, D "Managing Computer Impact - an international study of management and organisations" Ablex, Norwood, 1986.

23 Voss, op. cit.

24 Mueller, W S; Clegg, C W; Wall, T D ; Kemp, N J and Davies, R T "Pluralist Beliefs about New Technology within a Manufacturing Organisation" *New Technology, Work and Employment* **1** (2) pp127-139, 1986.

25 Buchanan, D "Technological Imperatives and Strategic Choice" pp 72-80 in *Information Technology in Manufacturing Processes: case studies in technological change,* edited by G Winch, Rossendale, London, 1983.

26 Thompson, J D "Organisations in Action - Social Science Bases of Administrative Theory" McGraw Hill, New York, 1967.

27 Gerwin and Tarondeau, op. cit.

28 Gerwin, op. cit.

29 Ebers and Lieb, op. cit.

30 Cyert, R and March, J G "A Behavioral Theory of the Firm" Prentice Hall, Englewood Cliffs, 1963.

31 Galbraith, J R "Organisation Design" Addison-Wesley, Reading, 1977.

32 Gerwin 1988, op. cit.

33 Banbury, J and Nahapiet, J E "Towards a Framework for the Study of the Antecedents and Consequences of Information Systems in Organisations" *Accounting, Organisation, and Society* **4** (3) pp 163-177, 1979.

34 Hetzner, W A; Eveland, J D and Tornatzky, L G "Fostering Innovation: Economic, technical, and organisational issues" pp 239-255 in *Managing Technological Innovation. Organisational Strategies for Implementing Advanced Manufacturing Technologies,* edited by D D Davis and Associates, Jossey-Bass, San Francisco, 1986.

35 Ettlie, op. cit.

36 Rosenthal, op. cit.

37 Rosenthal, op. cit.

38 Graham, M B W and Rosenthal, S R "Flexible Manufacturing Systems Require Flexible People" *Human Systems Management* **6** pp 211-222, 1986.

39 Ettlie, op cit.

40 Mueller *et al.,* op cit.

41 Ebers and Lieb, op. cit.

42 Mueller *et al.,* op. cit.

43 Mumford, E and Welter, G "Benutzerbeteiligung bei der Entwicklung von Computer-Systemen" (Schmidt, Berlin, 1984).

44 Wildemann, H "Einführungsstrategien für neue Produktionstechnologien - dargestellt an CAD/CAM Systemen und Flexiblen Fertigungssystemen" *Zeitschrift für Betriebswirtschaft* **56** (4/5) pp 337-369, 1986.

45 Wainwright, J and Francis, A "Office Automation, Organisation and the Nature of Work" Gower, Aldershot, 1984.

46 Ebers and Lieb, op. cit.

47 Gerwin, op. cit.

48 Gerwin, op. cit.

49 Rosenthal, op. cit.

50 Bessant, J "Management and Manufacturing Innovation: the case of information technology" pp 14-30 in *Information Technology in Manufacturing Processes: case studies in technological change* Edited by G Winch. Rossendale, London, 1983.

51 De Meyer, A "The Integration of Information Systems in Manufacturing" *Omega* **15** (3) pp 229-238, 1987.

52 De Meyer and Ferdows, op. cit.

53 De Meyer and Ferdows, op. cit.
54 Leonard-Barton, D "Implementation Characteristics of Organisational innovations" *Journal of Communication Research* **15** (5) 1988.
55 Wildemann, op. cit.
56 Leonard-Barton, op. cit.
57 Gerwin, op cit.
58 Hedberg, B L T; Nystrom, P C and Starbuck, W H "Camping on Seesaws: Prescriptions for a self-designing organisation" *Administrative Science Quarterly* **21** (1) pp 41-65, 1976.

10

The Shifting Locus of Control

Lynne Baxter and James McCalman

The development of the electronics industry has been one of the major industrial success stories of Scotland in the 1970s and 1980s; in a region which has been characterised by rising unemployment levels and a decline in traditional industries. The emphasis of government agencies, such as the Scottish Development Agency (SDA), towards the electronics industry has largely been concentrated on the attraction of inward investment, which it has managed to achieve very successfully. However, the presumed indirect benefits of a cohesive indigenous sector which develops potential of its own have not been forthcoming. The level of local sourcing by foreign-owned firms has been falling during the 1970s and 1980s and there is little evidence of policy initiatives aimed at reversing this decline. Despite efforts on the part of both the SDA and the foreign firms themselves the local content continues to decline. However, developments in the strategies of multi-national enterprises (MNEs) and in government policy towards the encouragement of enterprise have created an increasingly attractive environment for the successful development of indigenous spin-offs. [1]

Van der Klugt argues that there are three main conditions for the survival of an electronics company. [2] These relate to development and maintenance of technological expertise in component and application technology:

- high R&D investment costs which dictate world-wide marketing of products
- market presence in the USA, Japan and Europe with associated product development, manufacture and distribution operations
- strategically placed production centres to supply global products to the three main areas

If one accepts van der Klugt's argument, this would indicate a more global approach to manufacturing strategy being taken by multi-national electronics firms; this is indeed the case with those located in Scotland. Increasing attention is being given to quickening the time to market of products, as well as meeting perceived customer needs. In order to cope with this, a variety of internal changes are being implemented. There are growing indications of flatter hierarchies within the MNEs as a whole. This has been accompanied by a change in the role adopted by multi-national subsidiaries located in Scotland.

There has been a change in emphasis, away from concepts such as the 'branch plant syndrome' which characterised foreign-owned entry in Scotland during the 1960s and 1970s. Instead of having a purely subservient manufacturing role, subsidiary sites are increasingly called upon to take responsibility for the development, marketing and manufacture of specific products for European and/or global markets. The level of responsibility and autonomy has increased. This brings with it a series of advantages in terms of the propensity for spin-offs and the growth of stronger links with indigenous suppliers. [3]

Wallerstein, commenting on the oil industry in Venezuela, noted that the area was becoming impoverished by the way natural resources were being exploited. The concentration on accumulating oil revenues resulted in the secondary aspects of the industrial process being dominated by foreign multi-nationals. The illusion of wealth in the area helped to create an inhospitable climate for other types of industry, they had to face increasing costs without government support. No local companies grew up to rival the world leaders in the oil fields and no locals progressed very far up the corporate structure. The cumulative result was that when the resources ran down and the area became a less attractive area to exploit, the MNEs moved out. Other industries had left previously or did not have the ability to compensate and the area became impoverished. [4]

This analogy has been successfully applied to the Scottish oil sector. Inward investment might be viewed as a good way of improving local economies, but these examples are used to demonstrate how inward investment could ultimately result in a pyrrhic victory for government agencies who strive to improve the economy by focusing on this method. The prospects for the electronic industry in Scotland appear to be a lot better because of the shifting locus of control and increasing use of IT to support global manufacturing strategies.

The foreign sector has progressed from the branch plant image of the 1970s, particularly in both the development of products for the European market and the level and sophistication of R&D. Haug *et al.* suggest that

148

'the emergence and growth of R&D activity was seen to be largely induced by the need for response to market signals ... [and] ... seemed to provide a mechanism for facilitating technology transfers from the parent multi-nationals, and the proportion of commercial applications from the research results was high and tended to be based in the affiliates themselves.' [5]

Growing R&D intensity at the level of the Scottish affiliates offers the opportunity for new enterprise spin-offs.

The result of these functions being passed down the company is that there is a change in the pattern of control. The branch plant syndrome which typified entry strategies in the 1960s and 1970s, has shifted towards more localised control and wider product responsibility. Firstly, there has been movement within these companies towards the decentralisation of day-to-day operational control. Secondly, there is an increasing awareness of the ability of subsidiary operations to undertake more prominent product development roles for European and global markets. Lastly, there is a growing awareness of the capabilities of new manufacturing techniques and process support technologies which encourage greater degrees of autonomy. Young notes that the incidence of R&D in foreign-owned firms in Scotland has increased rapidly. [6] Using Ronstadt's categorisation of R&D activity, Young suggests that 'what seems to have occurred is a significant increase in the number of companies with relatively low level R&D units.' [7]

However, it would be wrong to put too much stress on this point as the principal emphasis in foreign-owned subsidiaries remains production, and this distinguishes electronics in Scotland from that in south-east England. Sayer and Morgan argue that 'the overseas sector remains poorly intergated with multiplier effects which afford little secondary employment and, perhaps most important for longer-term prospects, a significant indigenous sector has not developed.' [9] What is notable about indigenous firms (e.g., Rodime) is that to keep abreast of international leading-edge innovation, they feel obliged to expand outside Britain soon after birth, in the case of Rodime this has been in the USA and Singapore.

There is evidence that several Scottish-based MNEs are moving in this direction and this should give hope for the future. [10,11] What is needed, therefore, is a change in what the SDA describes as the 'cultural and management weaknesses' in the indigenous sector to be able to take advantage of opportunities which currently exist and may increase in the near future. [12]

Support for business strategy

It is difficult to imagine that the developments outlined above could have taken place without the enabling factor of highly sophisticated information technology. The Scottish MNE sites are linked very closely with their parent companies. All types of information flows through the various networks, ranging from complex technical drawings to simple messages. Typically the information is batched together and transmitted to sites over the world. There is a movement to ever increasing immediacy in these complex communications.

If there has been a shift in, and widening of, the locus of control, only an extremely naive position would hold that steps to achieve this state of affairs would have been taken if those at corporate headquarters did not think they had adequate knowledge of, and control over, what happens in the company. Information technology and the astute management of this have been key factors in the ability to pursue this strategy. The information gathered, and fed out at the various terminals gives the head office sufficient knowledge of what is going on, to be comfortable in co-ordinating the world company and with devolving responsibilities.

Electronic Data Interchange (EDI) systems which exist within the MNEs cater for the transmission of performance data, financial data, technical data and simple written communications. For example, this means that head office can be aware of what is going on in subsidiary sites, in fairly close detail, very quickly. An example would be where technical drawings would have been updated in one location, but frequently this was not adequately recorded or 'flagged' to other sites, who found that they were repeating the original mistake in their ignorance. Nowadays the possibilities for this kind of error are minimised. In addition MNEs in this sector foster strong corporate cultures, which have the effect of socialising the person into operating along corporate guidelines, without much requirement for overt control systems.

If the control relationships in these companies can be said to have altered together with the proliferation of information technology, Foucault's work on social control and regulation is applicable here. Conducting an historical analysis of institutions he noted a perceptible switch between overt to covert forms of control. For example, in the penal system, capital punishment gave way to different forms of discipline which attempt to reform the wrongdoer or to get the wrongdoer to contribute to society. Institutional forms of regulation, such as timing, monitoring and prescribing activities are all designed to get the individual to behave in the intended way without overt punishment on the body. A set of technologies were developed to compliment these ideas. The layout of prisons in that era was designed to give the custodians the maximum opportunity to view what the prisoners were doing, hence knowledge, and the prisoners were made aware that they were being watched. These were the principle methods of creating discipline and controlling the prisoners. [13]

It can be argued that these are the type of changes happening to the control systems of MNEs. Instead of fairly overt forms of control and restrictions being applied to subsidiaries, the technologies exist to support a more covert, subliminal form, which fits into modern strategic business requirements. Strong corporate cultures and detailed information systems create the framework to control the way people operate whilst not appearing repressive. In later writings, Foucault gave more emphasis to the idea that power/ knowledge could be enabling as well as controlling and this is the aspect we would also to emphasise.

> 'The 'colonisation of the penalty by the prison' is explicable less in terms of developments in penal philosophy than as a significant dimension of the emergence and exercise of a new type of power, a power of normalisation which operates, in addition, in such nonpenal institutions as the school, the hospital, the factory and the military academy.' [14]

The newer systems of control emerge in everyday practice as if they are not systems for this purpose at all. The technologies of these systems, do not appear to be tools of control. Nor are they in a conventional sense, as they can enable the people who are monitored to gain access to information and knowledge. The systems may be used to monitor activities more effectively, but access and training on the use of these systems also gives the people in the subsidiaries new knowledge and means of communicating to other sites. This transfer of knowledge can prevent the long term negative effects identified by Wallerstein. This has happened within the MNEs, and is likely to happen when EDI networks are set up with suppliers; a specific example is detailed below.

Manufacturing strategy

The following sections are devoted to looking at more localised shifts of control, examining firstly the implementation of internal manufacturing strategies within subsidiary MNEs and related information technology; and secondly the external ramifications of these strategies in the shape of other strategies developed to manage the supply chain, focusing on indigenous suppliers. At present the development of IT strategies appears to be lagging behind business strategies.

Manufacturing strategies with various labels such as 'Just-in-Time' and 'Total Quality Management' together with 'Vertical Disintegration' are being pursued with the overall aim of ensuring three things: better customer service, shorter time to market and securing optimal value adding operations. Marketing strategies such as giving customers greater input in the product they receive and bringing innovations to the market place before a competitor necessitate the process used to make products being faster and the outputs of this being of higher quality. The organisational implications of these strategies can be quite radical. The control processes in the factory are advocated to move from a restrictive, non-participatory system towards a more positive, less overt, more inclusive type of system.

The strategies can be summarised as advocating a switch from product to process fixation, which ultimately serves to improve the product; as well as one from centralisation to decentralisation of organisational responsibilities.

Internal business strategy

The 'Just-in-Time' set of manufacturing strategies advocated by Schonberger and others are a way of effecting the above. [15] Instead of 'pushing' a large batch of units down a production line, ever reducing batch sizes are 'pulled' down the line when sub-sectors indicate there is a customer for the output. This results in shorter product cycle times and gives greater visibility to areas where these could be further reduced and highlights materials deficiencies.

The whole notion that bigger must be better is reversed, with MNEs embarrassed at large warehouses built for economies of scale and production areas populated by small areas of activity with dedicated machinery, such as U-shaped lines and single cell manufacture.

Thus the layout and utilisation of machinery and human resources are the subject of different pressures. The ideal way suggested for operating is to give the workers more control over the process and responsibility for quality. Schonberger suggests that an effective way of operating would be to copy the *kanban* system used in Japan, where small buffer areas, such as marked squares on the floor or shelving, are used as visible signs that product is or is not needed further up the line. When there is a problem workers can stop the line. They also contribute to the discussion on how to improve the system and best effect the process. [16]

This is another way of changing the technologies of control. As was argued above, arrangements which increase the visibility of people's action and the flow of knowledge about what they do can act as a disciplinary force, which might not be the initial intention.

IT strategy

At present there is not what one might call a clearly defined strategy being pursued in this area. Some companies have attempted to go down the path of Computer Integrated Manufacturing (CIM), but systems are not particularly integrated at the moment. Computer numerically controlled (CNC) machines are operated to the requirements of computerised production schedules, some are self-correcting and interpret their own statistical process control data. Planning and scheduling are sometimes linked to materials and tooling tracking (done by chip or barcode). Information systems about customers and suppliers, some amounting to appraisal decision support tools exist. However, there are gaps in the chain which would mean that the 'information' or co-ordinating aspect of computing is not handled as well as the execution. (see Chapter 9)

Explanations for this centre round the difficulty of creating systems which were sufficiently flexible; the difficulty of coping with vast amounts of quite often irrelevant data and the difficulty of getting human co-operation. There is also the idea that restricting an employee to pushing a button to operate the machine leaves less margin for disruption than giving them access to the total system of the company; there is not the recognition of the controlling effect of computers, just the liberating ones.

External business strategy

The pressures for vertical disintegration combined with quality improvements and timely deliveries mean most MNEs have developed more sophisticated strategies to manage materials and in particular suppliers. Schonberger suggests that stronger relationships should be built with fewer suppliers as an integral part of the 'Just-in-Time' policies he advocates which are outlined above. There should be more recognition of the interdependencies, with sourcing based on a wider concept than unit price taking into consideration things like quality, flexibility and so on. The degree of service given by good suppliers when they are delivering perfect parts to the point of use several times a day, and the costs of breaking this relationship and going elsewhere, should bind the customer more tightly to the relationship.

These recommendations have been less popular than the internal ones. A range of approaches have been adopted where companies have attempted to achieve the results without moving from their quite distant relationship with the suppliers. They have tried to cut down the numbers, but they have not built stronger relationships with the remaining ones. A middle way which has been pursued is where detailed programmes or paths to improvement have been set up for the supplier to follow as a way of culling them and improving performance, with the customer not moving much closer to the good ones. The other extreme is where a lot of activity is centred on a fairly wide sample of suppliers, with training programmes, real life projects and a face-to-face mode of conducting business. This approach is the closest to the pronouncements of Schonberger.

The reasons for this are complex and not quite clear. In papers writen about customer vendor relationships there is a tendency to typify the picture before 'Just-in-Time' as one of adversarial relations based on cost fixing with 'acceptable' levels of defects. This is too simplistic. Baxter *et al.* note that 'no' is not in a vendor's vocabulary when dealing with a customer. [18] Cartels exist in many supply sectors, resulting in a carve-up of the pitch before the customer has entered the discussions. Customers who have been in the sector or geographical location and have sourced externally have built up relationships with local suppliers; perhaps a limited number of personnel have been conducting the relationship over a number of years. Every year or so there is some tinkering over price and deference to the customer and the relationship continues. However, the gap painted between previous and currently desired quality levels is more accurate. But it would be correct to say that the distance between customer and supplier both in the sense of contact and in the sense of status is being maintained.

The role of IT

One would imagine that the increased speed and quantity of transactions between customer and supplier would lead many companies down the path of setting up links similar to those developed in the motor industry; at present this is not the case. Electronic Data Interchange packages are sold by MNEs but at present not utilised in any great way with local suppliers. Some have plans to implement links, but most consider the business relationship to be too immature in terms of modern requirements. They are taking the advice which they are giving to prospective customers themselves; the DEC video about EDI contains a passage describing how 80% of the problems associated with EDI come from business areas, the technical ones account for only 20%. [19] Establishing just what is transmitted, when the data is gathered and who has access to the system can be the source of much attention. EDI systems are currently designed to take information in a language structure suitable for industry sectors such as electronics in the design, financial, logistics and production information. (see Chapter 11)

One would imagine that this would be an area where a customer who had pursued a strategy of closeness with suppliers would be one who would also be thinking about close electronic meshing. This has not been the case, rather the business relationship is considered insufficiently advanced to merit this. However, suppliers do have the opportunity in one company of making use of the intra-organisational system, as a supplier qualified to source locally has access to the MNEs world supply network, i.e. can be considered by all the MNEs manufacturing units worldwide as a source of supply. This is strictly managed by the local subsidiary and all contacts go through them. However, the benefits to the indigenous supplier are good, as they get an export distribution network for no expense.

The customer who is developing electronic links with their supply base is one of the most established in the sector, and have long-standing relationships dealing with large quantities of parts. However the types of links envisaged by most companies tend to be one way. The customer wants intimate knowledge of the supplier's business, production schedules, capacities, where they source the material and how that relationship is progressing, but the reciprocal degree of involvement is not forthcoming. Customers do not want suppliers to have access to their production scheduling, etc. and the electronics sector is not one where long term contracts are common.

The prognosis for suppliers

Although the supplier has increasing pressure to perform to strict maxims on the nature and process of the part it makes, it could be argued that through the testing time it is being given an opportunity to cut its teeth and learn from the MNEs with a view to having skills and products which the company itself can put forward at the global market place. The local supply base is in a position to take advantage of current maxims on local supplying, as they are geographically at least, best equipped to meet the needs of the MNEs. Once a supply base has been set up and is being managed smoothly it is highly costly and time consuming to try to change this. With the reduction of tasks undertaken by the buyer company, the less knowledge that company retains on the best possible way of producing and sourcing a part; presumably the specialist supplier will have more input in the design.

The power relationship between customer and vendor is not one way, nor can it be said to be a zero sum. Although tough standards are being placed on the supplier, the supplier who meets these demands is a valuable link in the MNEs supply chain. Suppliers who adopt a proactive strategy for EDI can further improve their position in global terms. Once the fundamental stages are succesfully completed, it is possible to argue that having strong computer links mesh the customer into the relationship, and provide a substantial barrier to others who have not set them up. It remains to be seen whether small companies in Scotland avail themselves of the teaching on offer and the opportunities which exist.

Conclusion

There is a tendency to take minor alterations in corporate and government strategy out of proportion to the likely development trends of the electronics industry in an attempt to predict a more optimistic picture for the development of indigenous enterprise. However, there have been a number of key alterations in recent years which do give cause for such optimism. If we take as a starting point two specific factors, the changing role of subsidiary operations and the development of advanced manufacturing and manufacturing support technologies in the electronics industry there is a reasonable case to be made for increasing subsidiary authority and subsequent spin-off potential and indigenous linkages.

Electronics MNEs operate global strategies. However, there are within these global strategies margins of flexibility to individual subsidiaries based on the changing face of global markets. The electronics industry is faced with ever-decreasing product life cycles, and more demanding and sophisticated customer demands based on quality, specification and delivery. Increasing levels of competition make the speed of change a crucial factor in the success of many electronics manufacturers. To ensure this flexibility for change means delegating to subsidiary operations a responsibility for manufacture and market strategy hitherto unknown. Subsidiary operations are the first to see changes in product or market demand and are in a position to react faster than the centrally-controlled global corporation. The European market is a prime example of the development of such a strategy and as European revenues account for an increasing proportion of multi-national sales, so the importance of being able to react to the needs of the European market becomes crucial.

Therefore, corporate strategy towards European subsidiaries is becoming more flexible by allowing these operations to undertake responsibility for the marketing and manufacture of specific product ranges aimed at the European and sometimes global market. The movement away from final assembly and testing towards outright responsibility has two implications in terms of the shifting locus of control. First, subsidiaries need to be able to gear products to their markets and this includes changes to design and future product development. This warrants the growth of related R&D activity at the subsidiary site. Although this is minor and does not entail basic research and development of new products there are implications for the management of such operations. Product design and quality departments would be one such example of the growing extension of subsidiary responsibility. An increasing level of R&D activity at the subsidiary level also requires highly skilled staff and management which increases the potential for spin-offs enterprises to develop. [20]

Added to changes created by the growth of European revenues, faster product life-cycles, and the need for speed of change emanating from the subsidiary operation, there are implications of the use of advanced manufacturing and manufacturing support technologies. The continued use of Materials Resource Planning and 'Just-in-Time' manufacturing techniques creates a need for closer subsidiary control over day-to-day manufacturing operations. This control extends authority not only in the scale and pace of manufacturing, but also in areas, such as product design and procurement. As the managing director of Prestwick Circuits, one of Europe's leading printed circuit board (PCB) manufacturers, commented

'The only way that proximity to the plant works with "Just-in-Time" is if the plant has design authority. You're not really talking about a good working relationship that is restricted to purchasing. It is the total engineering relationship that is affected with feedback of what is possible to manufacture, to get designs that reflect what is possible so you can get the lowest relevant cost and improvements in manufacture can be fed back into the design. If the design cannot be responsive because there is a gap in communications then you don't get any benefit at all with "Just-in-Time" relationships in a satellite organisation. There is an organisational problem for the multi-national in that sense.'

The organisational problem reflects the need to devolve more autonomy to the subsidiary operation. Global sourcing policies are likely to remain where standardised components are required and products remain unchanged over time. However, if the scenario is one of shorter life cycles, matching customer wants through smaller batch sizes, and developing new products according to market information, then the need for control over operations at local level is enhanced. Basic R&D and product design is likely to remain the prerogative of corporate headquarters, but as subsidiary operations develop these products for the European market the need to alter design, and establish a local supplier base so the opportunities for linkage creation and spin-offs are enhanced. Again the managing director of Prestwick Circuits noted that

'The five hour gap over the telephone is enough to make it very difficult for the people over here to be as free and innovative as their opposite numbers at head office. I suspect that is not specific to Scotland but happens in any satellite operation. Another area of difficulty resides in the fact that there may be corporate purchasing policies to reduce the total number of supply sources. It is only natural for the people who are making the key decisions to be located at head office and for them to favour their own orbit of knowledge. I wouldn't say that this has been a major problem but it will become one as "Just-in-Time" and total quality management techniques are applied. There is a need to have very close customer/supplier relationships along the Japanese style and it is very likely that the reduced supplier base will be one that the headquarters group understand.'

Information Technology can help execute modern supply relationships and provide head offices with some of the knowledges they need to control operations on a global basis. The shifting locus of control in each of the three ways described in this chapter offers indigenous companies and individual opportunities for development far superior to those which existed before.

References

1   McCalman, J "What's Wrong with Scottish Firms? Local sourcing in Electronics" Fraser of Allander Institute, *Quarterly Economic Commentary,* University of Strathclyde, February, 1987.

2   van der Klugt, C J "Japan's Global Challenge in Electronics; the Philips response" *European Management Journal* **4** (1) pp 4-9, 1986.

3   Young, S "Scottish Multinationals and the Scottish Economy" Working paper for the conference on Scotland and the Multinationals, IRM and Strathclyde International Business Unit, Glasgow, 1986.

4   Wallerstein, I "Processes of the World-System" Beverly Hills, London.

5   Haug, P; Hood, N and Young, S "R&D Intensity in the Affiliates of US-Owned Electronics Companies Manufacturing in Scotland" *Regional Studies* **17** (6) pp 383-392, 1983.
6   Young, op. cit.
7   Ronsadt, R "Research and Development abroad by US Multinationals" Praeger, New York, 1977.
8   Young, op. cit.
9   Sayer, A and Morgan, K "The Electronics Industry and Regional Development in Britain" in *Technological Change, Industrial Restructuring and Regional Development,* edited by A Amin and J B Goddard, 1984.
10   Buchanan, D A "Job Enrichment is Dead: long live high-performance work design!" *Personnel Management* May 1987.
11   Young, op. cit.
12   Scottish Development Agency "Electronics Scotland" Newsletter of the Electronics Division of the SDA, Glasgow, 1986.
13   Foucault, M "Discipline and Punish" Penguin, Harmondsworth, 1979.
14   Smart, B "On discipline and social regulation: a review of Foucault's genealogical analysis" in *The Power to Punish,* edited by D Garland and P Young, Heinemann, London, 1983.
15   Schonberger, R "World Class Manufacturing" Free Press, New York, 1983.
18   Baxter, L F *et al.* "Getting the Message Across? supplier quality improvement programmes: some issues in practice" *International Journal of Production Management* **8** (5) 1989.
19   Digital Equipment Corporation "EDI: Making it Work" video, Digital Equipment Corporation, Reading, 1989.
20   Young, op. cit.

Part IV
Value Added Networks

11
Strategic Implications of Inter-organisational Systems

Yannis Bakos

Information systems linking different organisations offer significant opportunities both to create economic value and to allow strategic manipulation. Theoretical analysis and practical understanding are complicated by the involvement of several organisations, each pursuing its own self-interest. The increasing use of these information systems as an element in the competitive game creates strategic problems for firms in industries where such systems have been, or are about to be, introduced. These problems include unseating competitors with entrenched systems, finding appropriate responses for captive customers, and identifying opportunities to act as an information broker. (see Chapter 2)

Inter-organisational information systems

Inter-organisational information systems (IOS) are systems based on information technology that cross organisational boundaries the purpose of which is the exchange of information-based products or services. A typical IOS is an information system which links one or more firms to their customers and/or their suppliers. Traditionally information systems have been restricted to a single organisation because of organisational and technological limitations. This situation is changing as organisations improve their ability to understand, utilise and manage information technology and as they become aware of its potential to create and exploit inter-organisational efficiencies. As a result, we are witnessing an increase in the number and functionality of inter-organisational information systems.

This chapter presents insights derived from economic models employed to study inter-organisational systems in vertical markets. Two types of such systems, information links and electronic markets, are examined in a vertical market setting and their payoffs and implications for industrial structure and strategic conduct are assessed.

It should be pointed out that inter-organisational information systems are not a new phenomenon. Depending on the definition of information technology used, the mail and telephone networks can be considered as long-standing examples of inter-organisational systems. These systems have become indispensable because inter-organisational transactions play a central role in our economic system. The difficulty in administering control and coordination mechanisms across organisational barriers often makes these transactions subject to substantial inefficiencies, creating opportunities for successful applications of IOS. [1]

Information links and electronic markets

IOS are usually encountered between two stages in a linear value-added-chain, and thus can be thought of as having two primary types of participants, which we call suppliers and customers. We can also think of each system as being operated by an intermediary responsible for at least part of the added-value and intermediating functions. It is also possible that a customer or a supplier functions as an intermediary. This view of IOS in a vertical market involving customers, suppliers, and one or more potential intermediaries describes the industrial setting central to our approach. Two types of vertical market IOS are of particular interest: information links and electronic markets.

An inter-organisational information link is an IOS at the boundary between the value-added chains of two firms in a vertical market. Information links improve the economics of gathering and communicating information; this effect can be modelled as an increase in the performance of inter-organisational information channels. The introduction of an information link as a stand-alone system or as part of a market system can improve coordination at the interface between a customer and its suppliers, creating efficiencies such as better management of inventory levels or improved data exchange between the organisations involved.

An electronic market is an IOS in a vertical market which allows the participating buyers and sellers to exchange information about prices and product offerings. Economic theory suggests that the cost which buyers incur to acquire price and product information enables sellers to extract monopolistic rents in otherwise competitive markets. Information systems for market intermediation are likely to reduce the cost of price and product information; electronic markets may thus promote price competition and reduce sellers' market power.

Information links and vertical markets are not mutually exclusive; individual systems may exhibit characteristics of both an information link and an electronic market, as is the case with market intermediation systems that offer inventory management features. Furthermore, the potential of such systems to affect the efficiency of inter-organisational transactions and the market power of individual sellers and buyers ensures their strategic relevance.

Modeling IOS in vertical markets

Economic models of IOS can highlight the characteristics that distinguish them from other types of capital investments. IOS typically offer substantial economies of scale. An intermediary must incur large system development and maintenance costs but will then face relatively small incremental costs for each additional transaction. A second characteristic of these systems is that the benefits realised by individual participants increase as more organisations join the system. This property, known in industrial economics as network externalities, can affect the dynamics of IOS introduction and adoption, e.g., by favouring the first intermediary introducing such a system. [2] Finally, IOS are likely to reduce the cost of comparing the offerings of different suppliers in an electronic marketplace and they can be used to impose switching costs on customers or suppliers.

There are three ways in which inter-organisational information systems can affect the structure and efficiency of a vertical market:

- the introduction of an information link as a separate system or as part of a wider market system can increase the capacity and decrease the response time of inter-organisational communication. This improves the coordination at the interface between the value added chains of a customer and its suppliers allowing, for example, better management of inventory levels or a switch from inter-process inventory management to a 'Just-in-Time' system.
- a market intermediation system can reduce customer costs of locating alternative suppliers or supplier costs of locating additional customers. This reduction is likely to affect the monopoly power of the suppliers or the monopsony power of the customers in a vertical market which is moved 'on-line' by the introduction of an inter-organisational information system, and will also have implications for the efficiency and structure of that market.

the economics of developing, introducing and operating inter-organisational information systems may have implications for the structure of individual markets. For example, by causing a shift from decentralised markets without significant intermediaries to more centralised markets where a few organisations intermediate the information exchange between customers and suppliers in that market.

Inter-organisational information links

An inter-organisational information link is at the boundary between the value-added chains of two firms in a vertical market. We refer to these firms as the supplier and the customer, or as the upstream and the downstream firm. Such an information link can be modelled as a communication channel between a customer and a supplier, which is characterised by a certain capacity and response time. In this setting, the use of information technology is assumed to result in reduced response time and increased capacity of this communication channel. The first effect comes from the ability of IOS to speed up the information processing component included in the response time of the system, as well as their ability to set-up a connection faster than systems based on conventional technology such as mail or telephone systems. The second impact comes from the superior capabilities of IOS to transmit information with speed and accuracy.

Inventory and monitoring models

Efficiencies resulting from the introduction of IOS can be modelled in terms of reductions in the cost of inter-organisational coordination. In many vertical market settings, inventory and monitoring costs can be used as a proxy for coordination costs. In this section we discuss the implications of such models. A detailed description of a possible formulation and the ensuing analysis can be found in. [3]

In considering inventory or stock control, increasing the capacity of the information link and improving its response time results in shorter order lead times, decreased total inventory and reduced coordination costs. Given certain realistic assumptions about the physical characteristics of the system, if the lead time becomes small enough, the optimal inventory capacity of the downstream firm eventually becomes less than the in-process inventory. At that point, the downstream firm may dispose of its inter-process inventory buffer altogether. The coordination between the two firms has changed from a buffered inventory link to a 'Just-in-Time' system. IOS may thus promote a substitution of information exchange for inventories, resulting in higher levels of inter-organisational communication and lower overall coordination costs.

Alternatively, information links can be studied in a setting emphasising the monitoring of organisational processes. When monitoring a stochastic process that satisfies certain realistic requirements it can be shown that the performance of the information link becomes a valuable resource. Increasing this capacity beyond a certain point results in logarithmic decreases in monitoring costs. Hence, as the information processing and communication capacities of the information link increase, the cost of coordination decreases, in the same way as the inventory example. These results lend theoretical support to an intuitive conclusion, that coordination and monitoring are information-bound.

Implications for vertical markets

Models like the ones discussed above demonstrate the potential benefits of inter-organisational information links in vertical market settings, where we identified a macro-level trade-off between information exchange and inventories. IOS are likely to increase inter-organisational communication and lower overall coordination costs. Information technology may improve the efficiency of inter-organisational information exchanges by several orders of magnitude, allowing the complete elimination of inter-process inventories and a switch to 'Just-in-Time' systems based on timely delivery of intermediate goods, or *kanban* systems driven by the vertical flow of information about demand at each stage of production. [4]

Naturally, inter-organisational information links are not always the best way to reduce coordination costs between suppliers and customers. Substantial gains may be realised by restructuring and streamlining operations to reduce the need for information processing or by redesigning systems and improving coordination strategies to make better use of the capacity of existing information links. This strategy will be cheaper to implement and, before resorting to technology-intensive solutions, a re-evaluation and redesign of existing systems and procedures may be appropriate. The analysis shows, however, that there is an information-theoretic frontier which will be reached at some point, and IOS can shift the limits imposed by that frontier.

Electronic markets

We now focus on the impact of IOS on vertical markets. Inter-organisational information systems can create 'electronic marketplaces' by serving as intermediaries between the buyers and the sellers in a vertical market. In that capacity, they are likely to reduce the cost which buyers must incur to acquire information about sellers' prices and product offerings. Furthermore, the economies of scale and network externalities exhibited by IOS are likely to favour large centralised intermediaries and early movers.

Search costs in differentiated vertical markets

The economic literature on search costs suggests that heterogeneity of consumers and product offerings is central to the ability of sellers to exploit buyer search costs and thus obtain monopolistic rents. [5,6] A model for the costs of search in a differentiated market can be used to analyse the effect of introducing electronic intermediation to a market with differentiated products. That model requires buyers to incur a search cost in order to be informed about the product offering and the price of some seller and then to decide whether to purchase, keep searching or give up.

In this case, the cost of information acquisition allows sellers to extract some monopolistic rents. Reducing the cost of search, e.g., by introducing an electronic market system, results in lower prices and reduced seller profits. Social welfare is increased by reducing the cost of buyer searches and enabling them to locate products better matching their needs. If the search cost is low enough, buyers look at all product offerings and purchase the one best serving their needs, resulting in a socially optimal allocation. Very high search costs, on the other hand, lead to efficiency losses and eventually cause the market to break down.

Implications for market intermediation

Our analysis suggests that electronic markets are likely to promote price competition and reduce sellers' market power. Buyers are likely to benefit from these systems in two ways: firstly, they may enjoy lower prices because of the increased competition among sellers; and secondly, they will be better informed about the available products and thus may choose sellers which better suit their needs. Such efficiencies would make the introduction of electronic market systems socially desirable for markets with high information costs and create a profit potential for the right intermediaries.

Conversely, these systems can put sellers in a 'prisoner's dilemma'. Sellers as a group have no incentive to introduce a system offering price and product information, which makes them all worse off. Yet each of them would like to introduce such a system individually since the revenues that can be derived by charging buyers for the services of such a system outweigh the loss of individual monopolistic rents. This may account for the puzzling observation that sellers are the ones most likely to precipitate the introduction of electronic market systems in concentrated industries despite the potential of these systems to reduce monopoly power.

Airline reservation systems in the United States of America fit well the above model of electronic markets and have played an increasingly important role in recent years. The three systems that have dominated the market are offered by American (SABRE), United (Apollo) and TWA (PARS). These systems have allowed the airlines to lower their operating costs through improved monitoring of their operations and through access to better demand data. Reservation systems have also been used as strategic tools in several capacities ranging from biased screen displays to the ability to administer a wide gamut of thousands of active fares and promotions. It was suggested that electronic markets would increase price competition, reduce seller monopoly power and lead to more demanding customers who are less willing to compromise on their preferred product. Airlines have experienced all these effects. [7]

IOS and corporate strategy

The increasing use of inter-organisational information systems as an element of the competitive game creates a number of related strategic problems for participants in industries where such systems have been or are about to be introduced.

Competing through IOS

A review of the literature on the competitive effects of information technology identified two major sources of competitive advantage, comparative efficiency and market power. [8] Search costs, unique product features and switching costs were identified as the main sources of market power, while internal and inter-organisational efficiencies

Figure 11.1 A causal model of competitive advantage

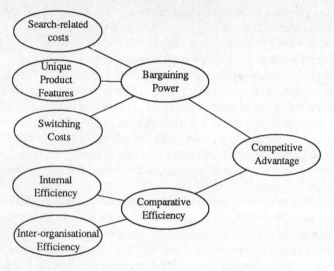

underlie comparative efficiency. (seeFigure 11.1) IOS directly affect the inter-organisational efficiencies as discussed earlier. These systems also affect search costs and switching costs, while they may allow information intermediaries to offer unique products associated with their systems.

The sustainability of competitive advantage should be a critical concern. Experience with information technology suggests that technological advantage is sustainable only in situations involving more than simple technical sophistication and which demand substantial organisational learning and complex organisational interactions. Advantage based purely on technological sophistication is difficult to sustain because of the open and rapidly evolving nature of the technology. [9] On the other hand, the exploitation of organisational complexities to create sustainable advantage through IOS is a promising area of research; as the number of organisations involved in a system increases, organisational problems increase disproportionately.

Information links

The efficiencies offered by an inter-organisational information link depend on the characteristics and needs of the participating customers and suppliers. A firm introducing such a system must closely monitor changes in its customer base, which could either enhance or reduce the opportunities for IOS offerings. Furthermore, the distribution of the benefits and payoffs derived from an information link among the system participants is typically determined by the strategic characteristics of the situation which establish the relative power of the IOS participants.

An important tactic for improving the strategic value of an inter-organisational information link (assuming it is supplier-owned) is to provide unique and valuable information and services which require idiosyncratic changes to the customer's organisation and, thus, make switching to a competitor more costly. IOS can facilitate unique information or service offerings previously unattainable and of great value to customers. The higher the perceived value of these offerings, and the more complex and idiosyncratic the interface is for the customer, the higher will be the imposed switching costs. Correspondingly, information links can increase a customer's power against its suppliers if they reduce the cost of locating alternative suppliers, dependence on unique supplier products and the costs of switching suppliers.

Every supplier is a customer of another supplier in an unbroken value-added chain. Thus, the opportunity to gain market power can be pursued by customers and suppliers to a firm's disadvantage unless tactics are devised to avoid the problem. Three specific tactics present themselves: avoid becoming dependent on customer and supplier-controlled information and services, create an efficient electronic marketplace between one's own organisation and its suppliers, and try to avoid such an electronic market on the customer side.

Electronic markets

Our analysis suggests that electronic market systems generally favour buyers and reduce seller monopoly power. How then should sellers react to technological developments that make a market system feasible, or even imminent? In the long run it may be impossible to avoid some loss in market power, especially when this power is based on high information costs. System revenues may compensate for this decline in the short-run but, as rival systems are introduced, their profits are likely to be lost through competition. Yet colluding to prevent an electronic market may induce buyers to introduce such a system themselves or invite a third-party intermediary to do so.

The best strategy for sellers may be to control the type of system eventually introduced; a system emphasising product over price information may allow sellers to keep much of their monopoly power while giving buyers access to the allocation efficiencies and for which buyers could be charged user fees. Introduction of such systems could provide a focal point for a relatively cooperative outcome, as other sellers may 'get the message' and introduce themselves systems that emphasise aspects other than price information and comparison. Established systems can raise the barriers of entry for third-party information providers and thus delay or avoid the competition from systems offered by non-industry participants.

Buyers obviously have the opposite incentives and would like to facilitate an electronic market that makes easier comparisons among sellers' prices and product offerings. A single buyer may be too small or may not have adequate interest to introduce a market system and may lack the clout to induce seller participation. Buyers may have to form coalitions and introduce jointly owned systems, or a third party organisation with the necessary technological sophistication may play that role.

Information intermediaries

The efficiencies of electronic markets aggregated over the entire economy make the provision of electronic intermediation services a market of vast potential, holding large rewards for the players that will be appropriately positioned at the right points in time. Information systems for market intermediation require large investments in start-up hardware, development costs and continuing maintenance. Once a system is in place, marginal costs are low. As traditional technology with low entry costs is replaced by systems based on information technology with large development costs, the new economics of intermediation are likely to favour more centralised markets and intermediaries with access to a wealth of resources who can exploit their know-how in different industries and defray their development expenses among several systems.

As electronic market systems and more general inter-organisational information systems become commonplace, competition among intermediaries is likely to increase, causing intermediation profits to decrease. This trend is already evident in the more mature electronic markets, as demonstrated by airline reservation systems. Experience from the long distance communication industry suggests that a few firms with large installed bases, intermediation expertise and proprietary data bases will become information utilities dominating the provision of intermediation services.

Early mover advantage

Information technology is characterised by uncertainty about the potential value of new systems and by network externalities which favour established systems with large installed bases. As a result, firms in an industry are likely to be hesitant. However, once a system proves successful its momentum rapidly increases. Unless the technology evolves rapidly in a way which penalises firms which deployed an earlier generation, late movers are at a disadvantage. On the other hand, being an early mover can result in offering or participating in a system that is inappropriate or which soon becomes obsolete; early movers will sometimes be stranded with a bad technology. This creates a conservatism on the part of potential intermediaries that favours those with sophisticated capabilities for technology assessment.

Another peril of an early system that becomes well established is that it may leave no alternative for other industry participants except to form a coalition and offer a credible competing system. Experience suggests that the advantage gained by moving early in offering an IOS system in any particular industry will most likely open only a window of opportunity. When IOS technology becomes commonplace, profits will be lost through competition from intermediaries who have not achieved some form of sustainable advantage. Firms can try to exploit opportunities for supranormal profits for as long as they last and attempt to control the transition to a more competitive environment by biasing the final outcome in their favour.

Conclusion

Inter-organisational information systems are a fact of life and they are becoming more prevalent every day. We have argued that these systems hold great promise for improving inter-organisational coordination in bilateral and market settings. Their economic efficiencies can create potential opportunities for information intermediaries, yet when IOS technology becomes commonplace, profits will be lost though competition by intermediaries who have not achieved some form of sustainable advantage. The underlying economies of scale may enable certain firms to exploit their system development expertise, installed networks, customer bases and proprietary databases thus becoming information utilities and possibly dominating the provision of intermediation services.

In the long run, bilateral information links are likely to be replaced by industry systems or specific applications running on top of these systems, except in the most idiosyncratic applications. Market systems will play an increasing role in the economy at large, offering efficiencies from improved coordination. In information-intensive industries, electronic market systems are likely to be introduced by existing firms. Such systems often start as links between a firm and its customers or suppliers. Other competitors, being put at a disadvantage, will typically respond with alternative systems paving the road to an industry-wide electronic market.

IOS will eventually become a strategic necessity and part of the industry's infrastructure. Systems involving an alliance with an information service intermediary are likely to gain advantage because of the latter's economies of scale and scope. Information intermediaries are likely to capitalise on their accumulated know-how and initiate the introduction of IOS in less sophisticated industries. Such systems will probably involve an alliance with a market participant because intermediation needs vary across industries, but may allow the intermediary to appropriate a larger share of their payoffs.

References

1   Williamson, O "Markets and Hierarchies" Free Press, New York, 1975.
2   Katz, M L and Shapiro, C "Network Externalities, Competition and Compatibility" *American Economic Review* **75** pp 70-83, Spring 1985.
3   Bakos, J Yannis "Interorganisational Information Systems: Strategic Opportunities for Competition and Cooperation" PhD Thesis, MIT Sloan School of Management, November 1987.
4   Aggarwal, S C "MRP, JIT, OPT, FMS? Making sense of Production Operating Systems" *Harvard Business Review* **63** (5) pp 8-16, September-October 1985.
5   Reinganum, J F "A Simple Model of Equilibrium Price Dispersion" *Journal of Political Economy* **87** pp 851-858, 1979.
6   Shilony, Y "Mixed Pricing in Oligopoly" *Journal of Economic Theory* **14** pp 373-388, 1977.
7   Copeland, Duncan G and McKenney, James L "Airline Reservation Systems: lessons from history" *MIS Quarterly* **12** (3) pp 353-370, 1988.
8   Bakos, J Yannis and Treacy, Michael E "Information Technology and Corporate Strategy: a research perspective" *MIS Quarterly* **10** (2) pp 107-119, June 1986.
9   Clemons, Eric K and Row, M "Structural Differences Among Firms: a potential source of competitive advantage in the application of information technology" pp 1-9 in *Proceedings of the Eighth International Conference on Information Systems, Pittsburg, Pennsylvania, December 6-9, 1987*, edited by L Maggie.

12
Using Minitel to Enrich the Service

Marie-Christine Monnoyer and Jean Philippe

Information technology is now part of the technological environment in all branches of activity. Technical improvement, cost reduction and simplification of the use of materials now means this technology is a base for activities in production as well as in marketing. This technological revolution has now affected a sector of activity which has long remained excluded from progress in productivity - the service sector.

Just as economists have been wondering for sometime about the future of this sector, because of its low output, the appearance of information technology now means that coded, batched data can be processed very quickly, as can the techniques which link computers and files, thereby transforming:

- production rhythm and therefore output and productivity
- the problem of reproducing the service
- the physical means of support for the service
- the nature of the relationship between the service supplier and the customer, as well as that between the service supplier and his own suppliers

These opportunities are likely to become reality in a very great number of activities, either by giving rise to the conception of new services, or by modifying the production process of the service.

These new services therefore arise from the implementation of new technologies. So far they seem to us to be limited in number and with rather feeble effect on economic life as a whole. Nevertheless the modification of the production process could reach almost all services upon the condition that the consequences of using IT can be included in the concept of the service itself.

Using IT in service companies supposes that a certain number of constraints have been removed - constraints which are linked to the necessity of identifying and coding the different types of information that play a role in the production process of a service or 'servuction', to use term coined by Langeard and Eiglier, as we will do. [1] There is an obligation here because this presumes there is a managerial orientation, by which we mean careful reflection concerning the organisation of production and this comes out as a multiplicity of different situations which are the result of analysis of each entrepreneur concerning the service that he offers.

We are particularly interested in medium sized companies in the service sector because, as Porter explains, the diversified character of this sector makes the strategic thinking more difficult. [2] It also makes it all the more necessary because there is a desire for growth. Until now these businesses seemed to be particularly isolated from the technological progress that computerised management brought into large firms in the tertiary sector beginning at the end of the 1960s.

In the companies under consideration we have concentrated on the consequences of using IT in management of the firm and for transforming the material means of support for carrying out the service. These are procedural innovations which without modifying the nature of the service (e.g., distribution of medicines and providing a maintenance service) transform the production organisation, enrich the relationships between partners and create new complementarities which can lead to the appearance of new services and are at the origin of a greater variety of strategic opportunities. They have given rise to a flowering of experiments which make the analysis of such cases necessary. The analysis of company cases makes up the first part of the current study of the field of service companies which are presented with the opportunities offered by IT.

Two companies

Among the many companies whose development we have monitored over the past three years, we have chosen two medium sized companies of between 200 and 300 persons, whose independence and autonomy are quite real despite the fact that one of them has belonged to a large national group for nearly 15 years. Each has been operating in the service sector for 30 years which shows that the services they offer are not, in themselves, particularly innovatory.

The first firm manages, on behalf of about twenty laboratories, a stock of medicines which are destined for 32 French wholesale distributors, hospitals and dispensing chemists. Its head office is in Marseille. The second company offers a maintance service in industrial fluids and heating equipment, with most of its work in Lyon.

A pharmaceutical depository

This company is organised around the office in Marseille and seven branches, covering the whole country. Its function is to deliver in as short a time as possible, under 24 hours, the pharmaceuticals from the supplying laboratories to the customers, namely:

- 220 branches of 32 wholesale distributors
- dispensing chemists (direct sales points)
- hospitals and clinics

The use of IT concerns the collection of orders from the customer. From now on, orders will be placed by telex, Minitel and facsimile, and not by telephone, mail or through representatives. The company has equipped each of its branches and the head office with a computerised device for managing telex transmission and reception. Ordering procedures have been standardised and all telexed orders from the wholesale distributors can be handled automatically, as can orders placed directly by dispensing chemists using their Minitels. Orders placed by mail or by telephone now concern only 'die-hards', some hospitals and clinics which account for less than 15% of the volume of business. The computerised handling of orders means that deliveries can be made a few hours after the orders have been received; generally in the afternoon for an order which is received in the morning.

The setting up of the computer network between the head office and the branches means that the job of managing the branches can also be centralised. The operations linked to customer orders, such as billing the customers, accounting and local stock movements, can be carried out at the head office every afternoon. In the same way, this device means that the management of the purchases necessary to supply each of the seven branches can also be centralised. Thus, every evening, around 9 pm, using its Minitel, each branch can check the exact situation of its stock and the orders placed with the supplying laboratories.

The efficiency of the handling process which has been set up ensures that all the obligations of pharmaceutical product distributors can be carried out efficiently. The company is the sole distributor for the laboratories which have entrusted their products to it. It has available all the information relating to their sales and can therefore supply answers to GERS (a group for the collection and study of pharmaceutical statistics) which, once a month, assembles data relating to the consumption of pharmaceutical products in France.

The efficiency of the information processing methods also allows the firm to give a daily individual update to each of its partners concerning the marketing of their products and the forecasts which it is possible to deduce from them. The availability of this information allows the laboratories to adapt their own production management to this data: calendar, manufacturing rhythm, integration of seasonal factors or epidemics. This information service is available daily, from 9 pm for the different laboratories:

- either by Minitel for the sales and accounts departments
- or directly by the laboratories' computer, which is automatically supplied with the day's information.

IT has also been introduced into all the communication systems within the company and with its partners. Meetings with the branch managers take place each week by teleconference, while facsimile has largely ousted traditional mail. The extension and development of the network of branches, which would allow a reduction in the distribution costs to the end customer, no longer poses problems of organisation and standardisation of methods of collecting information and in the distribution department. The free time made available by the automation of processes is mainly used for improving commercial relations with the chemist customers who are the best sources of information on user reactions and the evolving patterns of consumption.

A tele-maintenance company

For twenty-five years, this company has carried out maintenance of domestic heating installations, and has now turned towards a market of maintaining the equipment used in the hydraulics industry. In order to do that it has set up a system of tele-maintenance which means that no human presence is necessary on the site under surveillance. Instead, from a computer located at the company headquarters, they can follow the value of the characteristic parameters of an installation, using transducers placed on the equipment. Not only do the transducers replace the technicians, but the operator of the control desk can adjust the value of parameters on defective equipment, and in most cases ensure, from a distance, the repair of equipment.

This transformation in surveillance and intervention has meant that the company could expand over a larger area, at the request of certain customers. It is no longer strictly limited to the Lyon conurbation, but is already extending South-West towards Le Puy and South-East towards Grenoble, towns whose distance from Lyon no longer requires costly trips which increase the final cost of the service.

Instead of waiting for a telephone call if there is a breakdown, the company now has the means, minute by minute, to collect data on the state of the equipment under surveillance. It can also supply its customers with a detailed report of the all the maintenance work carried out as time goes by. Consequently, maintenance activity loses a lot of its manual character and becomes a largely computerised service, which is becoming progressively more complex.

At first, the service company offered its customers access using Minitel to the control of its equipment in real time. On the central computer the maintenance engineer in a factory can therefore observe the value of the parameters transmitted by the transducers fitted to the equipment. He can even give orders and carry out modifications. The industrial client is therefore not entirely dependant on the service company that it has chosen.

The service company proposes its network of information flows to prospective customers who would like to keep control over the maintenance of their activities and who are interested in the advantages of tele-maintenance, either continuously or simply at certain times of the day. The company therefore strictly limits its service to the information part of the surveillance activity. It also deals with the installation of control equipment (transducers, data flow network, etc.) and the computer acts only as a communication server which allows the industrial customer to interrogate his own equipment using his own computers via the central computer of the service company. This possibility appears to be particularly interesting for equipment which is geographically dispersed and not very well integrated into a production tool (e.g., pumping stations) or for companies or organisations which do not wish to pay the cost of having surveillance outside normal working hours.

Finally, the service company, aware that it possesses an original way of collecting data on the life and activity of equipment, has reached a partnership agreement with another company in order to organise preventive maintenance of heavy plant which function continuously using the analysis of the profile of the machine's vibrations. The parameters directly received from the transducers placed on the machines are directed via the service company's central computer to a specialist who can then inform the industrial customer of the result of the analysis, and set up certain elements to prevent a breakdown. By now, we are a long way from traditional maintenance.

From procedural choice to strategic analysis

We have chosen to present these two companies because they seem to us to be fairly meaningful as regards the way that IT is introduced into the production process and at the same time into the thinking process that leads the head of a company to consider the future and the evolution of his service. In the current state of technical distribution, the use of IT does not show an immediately strategic character. Our goal is therefore to analyse the elements on which a strategic element might lie and when it exists to study the different potential axes.

The determining elements in choosing IT

Medium sized service companies, which are less directly concerned than large companies with the problems posed by the management of large amount of data and the complex problems of communication between several points, are beginning to become interested of IT. They are doing so, motivated by the need to make productivity gains in a much less stable and more competitive market. Such an evolution should not be too surprising when we remember that a technology like IT was conceived without any clear idea of who might be its users or promoters.

Small and medium sized enterprises are discovering that it is possible to reduce the cost of:

- the processing of internal information, such as accounts cash flow
- the processing of information concerning the partners: handling orders, managing purchases and processing data concerning suppliers and customers

The tele-maintenance company previously mentioned has 'discovered' telematics thanks to one of their customers who proposed an order system using his Minitel. When faced with the efficiency of the system, e.g., search for the availability of the product, and reduction of waiting time, the company sought to develop its own uses of Minitel.

Small and medium sized service companies often play the role of middleman between the producer of goods and the final customer, or the role of a partner during a precise phase in production or distribution, using IT as a new means of communication which completes an existing system.

Innovation could stop there. Some companies, faced with the apparent failure through the inefficiency of this new medium, only keep it because its modern character is good for their image. However, the quest for high performance contains a latent marketing approach which could lead the head of the company to seek:

- application for a new technology
- markets for a new service, or for redefined service
- synergy of efforts devoted to research
- distinction from competitors which is to, say, a certain number of paths towards strategic thinking

Information: the raw material for servuction and the base for strategic re-orientation

Whether it is a question of managing files, memorising the state of the information, or carrying out calculations, the use of IT requires, a previous coding of the data to be handled. Once, this operation has been done, it means the company can realise that there is no real difference between the handling of a breakdown, of an order or a payment. These are just information which arrives in the company and which must be sent to the person in charge of handling the corresponding file. Each of these pieces of information is a 'vector' where the number of the 'dimensions' can vary from 1 to n, according to its complexity.

Thus, the breakdown for the maintenance company is the variation of one or several parameters of the equipment in relation to their reference value. An order for the distribution of medicines is for a number of products destined for a customer with a name and an address.

It therefore seems possible:

- to handle certain production jobs by means of IT
- to bring together the handling of all the information data that a company needs to analyse

This new appraisal of the tasks carried out by a company leads to the identification of their information content and in the same way to the discovery of the information load that the company possesses. This discovery can be the basis of a managerial exploitation of the information.

Towards strategic thinking

The use of IT in service activities gives rise to a multiplicity of possible strategic re-orientations as our two case studies have suggested. IT can intervene in the three phases of servuction: conception, production and availability of the service.

Information and communication technologies include a primary constraint, which is the obligation to encode the information so that it can be handled by the machine. However, this intermediary step can prove to be extremely fruitful for the company since it obliges the service provider to analyse the concept of his service under a new light, that of information. This seems to us to be at the origin of four axes of strategic redeployment.

Standardisation

Information in the world of services is neither formalised nor stabilised. In order to be able to encode information, the concept of a service must be analysed, its constituent elements broken down, in order to separate them from each other, and to release the information which goes with them. This procedure has considerable organisational side-effects since it leads to the isolation of different sequences in the procedure of the production of a service.

Information encoded is information analysed. Thus, when a computerised system for handling orders is created, we see the need to classify products, as well the organisation of their place in the warehouse.

Encoding information also leads to the encoding of the human work which is necessary to carrying out the service. Coded work thus means that the service can be reproduced identically, as can each of its components. The cost of producing the service, as well as that of linked services, is thereby considerably lowered. The unique character of the service, which could seem to make its identical reproduction impossible is seriously diminished. The resulting standardisation is still compatible with the maintenance of various individual stages in the service in order to satisfy certain demands made by the customers. According to the degree of the standardisation adopted, the service comes to resemble an industrial product.

By giving each customer the possibility of 'keeping an eye on' the equipment which the maintenance company is responsible for, the firm is in fact realising an individualisation (by means of a calling code), which is to say with no real marginal cost, of a piece of communication software set up between the central computer and the equipment and the surveillance.

Enriching the service

By breaking down the service into units of information, the information content of the company stands out clearly, this content is largely unexploited. Now, as soon as the encoding of this information has taken place, it becomes clear that:

- a further exploitation is not much more expensive and can give rise to complementary internal services (circulation of information, updating of documents or of knowledge, etc.) and even of external services aimed at the customer which will thereby improve the quality-price ratio of the service
- new methods of exploitation can make up new service-products for which customers need to be found, among the existing clientele or by opening up new markets

The use of an automatic system of telex management by the pharmaceutical warehouse agent has considerably reduced the cost of handling orders. The use of computer networks allows the telemaintenance company to bring to its customers' attention the different anomalies which were the reason for their intervention. The company did not previously do this because the cost of the service was independent of the number of the minor interventions. By offering its customers this complementary service the company makes the preventive maintenance of their equipment easier and reinforces its position as a provider of services in relation to its competitors.

Geographical widening

Until now, service activities seemed to need some kind of personal contact between the service provider and the customer. However, this necessity is diminishing, since information can now be moved along a network. The use of IT favours the appearance of new means for the circulation of information, which reduces the special position of paper work and personal contact. The service company can now ensure its freedom from its previously restricted position by getting rid of the permanent contact with the client. The geographical expansion of the market becomes potentially huge.

Even if, in the case for setting up the equipment or of a serious breakdown, the tele-maintenance company still has to send specialists to do the job on the spot, daily maintenance can be carried out from a distance.

This expansion is not so widespread as for an industrial product, but it can concern at least the information part of the service. The management of the service company can thus be centralised simply by setting up a network of sales points for the service. The management of this network then becomes possible at reduced cost and opens up important possibilities for expansion of the markets, even for services which supposedly require a permanent contact with the customers.

Increasing the customer base

The rapid circulation of information, either as a constituent of the main service or of a connected service, and the interest that this information might have for the immediate partners of the company mean that the company appears not just as the source of products or services, but also as a source of information for the suppliers of the final customers. This information can be exploited in the heart of the immediate surroundings of the firm, as the pharmaceutical products stockist tell us. He offers his suppliers a detailed analysis of his customers' purchases.

However, this analysis can also be offered to others customers who are interested in basic company information (e.g., GERS) or with whom it is possible to realise new services based on existing information, as can be seen by the collaboration set up between the maintenance company and the company studying the vibration of heavy plants.

Information becomes a service sold by the firm on the same basis as its original provision of a service.

Conclusion

Through the analysis of these two company situations, the use of IT has shown company heads the largely informational nature of their activity, and the possibilities of strategic redeployment centred around four axes:

* standardisation of the service-product
* enriching the service through information
* geographical widening of service provision
* definition of new partners

For service activities, these new strategic formulations seems to be the means to conquer the traditional dispersal of the sector.

References

1   Langeard, E & Eiglier, P "Servuction, le marketing des services" McGraw-Hill, New York, 1987.
2   Porter, Michael E "Competitive Strategy" Free Press, New York, 1980.
3   Monnoyer M-C et Philippe, J "Modernisation des Activities de Service et Technologies de l'Unification" Université d'Aix Marseille III, Centre Economie Regionale, 1986.

13

Strategic Management in Telecommunications Firms

Gillian Marcelle

Many theoretical and conceptual studies suggest that organisations adapt and respond to rapidly changing economic and technological environments. The effectiveness of this adaptive response will, to a large extent, determine the success with which these organisations survive and take advantage of the environmental changes. [1,2,3]

When one attempts to identify the sources of industrial change in the telecommunications industry it is useful to group economic and regulatory changes together and to make technological changes a separate category, among the many causes of industrial flux. However, it is not the sources of change upon which attention is focused here, but rather on the responsiveness of industrial players to the changes.

A two-tiered approach is adopted in investigating the adaptive reponses of firms to changes in the telecommunications industry. The product innovation process is examined, then the focus is put on the changes in organisational form and behaviour which accompany the growth in product diversity.

The methodology employed was one of comparative case studies of three firms: SEL, IBM Deutschland and Siemens. The objective was to generate and then analyse primary data elicited through field interviews. The participants included persons responsible for financial planning, strategic marketing, corporate planning, and technical management at various levels within their respective firms. As far as possible, the financial figures reported were reconciled with secondary sources and published company reports. The advantage of the elite interview technique was the richness, diversity and relative candour of the opinions, strategic policy statements, speculations, and hunches it provided. An additional interview was conducted with research economists in the Deutsche Bundespost (DBP); with their published literature providing useful background information. Finally, the author participated in a seminar presented by a member of the board of one of the companies, during which that company's international business strategies were discussed in considerable detail.

Considerations of the use of case study approaches are given in by Reid [4], while Johne [5] provides many expanded examples where similar methodologies are used in the study of product innovation for manufacturing firms.

The working definition of product innovation used in this discussion is as follows: the processes by which the product ideas generated in search, acquisition and development phases are transformed into saleable offerings and delivered to customers and clients. By adding the qualification of strategic product innovation, emphasis is placed on the strategic management of this process. Strategic behaviour is interpreted as the interaction of policy and action which aims to achieve particular defined objectives even when contextual constraints and other environmental influences are taken into account.

Effective performance as a service provider can be conceptualised in terms of: profitability, cost effectiveness, technological capability, range of service offerings, quality of services and support to users. By technological capability is meant:

- the extent to which the service provider offers state-of-the-art solutions to particular client needs (where this is most effective and appropriate)
- familiarity with and competence in the technical dimensions of the service product
- the ability to design, install, operate, and manage both the infrastructural and infostructural elements of the service
- the ability to provide services or systems which are 'future-proof'

These then are the variables used to address the main interest of this study which is the examination of the nature and extent to which modifications of organisational form and behaviour were incorporated into effective performance of value-added service providers and their strategic management of product innovation.

The West German telecommunications system is undergoing a major redevelopment in which reorganisation of the Deutsche Bundespost (DBP) is at centre stage. [6,7] As Figure 13.1 shows, the proposed restructuring of the DBP will have the effect of retaining its monopoly for the basic voice telephony service, will establish limited competition in services such as telex and will introduce full competition in the markets for other service areas, such as mobile communication. The new form of asymmetric regulation of the telecommunications industry was proposed by the Witte Commission early in 1988 and was implemented with Parliamentary approval.

Figure 13.1 Proposed re-organisation of the Deutsche Bundespost [8]

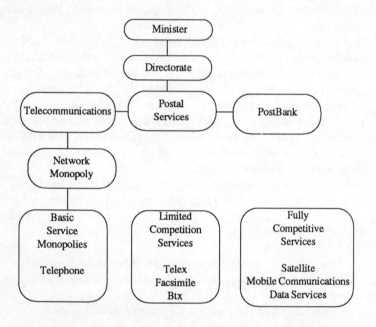

Product innovation trends and performance which will be examined are certainly a response to this changing regulatory environment which introduces competition and provides market access to areas which were previously the preserve of the public carrier. Both corporate players and the telecommunication administration itself are in a position to respond to the altered rules of the game, therefore enhanced levels of product innovation is one of the possible outcomes. Wieck has developed this idea in theoretical discussions of the strategic behaviour of established telecommunication companies after deregulation. [9] However, when product innovation is viewed as an expansion of the commercially available solutions to specific problems, in this case communication needs and requirements, it is clear that it is also a cause of industrial change as well as a response.

The generation of solutions and their transformation into commercially available products requires committment of resources for generating the product ideas-solutions and for their transformation (tailoring of the ideas; design of a service concept; choice of service delivery nodes; design of service delivery apparatus including network access devices and terminals; manufacture or procurement of the same). Changes in either the generation of solutions or in the transformation process will affect the product innovation process and the firm and industry level context in which it is located. In this lies the catalytic potential of product innovation.

In further developing the issue of product creation, it is useful to consider the following elements of the generation and transformation phases of product innovation.

Generation of solutions:

- basic research
- application oriented research
- communication with users
- product ideas

Transformation of solutions into saleable services:

- product design and development
- product tailoring
- product delivery
- product improvement

Have any of these elements changed? The answer has to be a resounding yes. For example, user input into the definition of needs; the user is now sophisticated, technologically knowledgeable and is able to define his needs in a much more precise manner than a few years ago. Thus communication with users has altered decidedly.

The technological inputs which give rise to product ideas come from a wider spectrum of sub-disciplines. This has implications for the internal skills base of firms, the sources of external skills, and the nature and direction of inter-firm technological cooperation.

A final example is provided by the change in product delivery. While we have thus far described the product as a solution, it is possible to go further and suggest that the solution should be provided in a readily usable form.

The basic capabilities for solving problems were previously delivered in black boxes which meant that for customers to derive the benefits of the product, they had either to possess the requisite knowledge or to acquire the know-how and skills which would transform these black boxes into productive resources. Increasingly, and as the necessary knowledge grows both in absolute terms and in specificity, the service product is delivered as a ready-to-use solution.

It is even misleading to speak in terms of delivery since this may conjure up notions of physical transfer while the core of the communications business is becoming concerned with provision of a capability and can, as a result, take the form of the exchange of the intangible. This has the implication of changing the industry from one consisting of firms which manufacture and supply black boxes into firms which unlock the productive capabilities of those tangible elements and make those intangibles available to the customers of their services.

Case studies

We begin by examining the three firms by describing their existing organisational structures as a hybrid of forms. (see Figure13. 2) Following this discussion, the details of the changes in the organisational form associated with the provision of value added services are considered.

In the older generation of organisational design of telecommunications divisions there was a basic separation of public and private network based systems since the firms were entering the markets as hardware suppliers. Very often the lines of reporting between these telecommunication divisions and top management went through general managers with direct

Figure 13.2 Hybrid organisational structure

Product & Operating Divisions		Central Departments	
Telecommunications	Components	*	Finance
		*	Sales
		*	Personnel
Business	Energy and	*	Legal
Systems	Automation	*	Commercial
	Systems		Management
		*	Corporate
Consumer	Medical		Development
Electronics	Technology	*	Public
			Relations
Data Processing	Automotive	*	R&D
Equipment	Equipment	*	Tax

responsibility for particular lines, e.g., business systems. There were other linkages to staff divisions such as personnel, corporate development and planning and to central line divisions such as finance and production. Since research and development divisions were typically large and powerful, these operated as independent divisions whose services were provided to the telecommunication divisions as needed. In addition, the firms often operated in other segments of the electronic industry producing systems, components and computer electronics. However, Siemens and SEL have positioned themselves strategically as telecommunication firms rather than as electronics firms.

New organisational forms

The first changes in corporate design established closer links between public carrier and private network divisions. This was done, for example, by integrating these two divisions into a communication networks division. Where the full-scale integration of customer premises networks and public networks has not been made, there is still some attempt to reduce the emphasis on the major role of public telecommunication administrations as clients. This is certainly not simple semantics because the conditions in an industry in which there are few suppliers and one client are very different from those which exist in the emerging telematics industry. By orientating decision-making and operations to changed conditions, the revision of organisational form is a necessary preparatory step.

For IBM Deutschland, reorganisation took the form of grouping the telecommunication equipment and service segments into a single business area designated as communication systems. This newly created operational unit was responsible for discrete hardware elements (e.g., terminals, modems, modulators and protocol converters) and for services such as network management and system components for control and switching. It was separated from the personal systems group, the application business systems group, the technology products group and the newly formed centralised marketing group.

The second consideration was the design and positioning of value-added service units within the corporate structure or appropriate alternative forms.

There was no evidence to suggest that the firms surveyed consider value-added services to be simply a new product-line which can be offered as any other product-line by extensions within existing divisions. Neither did the change in organisational design involve the formation of additional divisions or special units which provide value-added services through retention of the form and character of previous divisional systems of the corporate organisation. The opinions expressed by the companies and by the DBP indicated that the provision of value-added services required fundamental re-organisation. Some of the alternative forms with which the firms experimented are discussed below.

Siemens launched Vascom, an independent spin-off, in which it maintained a controlling interest. It was intended to cater for this new market, functioning as a fully fledged service provider. In the first instance, it provided the full range of internal communication services for the parent group but was expected to make a quick transition to offering these services on a commercial basis. The plans for Vascom include the formation of strategic alliances with industry groups viewed as potentially large clients. For example, major players in the insurance industry will be approached to participate as shareholders in the new venture. It is hoped that this arrangement will yield dividends in terms of cementing existing relationships and will help in for the acquisition of industry-specific knowledge.

Another option, suggested by SEL, is the acquisition of a firm which has already established itself as a value-added service provider.

Some general considerations involved in the design, selection or acquisition of an entity which would provide value-added services emerged from the sample, these are discussed below.

There is a need to establish simple direct lines of reporting to top management so as to facilitate responsive and rapid changes in product design and product capabilities. When the option of forming a subsidiary was considered, the benefit of having simpler organisational channels than those of the parent sponsor proved to be important. In some cases this was achieved through the formation of special project divisions which operated with modified lines of reporting to top management outside the regular system. There can also be hybrid forms such as that used by IBM, which assigned the provision of value added services to be one of the priorities of the communication systems group. Although not a temporary organisational form, it dramatically reduced the layers of management between top level and the reorganised business areas.

One also needs to consider the size of the value-added service provider unit since this has implications for the insertion into and articulation with the sponsoring firm. In the case of Siemens, which selected the subsidiary option, it was felt that the new service organisation would be too large to be made part of an existing operating division.

Organisational culture will also affect the choice of organisational form. There is a need for aggressive marketing, speedy decision-making, reduced bureaucracy and a change from the 'procurement mentality'.

The value added service provider should have responsibility as a profit centre, since there is a need for monitoring and evaluation of performance. The service provider, either as a separate legal entity or as a reconfigured business area, would be expected to show measureable results.

There should be independence in terms of sourcing of technology and use of multivendor equipment and network attachment devices for encouragement of increased flexibility. It was evident that corporate executives were prepared to allow the service providers greater scope in this regard by not mandating 100% use of the sponsoring firm's equipment. Two firms explicitly advocated use of multi-vendor technologies (if and when necessary) for provision of particular services or networking capabilities. In one case it is unlikely that this approach to compatibility will be taken even in the value-added services segment.

A final word on technological independence is required especially when considering the acquisition option. One should consider carefully this criterion when selecting among possible candidates for acquisition, so as to ensure that the value-added service provider brings to its sponsor capabilities which are not already present. An example of the importance of this consideration is provided in the case of Siemens who made substantial efforts to develop an inter-disciplinary skills base by adding important software skills and know-how to its existing expertise. Another area of required competence for the service provider is that of logistics management. There is also a greater need for familiarity with technological standards and compatibility requirements than in traditional equipment manufacturers. All three firms recognised these characteristics and reported changes in their recruitment policies to reflect these needs. As a result, the distribution of skills and training, particularly among technical specialists, has changed considerably. However, while independent skills are crucial, the need to integrate with the corporate sponsor cannot be overemphasised.

Since the service provider or unit will also gain from having access to and can utilise the sponsor company's know-how and expertise an appropriate balance needs to be found. The technological assets of the sponsors will be quite substantial as they are the results of cumulative R&D efforts particularly in switching and transmission, data processing, computer engineering and manufacturing technologies. In addition to the technological assets, the newly organised unit or firm can benefit from the ongoing commercial relationships of its sponsor.

The time tables adopted for the introduction of these changes differed markedly, allowing for two broad categories to be put forward: incremental versus radical organisational innovation. IBM undertook major organisational changes in February 1988, while Siemens launched Vascom in the second quarter of 1989. SEL has taken a longer term view of the restructuring process and was far more incremental in approach although expressing serious concern for these issues.

Product innovation strategies

All of the firms surveyed moved from first selling equipment through to selling systems and or providing services; this was the path of the service product innovation process. In this sequence several important changes can be identified.

Customer definition of service needs and requirments assumed a greater importance, to an extent where services can be said to be customer originated. While formal demand analysis appears to be in little use among the firms in this sample, there was a noticeable similarity in the occurrence of customer origination as the basis for service introduction.

SEL when discussing its approach to selecting from service introduction alternatives, described a loose categorisation in terms of 'must' services and 'possible' services, where the distinction was made on the basis of the riskiness of service or product acceptance. The channels for information concerning customer needs and requirements included: field reports produced by the sales and marketing personnel, tradefairs and exhibitions and published market research reports. One source of information which company executives regarded as central for planning were the directions of the Deutsche Bundespost. This requirement appears likely to continue into the future, despite deregulation, because many of the value added services are based on public networks and as a result there will be still be reliance on the infrastructure of the DBP.

The industry was propelled by a marketing rather than technological thrust ensuring that marketing activities were allocated greater investments of time and resources and provided the most immediate challenges. However, certain technological issues of a longer term nature, were also targeted as priority areas requiring careful consideration and investment. These included use of optical fibre technologies, multi-vendor compatibility and standardisation.

Product innovation among service products differed in complexity and character. The absolute size of the investment required for service introduction was considered to be an important determinant of the nature of the product innovation process. For example, the innovation process involved in delivering the new generation of digital and ISDN (Integrated Services Digital Network) switching systems differed from that used in providing specific value-addded services such as telemetry. SEL reported a difference in investment of a factor of ten and regarded the associated organisational differences to be substantial. For the digital switching conversion efforts, the central concern is mastery of the new technology and as such the process is spearheaded by the centralised research and development division. Following the introduction of these digital systems, the R&D division is required to be again closely linked to operating divisions and is mandated to provide greater accountability at the level of line general managers. Even with a specific product innovation, the organisation adapts its structure within the product life cycle.

In the smaller scale efforts, such as developing a telemetry system, special teams were established for the duration of the product innovation process. These teams often had direct contact to top management as well as responsibilities to particular divisional heads and this seemed to conform to the matrix style of organisation with mixed lines of reporting.

The firms sampled, expressed the opinion that product mangement for introduction of value added services does not require use of special techniques. The basic principles of operational product management were viewed as being adequate to the task. Product development was monitored and measured in terms of capital and material costs and human-resource input (measured in days). Typically, reports were generated on a monthly basis and the direct responsibility was that of the product manager. SEL believed that their dual product manager system gave a distinct advantage especially since the two managers often differed in functional specialisations and were drawn from marketing, manufacturing or R&D.

For the firms investigated, no disaggregated data was made available to assess the present contribution of value-added services to overall revenues and earnings. In two cases, SEL and Siemens, the proportion if calculated, is likely to be very small. While for IBM, the figure provided for the worldwide group, telecommunications revenues were 29% of total revenues, made up from 7% from services and 22% from equipment.

The telecommunication equipment sub-category includes customer premises equipment and public carrier equipment. Service examples included provision of BTX (Bildschrimtext) and remote computing. For comparative purposes it is useful to note the contribution of the other major business areas: software 12%, printers 8%, data processing equipment 24% and storage devices 15%.

Evaluation

On the basis of the methodology used, the observations which follow cannot be interpreted as being generalisable. The comparative approach is useful in that it provides evidence of varied responses to environmental change; what it does not do is provide a firm basis for determination of the ranking order in effectiveness.

To employ true measures of effectiveness of value added service provision, the services should be available and perhaps even in widespread use. This study was carried out before these requirements were met, so that there was no attempt at this stage to construct an effectiveness index and compare the three firms on this basis.

However, we can make qualitative forecasts on the basis of the actions implied by the strategic policy statements and the resulting market developments. In defence of the choice of firms, these were selected to reflect convergence between the computer and communication industries and also to investigate the responses of telecommunication equipment suppliers to industrial change. It is nevertheless true that the examination of product innovation by firms which are already established purely as service providers would have yielded additional insights. However, it is unlikely that the telecommunications industry will attain equilibrium where it consists of only these specialty players. Therefore, the two lines of enquiry are complementary, since firms from either segment will be operating in this hybrid market.

The investigation provided evidence of organisational flux at every level of the firm; divisional, corporate, and inter-divisional. While there is certainly an element of trial and error, much of this reorganisation conforms with our definition of strategic behaviour. This leads to the assertion that organisational redesign is one of the responses and results of industrial change. In line with the concept of product innovation there is evidence that the flux was related to the product innovation process and the management of this process.

One unfortunate outcome of this research is the dearth of measureable indices of performance in product innovation which it generated. While the sampled firms asserted that their management and monitoring of product innovation was close, tailored to corporate objectives and satisfactory, the firms provided no detailed data. Some of the areas for which answers were not made available include: average lengths of product innovation phases, evidence of shortening product life cycles, actual rates of product enhancements or improvements for particular product lines.

A good global measure of product innovation is reported by Siemens-for all its product lines. This states that for 1986, 56% of total revenues were generated from the sales of products introduced less than five years previously. However, this applies to areas other than telecommunications and cannot, without heroic assumptions, be considered to be equivalent for product innovation in this area.

Corporate perspectives on product innovation reflected considerable similarity in that there was an urgent need to introduce value-added services to the product mix of these information technology firms. The reasons advanced for entering the services component were the high growth potential relative to the stagnating equipment segment and the changing nature of customer demands. There is clear evidence that this decision is not trivial and has required almost textbook application of strategic redirection principles. As is also borne out by the case studies, the redesign efforts require involvement at every level of the enterprise but fundamental changes rely heavily on top level leadership.

One additional element of this repositioning by existing players is the determination of which value-added services to offer and the integration of these new product areas with existing core business areas. There was no clear-cut evidence as to whether or not, when the equipment manufacturer entered the services market, it would be accompanied by a streamlining of their product mix and associated organisational structure. Siemens, the most diversified of the firms indicated that their repositioning efforts would not include narrowing of their product range while SEL, the most specialised firm, has further tailored its product mix around communication services by selling off its consumer electronics division to Nokia.

The varied approaches to organisational design owed much to the industrial backgrounds of the firms which are competing in the converged market place for telecommunication services. The data processing firms possessed additional capabilities in terms of customer interaction and systems management, whereas the communication firms had mastered the switching and transmission technologies and were familiar with public networks and telecommunication administrations. These different comparative advantages can significantly influence the outcome of the competitive process in terms of effectiveness. However, it is not possible to say which of the competencies will be most important in the medium term.

It seems likely that a set of capabilities will be required and the firms which succeed in the value added services market will be those which exploit their inherent advantages and redress areas of deficiency. In this regard the alliances and relationships which the players form can be useful in providing the wider range of capabilities. Even this small sample provides examples of firms which made use of parent relationships, which acquired smaller firms and which used joint ventures to balance in-house with external but complementary capabilities.

One of the firms already provides value added services and its pricing policies for these services, given the level of access and related charges, is loss leading. By taking these anticipative actions the firm has established itself as a service provider even under restrictive market entry conditions. While timing was introduced in the examination of organisational redesign issues and treated in terms of incremental versus radical redesign, its consideration with reference to pricing strategies is another important element of the innovation process. For the larger and financially stronger firms, the adoption of predatory pricing strategies in the early stages will be feasible and defensible. However, this raises questions of the role of existing players *vis-à-vis* new entrants. Since the firms discussed here are all in the former category no definitve conclusions can be drawn.

The final issues to be addressed relate not to the corporate actors but to the DBP. Firstly, the DBP in assessing the effects of reorganisation on the competitive market for value added services seems to have made a misjudgement. The DBP's thinking emphasises the competitive threat of existing service providers while underestimating the changes the telecommunications suppliers are carrying out to enable them to provide value added serviceseffectively. The telecommunications equipment manufacturers operated in an environment where the most important competitive advantage was the strength of a procurement relationship, they are planning for a changed environment when they will compete directly with the DBP. [4]

The performance of the DBP in the newly liberalised marketplace cannot be assumed to be that of a loser failing againt its competition. Whither goest the DBP? Wieck suggests the deregulated environment will also provide opportunities for the former monopolies. [9] Many of the issues raised in the context of the private firms can be addressed to the reorganised DBP, particularly in the segment of operations fully open to competitive forces. However, since many aspects of organisational adaptation will be even more complex for the reconfigured public service organisation the DBP faces a stiff challenge.

Conclusion

Without doubt, the telecommunications industry in the Federal Republic of Germany provides fertile ground for examination of the 'winds of change' affecting information technology related industries. The present research has focused on one element of those changes which is both a response and a causative agent; the product innovation process and its strategic management.

The timing of the study did not allow testing of the many propositions which follow from the main findings. However, there are several testable propositions which, provided there is access to data as it evolves, can be taken up in the future.

The empirical extensions should include; construction of indices of effective service provision and correlation analyses between these proposed explanatory variables. It would be possible then to determine the relationship betweeen implementation of incremental versus radical reorganisation approaches; the influences of the form of value-added service provider and its relationship to existing players and the timing of market entry on effective service provision.

Finally, it is also necessary to examine possible relationships between effective service provision and the type of service offering at greater level of disaggregation than has been treated here.

References

1   Drucker, Peter "The Coming of the New Organization" *Harvard Busniess Review* **66** (1) pp 45-53, Jan-Feb1988.
2   Perez, C "Structural Changes and Assimilation of New Technologies in the Economic and Social System" in *Design, Innovation and Long Cycles in Economic Development,* edited by C Freeman, Frances Pinter, London, 1986.
3   Porter, Michael E "The Technological Dimension of Competitive Strategy" pp 1-34 in *Research on Technological Innovation Management and Policy Vol 1,* edited by Rosenbloom, JAI Press, Greenwich,1983.
4   Reid, G "Theories of Industrial Organization" Basil Blackwell, Oxford, 1987.
5   Johne, F A "Industrial Product Innovation, Organization and Management" Croom Helm, London,1985.
6   High Technology Europe, Survey Section V, *Financial Times* 13 April 1988.
7   Neumann, K "Models of Service Competition in Telecommunications" Deutsche Bundespost (WIK) Working Paper No. 28, Aug. 1987.
8   *Wirtschaft Woche* Special Report, Telekommunikation, No. 6, 5th February 1988.
9   Wieck, R "Comment" pp 285-292 in *The Law and Economics of Transborder Telecommunications,* edited by J Mestmaecker, Maker, Baden-Baden, 1987.

14
Investigating and Forecasting World Freight Trade

Nikolai Petkov and Filip Ivanov

The current state of the world market with rich and poor countries, transnational corporations, protectionism and discrimination, unstable exchange rates, energy crises, increasing competition and the heightened influence of political factors, predetermines the requirement for timely and reliable information. Such information is essential for making decisions in economic management.

The features of sea transport production are unusual. Firstly, it is sold before it has been produced and is consumed during the process of its production. Secondly, it is part of more than 80% of world-wide international trade. These characteristics make it a unique market both in operation and complexity. Market research for sea transport, i.e. concerning the international freight market, is distinguished from individual commodity markets by its scope; it verges on global economic problems in the complexity of its investigations.

In such an environment shipping firms actively use modern marketing methods, the so-called 'market management concept' based on complex market research.

Market research

Modern shipping companies operate in the complicated and rapidly changing environment of the international market. Market dynamics were developed in conditions of the relatively stable market structure which used to predominate, when anti-cyclical measures were used in strategic planning to invest at the lowest point of the economic cycle. Today this process is dominated by rapid changes in market structure resulting from the revolutionary changes in science, technology and communication. These circumstances predetermine the increased importance of market investigation, analysis and forecasting as a major part of strategic planning in shipping companies.

Market research is a sphere where the operational methods are well known. Yet through technical progress in management organisation and increased understanding of the dynamics of the market processes they can be changed and brought nearer to perfection.

Methodologically, freight market research should be based on the following main principles:

PURPOSEFULNESS: Freight market research should be closely connected with the aims and tasks of the shipping company. Namely the specific aims and tasks to achieve foreign trade of a given country and the 'export' of transport production of the international freight market are the conditions that should dictate the management, scale and depth of the market research performed.

COMPLEXITY: An analysis of all freight market elements is necessary, which presupposes investigation of a specific shipping market in its interrelationships and interdependences with the macro-economic processes and with other shipping and commodity markets. The complex approach necessary in market research requires investigation of the entire group of factors, both external and internal, which influence that part of the freight market under investigation. Market investigation processes require the forecasting of the researched market for a determined time period.

CONTINUITY: Only with continual market research is it possible to reflect all the changes in a timely manner and to draw the correct conclusions for shipping companies.

Market research in the shipping industry, without being different in its methods from similar investigations in other fields of economic activity, differs by the considerably increased volume of factors, processes and phenomena which must be observed to achieve reliable results. For example, producers are interested in technical and economic characteristics of their competitors' production; the effects of scientific-technical processes and development trends in production; the condition of the production and the research basis of the respective fields in the world scale; and other production and scientific or technical factors.

When examining the international markets, firms engaged in foreign trade are very interested in matters such as dimensions, dynamics, specificity, perspectives for development of demand, forms and methods of marketing, trade-political conditions for production at a given market, prices and price policies, financial-credit policies, etc.

The nature of shipping as an activity, integrating the production and marketing of transport, and appearing by its properties to be unique on the international freight market, requires the tracking and taking into account of all these elements.

Investigations

Conventional market research can be divided into two stages: investigation of the current market and study of long-term trends and problems of market development. The latter is divided into investigations of the whole and of its elements.

Given the character of the initial data used and the methods of analysis, market research can be divided into two main varieties; desk and field research.

Market research is the analysis of secondary information, acquired from:

- specialist periodicals
- information provided by representatives and agents of the company
- brokers' circulars
- statistical sources from different organisations (e.g., OECD)
- specialised information systems (e.g., Reuter's)

Desk research

Desk research covers market investigations. The methods used are the study of general economic factors, including major market developments and the analysis of trends in the world market.

According to Wegerland five major information sources exist for management decision making in market research for shipping: [7]

- intuition or personal experience
- statistical reviews of past and present market conditions
- extrapolation of the past trends based on statistical data
- market structure analysis
- theoretical-statistical simulation models

Historically, in the shipping industry most of the management decisions have been taken using the first three methods. Only recently has greater attention been paid to the more exact and complicated fourth and fifth categories.

The results of desk research helps to formulate the problem, to specify the direction of the next stage of investigation and to evaluate the overall state of the market.

Field research

Field research involves the processing of raw data, received directly from the market. This type of investigation is an important element of market research, because it ensures realisation of the major requirements of the market management theory for the results of its investigation. It can be used directly in practice, because of its orientation towards the individual aims and objectives of the company.

In shipping, these investigations are performed for markets about which long-term and investment policy is needed and especially in liner shipping or where an increase in fleet capacity is planned for the purposes of ensuring long-term engagement (time-charter or volume contract). Such investigations also appear necessary for the introduction of new tonnage onto spot markets and for the creation of a general development strategy.

Field research in shipping includes the arrangement of experimental voyages according to lines and destinations, direct contacts with shippers, stevedores, forwarders, brokers, agents, etc. The choice of method depends on different factors; terms for performance of the research, the volumes of the information necessary for problem analysis, potential volume of shipments and the availability of the necessary assets.

An important feature of market research is the investigation of segmentation. (see Chapter 2) The features of the international freight market mean that it is not profitable to carry out market research equally directed at all market sectors. A most important task is to separate and analyse the group of factors which influence the formation of demand in a particular market sector (cargo, tonnage group, etc). However, this does not concern investigations connected with the general market trends but only individual investigations.

Market analysis and forecasting can be carried out in two main directions. The first is the traditional one, based on the use of selected statistical indices, different evaluations of market developments, and thorough analysis of the entire complex mix of factors that compromise the market. This is the econometric method.

The second major direction is the utilisation of econometric methods of market investigation, ensuring a considerably improved accuracy of market forecasting and market development trends by means of mathematical models and simulation on computers. The econometric method of forecasting is most often used for development of prognoses and control of different freight markets and their segments. Although this forecasting method has been introduced comparatively recently, it is developing at an accelerating rate.

The extrapolation method has a special place in both cases. Extrapolation is based on the comparative inertia of the existing processes in the international freight market and on the tendency for the preservation of its basic historic regularities into the future. The continuity of the historical dynamics of market indices is determined by the persistence of factors which influence these indices with force and direction over periods of time and do not suffer apparent change.

At present, more than one hundred methods of forecasting are known which are generally distributed in four groups; extrapolation, expert evaluation, simulation and techno-economic estimation. Of course, for the purposes of submitting and reflecting the complex market connections and regularities and the tendencies for their development at a sufficient degree of reliability, it is necessary to use a mixture of methods.

Freight market research and forecasting require an existence and a clarification of:

* information flows
* methods of information processing
* technologies for preparation and distribution of data
* necessary technical equipment

Information flows

The development of the modern information industry has reached a level at which a great part of the information necessary for the successful performance of research and forecasting in freight markets can be achieved by the use of on-line inter-organisational information systems. (see Chapter 11)

International information systems provide access to data bases with information about existing market conditions and details for longer periods of time by different indices. (see Table 14.1)

Table 14.1 International on-line data bases

Database	Supplier	System	Contents
Freight Deals	Mardata	Geisco	Freight deals for bulk-carriers, gas-carriers and tankers. Existing freight and statistics.
PROMIT	Predicast	Dialog	Transport market information.
Monitor	Reuter's	Reuter's	Freight deals concluded during the day, shipping events, economic reviews, and political events.
Shipping Economic Service	Lloyd's	Chase	Global data on bulk-carriage and the international trade in bulk cargoes.

Systems of a bibliographic nature, providing access to data bases containing information about reports, articles in journals and magazines, conference proceedings, etc. (see Table 14.2)

These systems are both on-line and accessible world-wide on a subscription basis. However, international information systems serving brokers, e.g., Reuter's Monitor Shipping Service, are available only by election of the existing members.

The information collected from online data bases by the shipowners, Navigation Maritime Bulgare is an important source in their investigation of the freight market. The system collects and stores information for the purposes of decision making concerning the proposal and acceptance of transport contracts and the terms of those contracts. This system is used exclusively by the Bulgarian brokers' organisation and allows the simulation of different variants of decisions on the basis of optimising economic indices.

Artificial intelligence

The use of artificial intelligence (AI) in investigating and forecasting the freight market allows conclusions to be drawn from incomplete information. We are currently working on this, developing a prototype expert system for freight trade investigations.

Table 14.2 International bibliographic data bases

Database	Supplier	System	Contents
Balance of Payments	IMF	Data Resources	Monthly reviews of economic activities
BI Data	Business International	Geisco	International Reviews and forecasts of about 140 countries
Commodity	Interact	Chase	Reviews of bulk cargoes; sugar, etc.
OECD	OECD	I P Sharp	OECD published statistics
Economic Abstracts International		Dialog	World economic development in Europe since 1974
Time Series	Predicast	Dialog	Annual data on international production value of batches, consumption and foreign trade.
Forecasts	Predicast	Dialog	Published forecasts of different international markets.
Ship Movements	Lloyds	Chase	Movement of five major bulk cargoes
Steel Data Banks	DRI	DRI	Review of steel production and trade in the USA and the international market
FIRS	FIRS		Construction of ships, use of ships.

An expert system comprises a user interface, data base, knowledge base and inference engine. There are two types of expert system, based on production rules and on cases.

In an expert system using production rules, the knowledge base comprises a series of statements in the form 'IF ... THEN...' The inference engine determines whether all the conditions in the IF part are true. The rules can be conditions for other rules, in this way rules can be nested one inside the other. It is possible to use rules with forward chaining when, without an initial hypothesis, the expert system deliberates using given information and infers conclusions. Such an approach is convenient when the decision is made by means of selecting from a small number of possibilities.

However, we think that the method of backward chaining is more appropriate for application in expert systems connected with freight market forecasting. Here the action of the inference engine begins with the establishment of the aim. From this it starts by proving an hypothesis, testing the rules which determine the hypothesis in the 'THEN' sections. Backward chaining starts with a hypothetical decision and works back until it confirms the hypothesis.

We have found it expedient to use the rule-based deduction systems in the simulation of the econometric models. We use case based expert systems in the final stage of forecasting when the quantity of facts is greater and it is difficult for the experts to set out their knowledge in the form of rules.

Expert systems based on cases carry out an analysis of all the facts and draw deductions from all the cases available. We introduce the cases into the expert system in the form of large tables. Part of such a table is illustrated below, with only two parameters (see Table 14.3). The process under investigation is supposed to be a crisis in the international freight market. We assume that the critical situation could be identified by two main parameters: orders for the construction of new ships and the level of freight rates.

Table 14.3 Example of a case-based expert system

Increase in orders for new ships	Freight rates decline	Probability
yes	yes	0.3
yes	no	0.7
yes	n.a.	0.5

Expert systems are very important in areas where knowledge is essentially declarative and fragmentary. In these areas, the classical expert system has a considerable advantage when compared with traditional programming using mathematical models (e.g., Fortran). For the purposes of investigating and forecasting the freight market we consider it most expedient to examine a new mechanism for solving the problems of uniting the structural coding of procedural knowledge, corresponding to traditional programming with declarative representation, which is widely used in expert systems. It is necessary to create hybrid expert systems including the knowledge contained in econometric methods and models, as well as in the informal expert empirical knowledge expressed in the form of heuristic rules.

The inference mechanism in an expert system does not exactly correspond to an expert's deliberations. For example, in our work we find it necessary to allow for the possibility of breaking down the knowledge area into clearly differentiated problems and sub-problems to assist in the organisation of the inference mechanism. Knowledge structuring can be based on an analysis of the knowledge of an expert or of a group of experts, or on an analysis of a set of objects representing the area of expertise, and the application of a set of algorithms for the formation of natural classes. The structures obtained in this manner result in a better understanding of the problem than the semantic classes obtained from asking the experts.

In-so-far as we use both methods and the structures obtained from them which are not identical, it is necessary to transform the natural classes into semantic classes. As a basis of the inference mechanism we use approximate reasoning. Thus, the necessity arises of giving the rules appropriate weight coefficients because of the great difficulty in predicting and controlling the interaction between the rules. In such a case a systematic list of possibilities is obtained as the output.

The development and implementation of expert systems in the investigation and forecasting of freight markets is associated with considerable difficulties. The greatest difficulty in the development of prototype expert systems in this area is knowledge indeterminacy. One of the methods to solve this problem is the use of Zadeh's fuzzy set theory. [7]

A prototype expert system is under development using a Smalltalk-based expert system shell. The initial version contans 150 rules which are eventually expected to exceed 700. At the final stage of forecasting a set of about 200 cases is used.

Conclusion

Specificity of information associated with freight market inverstigations is defined as an integrity of incomplete and dispersed data. This makes it necessary to use artificial intelligence methods in order to facilitate management decisions which are as close as possible to economic reality. Furthermore, it is expedient to combine AI methods with econometrical models in the development of hybrid expert systems.

The use of the most modern information technologies is an important prerequisite for the preservation of freight market positions in the conditions of the present dynamic and difficult freight market. That is why the joint effort of specialists in market research on the one hand and specialists in information technology on the other are a necessary condition for further development in this direction.

References

1   Nan, D S "Expert Computer Systems" *Computer* **15** (2) pp 13-85, 1983.
2   Martius, G B "The Overselling of Expert Systems" *Datamation* **30** (18) 76-80, 1984.
3   Stefic, Marc *et al.* "The Organisation of Expert Systems - a tutorial" *Arch F Jutell* **18** 135-173, 1982.
4   Hayes-Roth, Frederick *et al.* "Building Expert Systems" Addison-Wesley, Reading, 1983.
5   Lagar, E R R "Fuzzy Set and Probability Theory" Aergamol Press, 1982.
6   Wegerland, Tor "Shipping Companies and Market Research" *Studies in Shipping Economics.*
7   Zadeh, F "Fuzzy Sets and Their Application to Cognitive and Decision Processes" Academic Press, New York, 1975.
8   Bibel, W and Jorrand, P (editors) "Fundamentals of Artificial Intelligence" Springer Verlag, Berlin, 1987.
9   Cercone, N and McCalla, G (editors) "The Knowledge Frontier" Springer Verlag, Berlin, 1987.
10   Holsapple, C W and Whinston, A B (editors) "Decision Support Systems - theory and application" Springer Verlag, Berlin, 1987.
11   Mumpower, J *et al* "Expert Judgment and Expert Systems" Springer Verlag, Berlin, 1987.
12   Litvinenko, A N "Main Principles of Estimation of the Industrial Goods' Competitiveness - problems of study of competitiveness of the goods' economic aspects" *VNIKI* **12** (1984).

Part V
Conclusion

15

Information Technology -
constraint or strategic resource?

Per Blenker and Andrea Pontiggia

The various contributions to this book relate to two major changes that
have taken place in the field of management.

Firstly, over the last thirty years there has been an increasing orientation
towards the strategic aspects of management. Almost every general
textbook in the field of management seems to have the word 'strategy' in
its title. Concepts such as: strategic management, strategic thinking, strategic planning, strategic marketing, strategic decisión making and competitive strategy seem to indicate that important changes are taking place
in management theory. Despite the popularity of strategy there seems to
be little agreement as to what it means.

Secondly, the development of information and communication technologies contributes substantial capabilities towards the rationalisation of
managerial decisions and actions. These new possibilities are supposed to
alter radically the way in which we do business.

Strategy and technology

Discussions about business strategy are complicated because the term
strategy has no single definition. In the literature on strategic management
the concept is used to refer to many different aspects of the managerial
process, such as:

- planning and control
- activities which are critical to success at a particular time
- long-term orientation
- definition of mission and objectives
- identification of resources

These activities take place in many different fields: economic results, technical efficiency, organisational outcomes, financial investment, etc. Strategy is often considered as a unifying label for these different activities, though in doing so the general meaning of business strategy is often forgotten. This might be a consequence of the relative newness of the idea and of the variety of approaches drawn from different cultural and theoretical perspectives used in business strategy. Consequently, the methodological hypotheses and analytical perspectives might not be adequately expressed. This question is central to the study of the relationship between information technology and business strategy and one that cannot be reduced to a simple problem of misunderstood definitions.

When we wish to examine the effects of information technology on business strategy, difficulties are increased because there is no single definition of business strategy.

The introduction of IT

The introduction of information technology establishes new and important assumptions about the effectiveness and efficiency of firms. Innovation processes related to the diffusion of information technology can be analysed by a variety of strategic approaches and models. From a general and perhaps slightly naive point of view, it seems that information technology facilitates new forms of organisational communication, such as telecommunication networks, while at the same time permitting a rationalisation of internal processes, such as increased access to information.

At this general level, information technology simply appears to contribute to the rationalisation of firms' goals; a rationalisation that starts from the new technological means. However, at a less general level it seems that the opportunities presented by information technology are often in conflict with existing organisational structures and processes.

Matching organisational characteristics with information technology is difficult because of the constraints that each organisation develops during its lifetime. The interpretation of these constraints redraws the organisational frontiers by building new organisational 'images'. The meaning of information technology is different for every organisation and the learning and cognitive processes at the organisational level are differentiated. Organisational specificity emerges and it will often determine the adoption of innovation.

Beyond different understandings of information technology, the advantages are limited by organisational inertia. Past experience in the field of information systems development shows that the most common reason for failure in innovation and implementation is due to organisational contingencies. Organisational change needs a certain amount of time and the stages of the change cycles are very different from those of technological evolution.

The effects of information technology are ambiguous and many tendencies can be found at once. On the one hand, there is the tendency to increase organisational efficiency, while on the other hand, information technology offers the possibility of moving towards market orientated forms.

Transaction costs analysis shows that the effects of information technology are not unique. The market failure due to related transaction costs is partially solved, but also the other form of managing transactions, resulted in more efficiency with the introduction of information technology. [1,2] The decrease in coordination costs, one of the effects of information technology, plays an ambiguous role in the determination of the most efficient form of managing transactions. [3]

Approaches to the relationship

These two developments, the increased orientation towards strategy and the development of information technology, were the common starting points for this volume. However, the many contributors differ on several points which we can divided into groups using two distinctions.

One distinction looks at the way technology is used to improve business strategy, from which it seems to be possible to isolate two general points of view. The first view concerns the internal use of information technology and is probably the most common; it is directed towards increasing efficiency within the organisation. The second view focuses on using information technology to improve the external relations of the firm, that is with clients and suppliers; these deal with the organisational environment.

The other distinction looks at the approach towards the relationship between business strategy and information technology. One approach is to see this relationship as being largely driven by strategy. The alternative is to see the relationship as being technology driven. The dilemma of choosing between these points of view is central and one which relates very closely to the dichotomy identified by Morieux. (see Chapter 2)

It is possible to relate the different views represented in this book and to extract different approaches to our common theme: the interaction between business strategy and information technology.

Figure 15.1   *Approach to strategy - technology relationship*

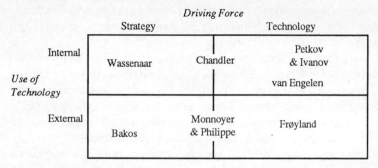

Of course the precise position of the chapters is open to discussion, but this is not our purpose. We want to devote less attention to the dichotomy of external versus internal application of information technology, which is dealt with by both Sutherland and Morieux. (see Chapters 1 and 2) Instead we direct ourselves to the question of whether the relationship is driven mainly by strategy or by technology.

Evaluation of the potential contributions of information technology to business strategy depends on how one understands technology and strategy. We must therefore remind ourselves of the meaning of 'technology' and 'strategy'; nothing is worse than to face new problems with old rather than current concepts. We shall therefore introduce and discuss different conceptions of both technology and strategy. We see the connection in the thinking of the chapters in this book as an attempt to move beyond one-dimensional ways of thinking about 'strategy and technology'. We need to open some windows to refresh the old air to help clear away stale concepts.

If approaches other than the traditional dichotomy of strategy-technology are available and useful, the next step must be to go deeper into alternative or integrative theories and thereby to transcend the one-dimensional approach to the strategy-technology relationship. We especially want to direct attention towards the organisational and environmental context which we consider mediates the relationship between strategy and technology.

The 'strategy - technology' relationship

The relationship between information technology and business strategy has been interpreted in different ways. We describe two points of view considering the relationship between strategy and technology as a direct relationship, one determining the other.

The strategy driven approach stresses the idea of technology as a resource or as an opportunity that increases freedom of action for the organisation. There is also a point of view which sees technology as a constraint on the organisation and the development as being technology driven.

Of course these two points of view may be too categorical, but as discussions and research on the relationship between 'information technology' and 'business strategy' often take one of the two positions, they help us identify common trends in the literature.

The technology-driven approach

One common approach is to see the developments in business strategy as a result of technological developments. Technology is seen as an autonomous force in society that has goals of its own and develops independently of business strategy.

From this point of view it is an illusion to believe that technology can be controlled; business strategists can have no real influence on technology. Technological development is seen as a one-dimensional and autonomous development that has a rationality of its own and cannot be stopped. Such an approach is carried to the extreme by, for example, Ellul and Marcuse. [4,5]

The potential influence of a single business on technological developments is non-existent or at best minimal. Thus what business strategy is really about is trying to adapt to, or hang on to, developments determined by technology. This is usually known as technological determinism.

Technology, from this point of view, is one constraint among many in the same way as resource scarcity and competitive games. The development and adoption of information technology is seen as a prior condition to operate in a particular industry (e.g., banking). This often means that comparison with competitors is stressed as a decisive measure of the potential success in the use of information technology. Competitive relations are viewed as a process of emulating rivals and the diffusion of innovation follows simple rules of imitation. The final effect is a kind of vicious circle; a firm's behaviour seems to over simplify the adoption and innovation process. This is directly linked to considerable organisational inertia resisting change, leading to a preference for evolution rather than revolution.

Information technology is viewed as a linear force that accelerates the organisational process; the result being an evolutionary change along the traditional development path. Neither inertia nor conflict can slow down the process induced by information technology. However, questions can be raised about this view, especially concerning the main hypothesis which is assumed implicitly. Can we be sure that new developments in information technology are similar to the innovations before? If organisational evolution follows a linear path, what are the reasons for investing resources in strategic planning?

The strategy driven approach

The other approach sees the relationship between business strategy and information technology as being strategy driven. From this point of view technology is simply a tool that can be used to achieve a business strategy that has already been formulated; it can be used to solve practical managerial problems. Technology has neither values nor a rationality of its own, but is seen as a kind of black box.

It is thus the business strategy that decides how problems are to be solved. Information technology simply opens up a broader variety of perspectives for business strategy. Despite the semantic limits indicated above, this approach assesses the potential effects of information technology and opens broader horizons for managerial decision making behaviour. From this approach, technology is seen as a resource which business strategists can draw upon and use as they please.

This is, as we shall see, the point of view that dominates traditional management theory. In this view firms formulate goals and strategies and then find or develop a suitable technology to achieve and fulfil the goals and strategies.

The need for a more dialectical approach

Of course neither of the positions viewing the relationship as direct, i.e. where one part of the relationship dominates or determines the other, are sufficient for a more thorough understanding of the relationship between 'information technology and business strategy' or indeed between 'business strategy and information technology'; they are too categorical. The question is not whether there is potential for influence or that technology is autonomous.

Nevertheless, one can argue, as Morieux has done, that the idea of business strategy rests on both these approaches. Morieux argues that the basis of strategic business analysis relies on two premises. First, 'companies enjoy irreducible degrees of freedom', which means that the relationship must be understood as strategy driven, and second, that 'the environment possesses irreducible levels of inertia', which stresses the technological environment as the determining force in the relationship.

This may sound conflicting, perhaps even contradictory, but indicates that information technology has what can be termed an 'ambivalent potential', that is, there exists a complex interaction between technology and strategy. It seems that information technology makes possible not only centralisation and standardisation of information, but also decentralisation and individualisation of information. Part of the technological development is relatively autonomous; other parts are more open to strategic action.

However, we must accept that the relationship between technology and strategy holds such contradictions. It is not a simple one-dimensional relationship. Our approach must be more dialectical, meaning that the development emerges as a result of many different interacting processes. From a dialectical point of view we cannot confine ourselves simply to analysing technology from a strategic point of view, i.e. to find technological means for strategic goals. Neither can we confine ourselves to analysing our strategy from an information technology point of view, i.e. assessing our strategic goals in the light of our technological means.

The choice of strategy and technology is interrelated and in order to understand this relationship better, we must focus on the factors which mediate the relationship.

We find that the very idea of strategic management suggests that the relationship between information technology and business strategy must be interpreted in a dialectical way. What we have to do is to see the relationship as being mediated by other factors in business and society. Thus we propose that, among other things, one must focus on the organisational and environmental contexts as the mediating forces of the relationship between business strategy and information technology. The organisational and environmental processes tie the relationship together.

This is our reason for considering the concept of rationalisation. The answers are not at all simple and must be orientated towards managing the process of strategic and technological change. In particular the phases of problem identification and implementation of new information technology require new capabilities, instead of the old idea of technology as a 'black box'.

From decision making to strategic management

In this part we describe the development in management from a traditional decision-making approach to the idea of strategic management. We do this in order to show that a dialectical approach, to the relationship 'technology and strategy', involves not only another view on technology, but also another percerption of business strategy or strategic management.

Management as decision making

The new emphasis on the strategic aspects of management, introducing business strategy and the concept of 'strategic management', has been a move away from the traditional philosophy of management as decision making, mainly dealing with analysis, planning and control. Within this philosophy, the central managerial activity was seen as decision making, and related to planning. In the traditional view of management, the gathering and analysis of information is the central activity for the rationalisation of managerial decisions and actions. Thus the rationalisation of managerial decisions and actions can be described as a complex information process. The key problem is seen as being how to make the right decision.

Traditionally, management deals with decision making as a question of the degree to which actions are able to fulfil certain criteria; it generally has to do with the means selected. Decision making can be regarded as the problem of providing information on two different aspects: [6]

- what means do we have, and how efficiently do they work? (empirical knowledge)
- is there consistency between means and decision criteria? (analytical knowledge)

Managerial decisions have to be rationalised in both respects. The rationalisation of means requires 'technically utilisable, empirical knowledge' and the rationalisation of decisions requires 'the explication and inner consistency of value systems and decision maxims, as well as the correct derivation of acts of choice.' [7] Rationalisation can thereby be characterised as a process of gathering, accumulating and analysing empirically and analytically true information and knowledge.

From this point of view information is seen as a resource or as the raw material that the decision maker needs in order to produce rational decisions, a need which is due to the complexity of the environment. In order to match this complexity, detailed information has to be produced. However, the production of complex information is itself insufficient; in some way the complexity of information must be reduced. Some sort of selection, treatment and analysis of the information is necessary in order to act.

Managerial decision making has generally been conducted by gathering the necessary amount of information and then analysing the consequences of different options for action. During the twentieth century the capabilities of this form of rationalisation have increased dramatically.

The development of the empirical-analytical sciences has contributed substantially to a further rationalisation of managerial means by an increase in the amount of accessible and utilisable empirical knowledge. The increased availability of advanced methods in the fields of operations analysis, cost-benefit analysis, decision theory and game theory has further increased the possibilities for analysing both the inner consistency between available means and the consistency between means and the decision makers criteria of choice.

There is little doubt that information technology has contributed substantially to the rationalisation of managerial decisions, by increasing the possibilities of storing, transporting and analysing information. The construction of large databases provides information which supports strategic actions. Communication technology has eased access to this information considerably and information processing has become much more efficient.

In the analysis of the consistency of means and decision-making criteria, the development of expert-systems and computer-based decision support systems has radically increased the possibilities of simulating future actions in such a way that the consequences of potential actions can be foreseen, without actually having to carry out these actions. These developments have contributed to a further rationalisation of decisions and actions because the outcome of potential decisions can now be made explicit more easily and related to the goals and criteria of the decision maker. There also seems to be little doubt that these developments will continue. (see Chapter 14)

The idea of strategic management

It appears that that traditional managerial theory studies a single problem, that is the problem of 'decision making' or 'strategy formulation.' However, it can be argued that the managerial activity is two dimensional. [8]

The focus on strategy formulation has often proved to be inadequate, producing unsatisfactory results, because the translation of strategic plans into reality has encountered difficulties. Ansoff has argued, that these difficulties are due mainly to the fact that, although it has long been recognised that the process of strategic activity consists of the three key sub-activities of 'sensing the need for action, deciding upon an action, and executing it', traditional research attention has been on the middle segment as the focus for strategy formulation. [9]

It was assumed that strategy formulation could be studied independently of the two other sub-processes, and that 'sensing-deciding-executing' is a natural sequence. The process has thus been seen as partitioned and serial. However, the serial approach seems to be only a special case of strategic behaviour. This approach has had its deficiencies since it has been shown that both the sensing and the execution activities have a determining influence on strategic action. Ansoff suggests that an alternative perspective on strategic behaviour should be based on the assumption of a dynamic interdependence of sensing, deciding and executing throughout the strategic act, and of a parallel, rather than sequential progress through the three stages. However, in the management literature there has been a transition from this decision-making approach towards an idea of 'strategic management' where:

> 'The strategic management activity is concerned with establishing objectives and goals for the organisation, and with maintaining a set of relationships between the organisation and the environment ...' [10]

We can describe the essentials of the strategic management concept using three main characteristics:

- due to a more turbulent environment, a complex and confusing field of instantaneous and simultaneous changes, the identification of strategic problems is now vital for success
- there is a focus on the implementation of strategy, the principal aim being 'to build a bridge between strategy formulation and implementation, rather than treating the two subjects separately as has been characteristic of much of the writing in the field.' [11]
- a more integrative approach is introduced. This is characterised by a greater emphasis on negotiation to initiate, build and maintain long-term relationships with key interest groups outside as well as within the organisation. Instead of optimising each functional unit within the organisation separately, strategic management focuses on an evaluation of the different strategic positions each functional unit takes within the organisation. This calls for another view on both management itself and its surrounding environment.

In the strategic management approach both the organisation and the environment are seen as consisting of other intentional and rational actors; it is recognised that these other actors have goals and strategies of their own. As these goals and strategies are often ambiguous and in competition, strategic management is orientated towards establishing commitment to mutual goals and actions. The concept of strategic management seems to open up some interesting questions that the traditional concept of management as decision making or planning has either not been aware of or has assumed away. From this point of view the introduction of strategic management is an extension of the traditional definition of management, this is the heart of our problem. (see Figure 15.2)

Figure 15.2 Intersubjective and objective dimensions of rationality [12]

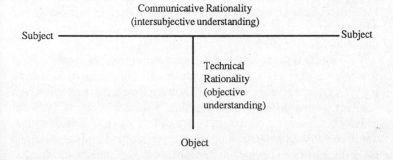

One dimension, the technical reason, deals with the physical world or a non-social context. It follows technical rules of action and can be evaluated in terms of estimating the efficiency of these actions in dealing with a series of conditions and events. Instrumental action might be related to social interaction, but is not itself a form of social action. Instead it represents individual maximising behaviour, orientated towards achieving individual success.

The technical reason is the kind of rationality typically engaged in the decision making approach to management. With the extension of management into strategic management it seems that a communicative person is engaged in the managerial process.

The communicative reason is orientated towards reaching understanding and deals with the social context. This type of action relates to the coordination of social intercourse, not through egocentric calculations of success for the individual actor, but through the mutual and cooperative achievement of understanding among participants in a group of actors.

The actors involved pursue their individual goals under the condition that, if they can reach mutually agreed definitions of the situation, they have to match their individual plans for action.

Strategic management involves both of these dimensions. Strategic actions are social actions, as they presuppose at least two persons, recognising each other as rational actors, and both pursuing certain interests through goal-directed behaviour. In strategic action, actors view themselves as competitive opponents and they are determined by the intention of influencing each others' decisions in a purposive-rational way. Strategic action follows rules of rational choice and can be evaluated in terms of efficiency in influencing the decisions of other rational social actors, each orientated towards success.

From this point of view, strategic management no longer concentrates simply on the formulation of strategy. There must be a closer connection between thinking and action. The formulation of strategy blends together with the social aspects, that is the identification of problems and the implementation of strategy.

If we accept this concept of strategic management, we cannot reduce strategic management to strategy formulation. It must also include sensing the need for a strategy and the ability to implement that strategy, which involves a quite different understanding of the environment. Both the activity of sensing the need for action (the process of problem identification, has to do with understanding and interpreting the social situation) and the activity of executing action (the process of implementation, that has to do with the motivation, legitimation and coordination of actions) specifically relates to the social aspects of strategic management.

The organisational and environmental aspects are thus the mediating factors of the relationship between technology and strategy. Therefore actions can no longer be seen as taking place in a non-social world. The environment must be viewed as a social world in which there are other strategic decision makers, each pursuing their own strategic interests. Thus the managerial decision maker can no longer be viewed as isolated from his social environment. Instead it can be argued that the essence of strategic management relates to the problems of:

- how to chose the correct direction for further growth from among many imperfectly perceived alternatives
- how to harness the energies of a large number of people in the new chosen direction [13]

Although, the strategic management approach proposed may seem more appealing and realistic, it nevertheless poses some problems as regards the rationalisation of strategic behaviour. Means can no longer be separated from ends, because strategic management changes from the traditional serial sequential processing towards a parallel dynamic process with interdependence between sensing, deciding and executing. Further, the subject must now be seen as social beings among other rational social beings, each having goals and strategies of their own. This makes the identification of strategic goals an important task and calls for social understanding of the managerial context.

However, if we accept this approach, and we find that the literature on strategic management has provided us with many good reasons for doing so, we must reconsider the concepts we use for the rationalisation of managerial strategic action. The traditional model of managerial decision making, based on the assumption of the individual decision or decision maker, is no longer sufficient. It is too narrow a conception, because actions within this framework can only be evaluated as regards an instrumental or means-end rationality. Instead we must search for other criteria for rationalisation, with which we are are able to cope with the rationalisation of goals and with the rationalisation of managerial actions taking place in a social context. One could say that we must search for a new kind of strategic rationality, which integrates both dimensions of rationality.

Consequences of the extended approach

Our main theme has been the effects of the business strategy-information technology relationship on management and organisation. We have argued that the concept of strategic management, involves a different view on management. This alternative view could involve other organisational structures (i.e. network) and other managerial processes (i.e. communication).

We shall try to show that an extended approach to business strategy and information technology requires management to be more orientated towards communication and learning.

New managerial roles

The managerial strategic situation opens up the possibility of realising several different actions if not, we would not be able to speak of a strategic situation. Therefore, there is an underlying claim for rationalisation. This is due to the fact that there is a range of different options open to the decision maker and that no spontaneous argument exists for realising one action compared to the other. Therefore the decision maker has a need to state a reason for his decision.

The claim for rationalisation can also be due to the fact that we are speaking of actions in a social context. Decisions and actions may therefore require some sort of rationalisation by the other participants in the social context.

In the typical strategic situation we must deal with both of these claims for rationalisation. We understand rationalisation to be the increase in rationality or reason in forms of action; this concept of rationalisation relates to the possibility of giving grounds for action.

The question is, what change is called for using the two-dimensional concept of rationality, focusing on the social context and on the rationalisation of goals? In Figure 15.3 some characteristics of the two dimensions of strategic management are listed.

The communicative dimension has to do with providing a *telos* for our *praxis* and is orientated towards establishing social standards that can link the expectations of those involved. Therefore it cannot be rationalised under the technical aspects of the means selected. Instead it must be rationalised under some moral-practical aspect and under the justifiability of the acting norm. In this process the barriers to communication must be transcended by giving grounds for action, with the aim of reaching an 'acting-supporting' consensus on goals and criteria for action. The rationalisation of communicative action therefore means 'extirpating those relations of force that are inconspicuously set in the very structures of communication and that prevent conscious settlement of conflicts, and consensual regulation of conflicts'. [15]

Such a concept of rationalisation is founded in language or human communication (communicative rationality). The rationalisation of purposive-rational action is founded in language, in the sense of language as representation. Language is seen as a means of communication by which information is carried or passed from one person (or machine) to another. However, in communicative action the focus is on another aspect of language, it emphasises language as an act or process. Human communication can thus be seen as a social action that by making explicit individual value orientations is able to create an agreed orientation, i.e. to establish common goals, norms and values. The concept of communicative rationality thus introduces human communication as the fundamental mechanism for the coordination of action as a means of making possible a motivational consensus that can lead to action in common.

Figure 15.3 A two-dimensional conception of strategic management [14]

1st dimension Decision-making approach to management	2nd dimension Communication-orientated management
Problem type: Uncertainty (What can we do?)	Problem type: Disagreement (What do we want?)
Information processing (analysis of facts)	Formation of will (genesis of norms)
'Objective' information on the coherence of effects	Intersubjective consensus on the coherence of meaning
Monological	Dialogical
Rational intercourse with objects	Rational intercourse with subjects
'Management technique'	'Management politics'
Building up strategic potentials of results	Building up communicative potentials of understanding
Utilitarian-strategic concept of rationality	Communicative-ethical concept of rationality
Rationalisation = improvement of control over things and persons (social-technology)	Rationalisation = improvement of the conditions for an argumentative formation of consensus with everyone involved (rational justification of norms)
Introduction of information, decision, organisation, management, control and PR techniques.	Developing a communication culture of the organisation inside (internal relations) outside (external relations)
Functional integration of systems (systems control)	Normative integration of social relations (legitimation of life-world)
State: Highly developed	State: Underdeveloped

Whereas the traditional focus of the decision-making approach was on information as the central means for the rationalisation of managerial action, the focus is now moved to communication. It is not possible to find a platform or a criterion for the analysis and evaluation of information inside the flow of information itself it must be found elsewhere. Common criteria and goals can only be established through a mutual understanding of the problem among the actors involved.

Thus the process of rationalisation is the process of communication that can produce a mutual understanding of the problem. Rationality therefore refers to an openness in the discussion concerning standards and criteria for action. From this perspective we have to view information and communication technologies as social communication systems. As means of communication, information and communication technologies can be seen as formalised systems that facilitate the exchange of meaning and knowledge among people who are engaged in strategic management.

It is from this point of view that we must evaluate how technology can contribute to the rationalisation of communicative action. The development of new forms of interactive communication technology promises easier transmission of information. It is less certain that technology will contribute to a further rationalisation of the process of communication and even whether such a development is desirable. Historically, technological developments in communication have often led to alienation and depersonalisation of the communication process as it seems to impose a higher level of structure on the communication.

Information and communication technologies are characterised by a high degree of standardisation of the information to be represented. Thus they produce information on facts and conditions, but involve more difficulty in bringing about the necessary interpersonal understanding of problems.

The possibilities of reaching a consensus supporting action might therefore be troublesome. A gap between the individual experiences of the actors and the representation of this experience in communication technology easily arises, as the technology and the standardisation of the information makes it difficult to represent the local situation of the individual actor. The possibility of reaching a mutual understanding of problems is probably rendered more difficult.

Structure, process and behaviour

Strategic action cannot itself secure conditions for motivation because each actor is following preferences and decision maxims that he has determined for himself, regardless of whether or not these are agreed by the other subjects. As a prerequisite, a strategic action system makes it necessary for the actor to agree on certain preferences. Therefore, strategic action must somehow be bound or institutionalised. Thus strategic action must be embedded in some form of organisation of consensual action, resting on socially recognised and binding norms that can guarantee the fulfillment of the motivational conditions. [16]

As a prerequisite for success there must be some sort of communicative understanding. It is worth emphasising that a concept of strategic rationality does not mean that purposive-rationality is totally neglected. Instead the scope of rationality is reconsidered and extended. Purposive rationality based on a means-end analysis is kept as a part of strategic rationality, but has to be transcended.

Strategic action can thus be seen as some sort of intermediate state, or perhaps better, strategic action must involve both purposive and communicative action. It is directed toward success and as such it must be evaluated or rationalised in terms of its efficiency as regards achieving desired objectives. But as it operates in a social context, the satisfaction of individual interests cannot be sufficient. Instead we would argue that a prerequisite for strategic rationality is to have communicative rationality. Rationalisation of strategic actions must deal with both the purposive and communicative aspects of rationality.

We thus suggest that managerial strategic action must be rationalised, not only in relation to the purpose, that is as technologies, strategies, formal organisations etc, but also in relation to the communicative aspect, for the development of normative structures for action.

By accepting that strategic management involves not just purposive-rational or instrumental action but also communicative action, we are better able to understand how the aspects of problem identification and implementation are to be integrated in the strategic management process.

The question is now how can information and communication technologies aid decision making by contributing to the rationalisation of managerial strategic action?

There seem to be two tasks for information and communication technologies in the rationalisation of managerial action. It must contribute to the rationalisation of purposive-rational actions by providing information on efficiency and consistency of means.

Equally, it must contribute to the rationalisation of communicative actions by increasing the abilities for communication in such a way that an easier understanding of mutual goals can be established.

In strategic management we thus need knowledge of social situations and social values. We have to communicate knowledge of conventions, habits and accepted world views which are generally expressed in ordinary language. The problem is to know how technology can contribute to a process of sharing meaning and knowledge, and how such an improvement in communication can be introduced?

Considering strategic management as action that has to be rationalised in respect to both purposive and communicative rationality, a central problem is whether it is able to profit from the technological advances in information and communication technologies. If it is, this benefit might surprisingly come from the information technology and not from communication technology. The increased possibilities of gathering, processing and analysing information should enable us to set free managerial resources that have traditionally been used for these time-consuming activities, leaving more time for the reflective aspects of management, such as the setting of managerial goals and evaluation criteria.

The organisational context

Another paradox emerges, linked to organisational modifications directed to the main organisational issues such as the effectiveness of organisational structures and changes in the communication, decision and control processes. We argue that the concept of strategic management involves a broader view of organisational design. Information technology offers different alternatives and defining the organisational form becomes critical.

Despite the variety of definitions of information technology there is a general agreement on many of its attributes. Less definable is the relationship that links or mediates information technology with the organisational structure and processes. The effects are often multiple, it is hard to discover what kind of evolution has occured and what are the changes that must be implemented. There is confusion and this is typical of the initial period when innovations are not understood and the opportunities or the constraints are hidden by limited comprehension.

The objective of the proposed conceptual analysis is not to cover every aspect of the complex problems derived from the introduction of information technology. Instead, our goal is limited to drawing some general conclusions about organisational changes. Many themes and hypotheses in the preceding chapters seem to skip the organisational dimensions. Yet, it is important to underline the strong relationship between strategic politics, decisions and the related changes to the organisational form. It emerges that a mediated approach is necessary. In the rich literature on organisational information systems there are numerous examples of conceptual frameworks that are borrowed from different disciplines. This richness is not at all apparent, but it confirms the necessity of finding a new 'mix' between descriptive categories and normative models. Among the different evolutions of information technology, diffusion of external information systems appears to be the most effective of strategic applications. [17]

In the design and implementation of information systems for managing the environment, all relations assume a new meaning and bring great change to the organisational forms, redrawing the frontier and the limits of organisations. The development of information systems moves from traditional internal applications towards a more complex evolutionary path, the effects are not limited to internal efficiency but cover the relationship between firm and environment. The development of information systems applications moves from a traditional objective of rationalisation and improvement of efficiency to a more complex evolution, covering the external relationship between firms and environment. The changes requested are not measurable using traditional techniques.

An example is in the field of methodologies for information needs analysis; when the focus moves from inside to outside the organisation the conventional design process is insufficient. In other words, it was necessary for a change in the information systems application field to occur to discover the complexity of the organisational implications.

It is very common to refer primarily to the effects on individual behaviour without considering the more important change in the nature of organisational forms. The transformation of the industrial structure is clearly dominated by the effectiveness of new forms of organising work and transactions. The 'putting out' or 'franchising' of contracts or the agreement to use common information resources are examples of information integration.

Firms face the problem of renewing their organisational frontiers and reformulating the 'make or buy' strategy. The traditional boundaries, physical, operational and technical, are changed by networks based on information exchange. The strategic decisions become more critical because of the necessity of facing complexity of information. Information technology generates new media and transforms the communication process and the organisational linkages between different firms (supplier and clients, etc.).

The concept of a management information system is very poorly defined and there are many different interpretations.

Finally this situation pushes us towards a new sort of theoretical integration, justified by the integration of information. Referring to an innovative concept of information systems permits us to recognise the global effects on organisations. There is a risk of thinking through a deterministic approach that stresses technology and puts aside the managerial consequences on firms' structures. First of all the analysis must be economical and the opportunities or the constraints are viewed in a holistic way. Strategy is essentially about the interaction between the firm and the environment and the main focus must be this interaction.

Achieving competitive advantage through information resources requires that these activities are based on a synthesis, on a clear business idea. At this level it is necessary for strategists to have more analytical frameworks in order to manage the paradoxes. It is necessary to accept the notion that information technology has moved out of the back room and became a relevant organisational resource that can be compared to human or capital resources. However, because of this we must recover the basic concept of information as an economically scarce resource.

The lack of precision of the terms information technology and information is critical, in fact they are often discussed interchangeably. The possibility of measuring information technology and the complexity of analysing information resources are the causes of the difficulties of defining them.

Organisation design theory underlines some of the trends and contradictions due to information technology.

Integration versus disintegration

The effects of information technology are often multiple and ambiguous. Using the transaction costs approach it is possible to show that information technology affects the organisational forms but that the direction in which it will do this is uncertain. The result may be towards the market form (buy) or towards the hierarchy (make). Changes in organisations follow an ideal line directed towards a higher level of efficiency.

At the same time in different industries the effect can be exactly opposite, market forces increase and there is the birth of an electronic market. Technological innovation forces organisational adaptation and becomes the starting point of deep organisational innovations. Different organisational forms, for example, more or less integrated, or more or less hierarchical, find their *raison d'être* in differentiated transaction cost levels.

Former organisational structures based on bureaucratic mechanisms are renewed by information systems. The organisational integration goes through an informational or perhaps even communicational integration. The organisational barriers are transformed and information processing activities allow a higher adaptability and flexibility. The traditional concept of an organisation declining into 'bureaucratic death' is removed by the use of information technology. We see two different prisons that force towards the opposite sides or limits of the 'continuum'.

Automate versus informate

The effects of information technology are thought of in two ways: on the one hand, the idea of automation is primarily directed at the reduction of cost through the substitution of manpower in operations and controls. Attention is directed towards decreasing production costs. On the other hand, information technology offers the opportunity to informate, that is to spread information and redefine the information structure, composed of the communication, elaboration and gathering processes. It is important to distinguish applications that influence directly the automation from those that affect the information processes indirectly, in terms of diffusion and modification of information routing the benefits are very different.

It follows that the strategic decision making processes have changed for two main reasons:

- there is a change in the decision maker's group, because information technology has changed the boundaries of the organisation
- new information support systems modify the decision models

The diffusion of a new generation of support systems is increasing the accuracy of the quantitative analysis.

Group decision processes are also influenced directly (through group decision support systems) or indirectly through the diffusion of information. But at the same time, information systems may permit a tighter control of performance and a reduction of the freedom to take decisions.

Conclusion

The general purpose of this book, our workshops in Brussels and this chapter in particular has been to trancend some of the simplistic, deterministic and one-dimensional approaches to information technology and business strategy. We have tried to achieve this by examining the most apparant contradictions and dichotomies in the field of technology and strategy.

The dichotomies presented are only the most striking and evident. If our question is to identify the apparent contradictions or paradoxes then the natural answer may be the difficulties of interpreting the change. The real paradox that synthesises all the others is somehow to accept the the paradoxes. The complexity of using not one or two theoretical models but many. Reality is complex and capabilities of integrating and, if possible, understanding the convergence or divergence of frameworks is necessary. Only by accepting and working with the many different paradoxes, using analogies and metaphors, is it possible to get a better understanding of the implications of information technology.

The number of approaches must not be considered as a limit, but as an opportunity to enrich our analytical tools. There are numerous 'images' of organisations and the environment, and in the same way, there are different 'ideas' of information technology and business strategy.

We find that the comprehension of organisational effects attributable to information technology requires a formula for fusing together different perspectives. From our point of view the organisational and environmental contexts become the central mediating factors between strategy and technology and we find that general mangement requires further development in order to deal 'rationally' with these critical aspects. In this approach the need to view technical change in organisational terms and to provide resources for managing it, including the key directing influence of their own time, prestige and attention becomes undeniable.

Information technology though it increases degrees of freedom at the same time reduces the degree of meaning and this is the essential problem.

The interaction between strategy and organisation leads to views of information technology as an integrative means that pushes towards rationalisation and organisational effectiveness or as a destructive means when it creates organisational crisis and establishes market and clan forms.

What seems to be required is more work on communications technologies which would increase the likelihood of reaching mutual understandings of problems.

References

1 Williamson, O E "The Economics of Organisation; the transaction costs approach" *American Journal of Sociology* **87** (3) pp 548-577, 1981.
2 Ouchi, W G "Markets, Bureaucracies and Clans" *Administrative Science Quarterly* **25** pp 129-141, 1980.
3 Ciborra, C U "Research Agenda for a Transaction Costs Approach to Information Systems" pp 253-274 in *Critical Issues in Information Systems Research,* edited by Boland and Hirschheim, John Wiley, Chichester, 1987.
4 Ellul, J "The Technological Society" Alfred A Knopf, Toronto, 1964.
5 Marcuse, Herbert "One-Dimensional Man" Beacon Press, Boston, 1964.
6 Habermas, Jürgen "Communication and the Evolution of Society" Heinemann, London, 1979.
7 ibid, p 117.
8 Ansoff, H Igor "The Emerging Paradigm of Strategic Behavior" *Strategic Management Journal* **8** pp 501-515, 1987.
9 ibid, p 508.
10 Habermas, op cit, p 183.
11 Porter, Michael E "Competitive Advantage; creating and sustaining superior performance" Free Press, New York, 1985.
12 Ulrich, Peter "Transformation der ökonomischen Vernunft" Fortschrittsperspektiven der modernen Industriegesellschaft, Bern, 1986.
13 Ansoff, H Igor "Implanting Strategic Management" Englewood Cliffs, New Jersey, Prentice-Hall, 1984.
14 Ulrich, op. cit, p 439.
15 Habermas, op. cit, p 120.
16 Habermas, op. cit, p 118ff.
17 Sutherland, Ewan and Morieux, Yves "Effectiveness and Competition; linking business strategy, organisational culture and the use of information technology" *Journal of Information Technology* **3** (1) pp 43-47, 1988.

Index